OUR DAYS
BY DEEDS AND
DREAMS

A DAYBOOK OF POEMS

BY

FLORENCE EARLE COATES

COMPILED AND ARRANGED

BY

SONJA N. BOHM

INCLUDING
POEMS ON WAR AND PEACE

WORLDS ASPIRE
SPRINGFIELD, VA

2024

WorldsAspire

Copyright © 2024 by Sonja N. Bohm. Published by Sonja N. Bohm

ISBN 979-8-218-51716-8

Our Days by Deeds and Dreams:
A Daybook of Poems by Florence Earle Coates.

All rights reserved. No part of this book may be reproduced or utilized in any form or by any means, electronic or mechanical, including photocopying and recording, or by any information storage or retrieval system, without permission in writing from the Publisher.

Library of Congress Control Number: 2024920200

Copyright Notice: All poems in this book are by Florence Earle Coates (1850–1927) and are in the public domain.

Compilation and Arrangement: © 2024 by Sonja N. Bohm

Cover Image: A mirror image detail from painting "The Muse of Painting" (1870) by John La Farge (1835–1910)

Cover Design: Sonja N. Bohm

A DAYBOOK OF POEMS

*"Our days by deeds are numbered,—and by dreams,
If we dream well and nobly…"* —FEC

January 1

RENEWAL

THESE sounds sonorous rolling!
  These vibrant tones and clear!
Listen! The bells are tolling
  The requiem of the year:
The year that dies, as mute it lies
  Mid fallen leaves and sere!

Now by the fading embers
  That on the hearthstone glow,
How sadly one remembers
  The things of long ago:
The wistful things, with flame-bright wings,
  That vanished long ago!

The self-effacing sorrow,
  The generous desire,
The pledges for the morrow,
  Enkindled at this fire!—
Enkindled here, O dying year!
  Where smoulders low thy pyre.

What hope and what ambition,
  What dreams beyond recall!
And look we for fruition,
  To find them ashes all?
Is life the wraith of love—of faith?
  Then let the darkness fall!

The sparks—how fast they dwindle!
  How faint their being glows!
Quickly the fire rekindle—
  Ah, quickly! ere it goes!
Woo living breath from the lips of death!—

From ashes bring the rose!
. . . .
Kind God! The bells, in gladness!
   The rose of hope hath bloomed!
For, consecrating sadness,
   Life hath its own resumed,
And welcomes here the new-born year—
   A phœnix, unconsumed!

                                          January 2

AFTER THE PAINTINGS BY GEORGE F. WATTS

I

LOVE AND DEATH

A MOMENT, Death!—only a moment more!
   She is my all; have pity! stay thy hand!
   Behold, a fearful suppliant I stand!
Take not away what thou canst not restore!

At thy approach the birds have ceased to sing,
   The roses of my lintel droop and pine,
   The genial sun itself doth coldly shine,
And in thy shadow all seems darkening.

That thou art merciless, as men declare,
   I'll not believe. Thy look is kind, not stern;
   And they who judge thee ill, of me shall learn
To know thee better, Death!—for thou wilt spare!

See, thou art strong! and I am weak—so weak!
   All beings that draw breath at last are thine:
   Thou wilt not covet this sole joy of mine—
Nor to deprive me of its solace seek?

Yet come no nearer! Shouldst thou pass this door,
    My heart that so importunes thee would break.
    Go back a little! for compassion's sake,
Go back! and hither—ah, return no more!

In vain, in vain! O awful Majesty!
    Thy very breath appalls my fluttering heart.
    Invader dread, what strength have I, or art—
What, save my anguish, to oppose 'gainst thee? . . .

Enter! the door is open. Yet thus much
    Let my submission of thy pity earn:
    When through the shaded portal thou return,
On me—me, also, lay thy easeful touch!

II

LOVE AND LIFE

THY hand I press,
    And am not much afraid:
    Though danger lie in wait in every glade,
Thou, Love, hast might to comfort and caress
My helplessness.

The way is steep;
    But thou wilt soothe its pain;
    And when at last the utmost height we gain,
To the soft shelter of thy wings I'll creep,
And sleep—and sleep.

The way is long;
    But though I wearied be,
    Still gazing upward, I shall gaze on thee;
And thy angelic voice, more sweet than song,
Will make me strong.

Whate'er betide,
    I, Love,—who may not know
      Whence I have journeyed, nor the way I go,—
Am still content to follow at thy side,
O deathless guide!

January 3

MUSIC

THE might of music, and its mystic fire,
    Will from no studied Art alone proceed;
The soul of Orpheus must infuse the lyre,
    The breath of Pan must blow the plaintive reed.

January 4

AFTER

AFTER the darkness, dawning,
    And stir of the rested wing;
Fresh fragrance from the meadow,
    Fresh hope in everything!

After the winter, springtime,
    And dreams, that flower-like throng;
After the tempest, silence;
    After the silence, song.

After the heat of anger,
    Love that all life enwraps;
After the stress of battle,
    The trumpet sounding "taps."

After despair and doubting,
    A faith without alloy,
God here and over yonder,—

The end of all things—joy!

January 5

HE AND I

HE and I,—and that was all,—
The boundless world had grown so small:
    So small, so narrow in content,
So single in possession sweet,
So personal, so love-complete,
    So still, so eloquent!

He and I,—and Earth made new!
The flowers blossomed for us two,
    And birds, to voice our rapture, sung
Divinely 'neath our northern skies,
As sung the birds in Paradise
    When life and love were young!

He and I,—O aching heart!—
Only a narrow grave apart!
    Yet seeking for his face in vain,
How changed, to me, the world has grown;
How cold it seems, how strange, how lone,
    How infinite in pain!

January 6

MIGHT I RETURN

MIGHT I return to that May-day of gladness
    When life is young, and all its promise fair;
Might I efface each memory of sadness,
    And put away the weary load of care,—
To pluck the rose that in Time's Eden blows,
    I would not go, were I to miss you there!

Might I ascend unto those realms of rapture
    Whose amaranthine joys fade not again,
Might I the secrets of Elysium capture,
    And find fruition for my longings vain,—
I would forego these dear delights, to know
    That you were with me, and to share your pain.

                                      January 7

MY DREAM

    THOUGH full of care
I tread the round
Of toil in which man's eager life is bound,
I faint not 'neath the load I bear;
For grievous though the burden sometimes be,
    I dream of thee!

    And when, at night,
I lie enwound
In silence that is sweeter than all sound,
The darkness, kindlier than light,
Shuts out the busy world awhile, and free,
    I dream of thee!

    Like to a breath
Of fragrance blown
From some shy blossom, hidden and alone,
Redeeming frost and wintry death,
So ever comes, like scent of bloom to me,
    My dream of thee!

    Like to a star
Amidst the clouds,
When angry tempest hurtles in the shrouds,
And darkling drifts the mariner afar,
So, out of storm and shadow, beams on me

My dream of thee!

January 8

OF FUTURE DAYS

   I DO not ask to know
Whither thy spirit after death shall go;
I only ask that I—where'er thou be—
     May follow thee.

   All torment and regret
Thou, with thy love, couldst teach me to forget;
And heaven—Alas! what hope of heaven for me
     Bereft of thee?

   Nay: faithless doubt and fear
I lose in Him who gave thee to me, dear!
He would not so unite to rend apart,
     Who made the heart!

January 9

LULLABY

DAY is stealing down the West,
   Tender, drowsy sounds are heard;
   Closer now each downy bird
Creeps 'neath mother-wings to rest.
In the fading sky afar,
   Kindled by some angel hand,
Twinkling comes a tiny star,—
   Baby's guide to Sleepy-Land.

Cooler, darker grows the air,
   Eerie shadows haunt the room;

In the garden, through the gloom,
    'Wildering bats and owlets fare;
But the lambs and birdies seem
    Happy now at home to keep,
And a darling little dream
    Smiles at baby in his sleep.

January 10

IN DREAMLAND

IN dreamland is a castle fair
    Wherein my love doth dwell:
Its turrets waver into air
    From fields where asphodel
And poppy keep not watch, but sleep,
    'Neath an enchanter's spell.

Pale offspring of a starlit sky,
    One rose—for need like mine—
Has over-climbed the ivies high,
    About her sill to twine,
And there, abloom, with rare perfume
    Makes exquisite her shrine.

Still, night by night, the wondrous bird
    That ne'er is heard by day,
Thrills, with my heart's unspoken word,
    Those mystic turrets gray,
And heavened above, sings to my love
    His plaintive roundelay.

Ah, would that I, through tender gloom
    Upmounting, lover-wise,
Might find her in the fragrant room,—
    Her virgin Paradise,—
But for one night behold the light

    Beam in her charmèd eyes!

Alas! I shall nor lead her down
    The steep and skyey stair,
Nor find her here in the dull town,
    The sunlight on her hair,—
Yet, could we meet, my heart would greet
    And know her anywhere!

                                            January 11

THE MIRROR

POET, why wilt thou wander far afield?
    Turn again home! There, also, Nature sings,
    And to thy heart, her magic-mirror, brings
All images of life: thence will she yield
Every emotion in Man's breast concealed:
    Love, hate, ambition,—hope, that heavenward wings,—
    The peasant's toil, the care that waits on kings,—
All, in thy heart's clear crystal, full revealed.

Hast thou forgotten? One there was who turning
    His poet-vision inward, through the years,
Found Falstaff's wit, and Prospero's high yearning,
    Shared Hamlet's doubt, the madness that was Lear's,
Saw Wolsey's pride, and Romeo's passion, burning,—
    Knew Desdemona's truth, and felt her tears!

                                            January 12

THE LOVE OF LIFE

"MY son is dead!" the aged woman wailed,
    "My son, who was the only help I had!
    My good, good son is dead—my faithful lad
Who ne'er in duty to his mother failed!"

Eager to comfort her distress, I spoke
    Words that have solaced many a soul bereaved
    Since kingly David uttered them when, grieved,
First to its final loss his heart awoke.

"Though he, indeed, shall not to you return,
    Yet, sorrowing mother, you shall go to him.
    Lo, even now, your lamp of life burns dim,
And you may find him soon for whom you yearn!"

Sudden the tears ceased on that face of woe
    As the poor creature turned my words to meet,
    And sighed, to my amaze:—"Still, life is sweet!"
Then I perceived she had no wish to go.

January 13

THE HERMIT

LISTEN! O listen! 'T is the thrush—God bless him!
    How marvellously sweet the song he sings!
All Nature seems to listen and caress him,
    And Silence even closer folds her wings
Lest she should miss one faintly-throbbing note
Of high-wrought rapture, from that flute-like throat.

The warbling world, itself, is hushed about him;
    No bird essays the amœbean strain:
Each knows the soul of Music—full without him—
    Could bear no more, and rivalry were vain.
So, Daphnis singing in the tamarisk shade,
All things grew silent, of a sound afraid.

The aspens by the lake have ceased to shiver,
    As if the very zephyrs held their breath:
Hearken how, wave on wave, with notes that quiver,
    It rises now—that song of life and death!

"O holy! holy!" Was it Heaven that called
My spirit, by love's ecstasy enthralled?

                                            January 14

RETROSPECT

HOW had it been, my belovèd,
Had Fate united us sooner,—
In the bright days when our hearts
First dreamed of loving?—

When, a thrice exquisite vision,
Hope, all her lute-strings unbroken,
Smilingly beckoned us on,
Wooed us to follow?—

When our youth, eager, expectant,—
Trusting the north as the south wind,
Hardly, its pulses a-throb,
Staid life's unfolding?

Had I been more to you, dearer,
Bearing my myrtle and roses,
Than, as I came, crowned with rue,
Weighted with sorrow,

Seeing both light and its shadow,
Taught both of truth and illusion,
Knowing earth's rapture and pain,
Sharing earth's travail?

More had I been to you—dearer?...
Deep in my heart a voice answers,
Healing the sense of unworth,
Whispering comfort:—

"Love takes no counsel of prudence;
Wherefore men, timid and doubting,
Marvelling oft at his choice,
Charge him with blindness;

"But—this believe!—not Apollo,
Clothed in his glory celestial,
Bears such a light in his breast
As that which Eros

"Holds in the heart of his darkness,
Guards as a torch never failing,
Given to guide him where waits
His sole desire!"

January 15

PERDITA

(ON SEEING MISS ANDERSON IN THE RÔLE)

SHE dances,
    And I seem to be
      In primrose vales of Sicily,
Beside the streams once looked upon
By Thyrsis and by Corydon:
The sunlight laughs as she advances,
    Shyly the zephyrs kiss her hair,
And she seems to me as the wood-fawn, free,
    And as the wild rose, fair.

Dance, Perdita! and shepherds, blow!
    Your reeds restrain no longer!
Till weald and welkin gleeful ring,
Blow, shepherds, blow! and, lasses, sing,
    Yet sweeter strains and stronger!
Let far Helorus softer flow

'Twixt rushy banks, that he may hear;
Let Pan, great Pan himself, draw near!

    Stately
  She moves, half smiling
With girlish look beguiling,—
A dawn-like grace in all her face;
  Stately she moves, sedately,
  Through the crowd circling round her;
    But—swift as light—
    See! she takes flight!
Empty, alas! is her place.

Follow her, follow her, let her not go!
    Mirth ended so—
    Why, 't is but woe!
Follow her, follow her! Perdita!—lo,
  Love hath with wreaths enwound her!

    She dances,
  And I seem to see
The nymph divine, Terpsichore,
As when her beauty dazzling shone
On eerie heights of Helicon.
With bursts of song her voice entrances
  The dreamy, blossom-scented air,
And she seems to me as the wood-fawn, free,
  And as the wild rose, fair.

January 16

LET ME BELIEVE

LET me believe you, love, or let me die!
  If on your faith I may not rest secure,
  Beyond all chance of peradventure sure,
  Trusting your half-avowals sweet and shy,
As trusts the lark the pallid, dawn-lit sky—

  Then would I rather in some grave obscure
  Repose forlorn, than living on, endure
  A question each dear transport to belie!

It is a pain to thirst and do without,
  A pain to suffer what we deem unjust,
  To win a joy—and lay it in the dust;
But there's a fiercer pain—the pain of doubt;
  From other griefs Death sets the spirit free;
  Doubt steals the light from immortality!

              January 17

WHY DID YOU GO?

DEATH called,—but why did you go?
  Did you not know
That life is better than death,
That snatches the breath
Out of joy?—that love is better than death?

  Did you not understand
  How guarded the Land
Where death leads?—that howe'er the heart yearn,
One may never return
  From the gloom
Of that dwelling-place lone that doth hold and entomb?

  O my sweet!
Might I follow your feet,—
Afar from the sun and the bloom-scented air,
  I would open once more
  The inexorable door,
And drink of dark Lethe, your prison to share!

January 18

A MAID'S DEFENCE

'TWERE little to renounce what now I hold:
    A treasure that makes poor, a pomp that tires,
    A vernal glow that kindles autumn fires,
A youth that, wasteful in its haste, grows old;
'T were little to relinquish pleasure doled
    In meagre measure to my swift desires,
    To give what nor delights me nor inspires,
In free exchange for Love's all-prizèd gold;

Yet there is something it were pain to yield,
    Which I should part with, Love, in welcoming thee:
    A shy uncertainty that dearer seems
Than e'en thy gifts, my firm defence and shield:
    The dim ideal of my waking dreams,
    The Love unknown, that distant, beckons me!

January 19

TO A POET

GIVE us one dream!—
One swift, authentic vision
Of perfect loveliness to snatch the breath:
One glimpse into unchartered realms elysian
Where never cometh death!

Sing us one song
Whose accent is immortal—
Enduring as the asphodel, the flower
That blooms unfading nigh to Hades' portal:
Sing us one song of power!

Brief, if you will,—

A word of life transforming:
A word hope's wearied vision to restore:
A vital word, our human heart-blood warming,
And . . . you need write no more!

January 20

JEAN-FRANÇOIS MILLET[1]

NOT far from Paris, in fair Fontainebleau,
   A lovely, memory-haunted hamlet lies,
   Whose tender spell makes captive, and defies
Forgetfulness. The peasants come and go,—
Their backs too used to stoop,—and patient sow
   The harvest which their narrow need supplies;
   Even as when, Earth's pathos in his eyes,
Millet dwelt here, companion of their woe.

Loved Barbizon! With thorns, not laurels, crowned,
He looked thy sorrows in the face, and found—
   Vital as seed warm nestled in the sod—
The hidden sweetness at the heart of pain;
Trusting thy sun and dew, thy wind and rain,
   At home with nature, and at one with God!

January 21

TO-MORROW

THE robin chants when the thrush is dumb,
   Snow smooths a bed for the clover,
Life flames anew, and days to come
   Are sweet as the days that are over.

The tide that ebbs by the moon flows back,

---

[1] Jean-François Millet died on this day in 1875.

    Faith builds on the ruins of sorrow,
The halcyon flutters in winter's track,
    And night makes way for the morrow.

And ever a strain, of joys the sum,
    Sings on in the heart of the lover—
In death sings on—that days to come
    Are sweet as the days that are over!

                                    January 22

THE MAN-SOUL

HE made it pure—
More pure than deep-sea water, or the dew
Distilled in mountain hollows: made it true
    As heaven's o'er-arching blue,
Or as that orb that doth the main secure,
The lonely mariner's guiding cynosure.
    He made it sweet
    As lover's lips that meet
For the first time, with tremulous delight;
Or as the tears that more than half requite
Their pain after long parting: made it brave,
    Fearless of wind or wave;
A tameless thing with aspiration filled,
That dares where eagles may not nest, to build!

                                    January 23

TO FRANCE (1894)

MOTHER of Freedom! Mother and fond nurse!
    Who, from thy mighty loins, with awful throes
    And cries of anguish bore her! what new woes
Encompass thee? What long-forgotten curse
Revives to chill thy soul and dull its seeing?

Veiled are thy falcon-glances, as in death:
   Thou bleedest, France! and, sobbing, drawest breath,
Sore smitten by the thing thou gavest being!

Is this thine offspring—once so nobly fair
   That at her look were riven human chains,
   And all men blessed thee for thy travail pains?
Behold! with serpents writhing in her hair
She stands, Medusa-like, the world appalling!
   Her bloodless cheeks bespeak the vampire's lust;
   Her victims fall before her in the dust;
Yet, unappeased, she still would see them falling.

Is this blest Liberty, this treacherous thing
   That hides its venom 'neath a mask of flowers,
   That smites its own defenders, and devours
The hands that feed it? This whose rancorous sting
Is uncontrolled by reason? Red and gory,
   The standard it uplifts on land and sea
   Reveals it truly, hell-born Anarchy!
Which borrows for its shame a name of glory.

Freedom disdains the cruel and the base,
   Their praise she deems inexpiable wrong,
   And in the homage of their savage song
She hears the voice of insult and disgrace.
Scorning the ransomed slaves who rule no better
   Than the oppressors they in wrath hurl down,
   Who make the Phrygian cap a despot's crown,
And others with their broken shackles fetter—

She leaves them to the evils they invoke;
   And listening to the voices of the wild,—
   As listens for the mother's voice her child,—
Courting the tempest and the lightning-stroke,
She opens to the void her pinions regal:
   The clouds, the skies, she knows to be her own,

And rising to the mountain-summits lone,
She rests where rock the eyries of the eagle!

> January 24

THE PILGRIM

ONCE a man set forth at morning,
Journeying with eager footstep,
Onward over fields new-wakened,
Where the dew lay on the blossoms,
Like to softly gleaming opals.

All the earth, refreshed by slumber,
In the early light and tender
Wore a green, benignant beauty;
And his heart sang high within him,
As the birds sang in the branches.

On he sped with fond impatience,—
While the world took on new wonder,—
Till he came unto a river
Where there waiting stood an angel,
Dark-browed, but with look celestial.

Then, appalled, the pilgrim started:—
"Death! Awaitest thou my coming—
Here where least I thought to meet thee?
It is Love that I am seeking!"

Very gently smiled the angel,
Dark-browed, with the look celestial:
"I am Love,—thyself hast named me;
Yet thou fearest! Lo! I leave thee
Till as now thou come to find me."
   . . . .
Once again the man, at sunrise,

Journeyed forth,—his step less buoyant,—
Passing over fields new-wakened,
Where the dew lay on the blossoms
Like to softly gleaming opals.

Once again Earth, fresh from slumber,
In the early light and tender
Wore her green and mystic beauty;
Yet his heart sang not within him
As the birds sang in the branches.

Onward still, without impatience,
Through a world whose charm half pained him,
Journeying,—behold!—the river
And the long-forgotten angel—
Dark-browed, with the look celestial!

As of old, the pilgrim started,
And his pale cheek flushed with anger:
"Death, thy pledge! Thou hast betrayed me!
Naught have I and thou in common:
It is Life that I am seeking!"

With transfiguring smile the angel,
Whose whole look now showed celestial,
Answered:—"Is it Life thou seekest?"
Be at rest, thou weary pilgrim!
Seek no further: thou hast found me."

January 25

PILGRIMAGE

WANDERER from a fading strand
   Unto shadowy shores unknown,
Thou whose sails are onward fanned
By flattering breezes,—hast thou planned

All thy course alone?
Canst thou tell, now clouds begin
    To gather in thy path of day,
To what harbor thou shalt win,
As the long night closes in
    On a wider way?

Pilgrim, no: I cannot tell.
    Strange my course, and stormy woes
    And darkness may obscure its close;
Yet I feel that all is well,
    For my Pilot knows!

January 26

SUPPLIANT

FATHER, I lift my hands to Thee:
    Reject me not!
Mine eyes are blind, I cannot see.
Be Thou the lamp unto my feet,—
Guide to the rock of my retreat;
O Light, my darkness cries to Thee!
    Reject me not!

Father, mine eyes with tears are wet,
    Reject me not!
Though Thou forgive, shall I forget?
Nay, though thy mercy fall like rain,
My spirit still must bear the pain
And burden of a vast regret.
    Reject me not!

To whom, unfriended, should I flee?
    Reject me not!
To whom, my Father, but to Thee?—
Ah! 't was thy child forgave the sin

Of the repentant Magdalen,
And blessed the thief on Calvary!—
   Reject me not!

January 27

A NARROW WINDOW

A NARROW window may let in the light,
A tiny star dispel the gloom of night,
A little deed a mighty wrong set right.

A rose, abloom, may make a desert fair,
A single cloud may darken all the air,
A spark may kindle ruin and despair.

A smile, and there may be an end to strife;
A look of love, and Hate may sheathe the knife
A word—ah, it may be a word of life!

January 28

WINTER-SONG

TO him who doth remember,
   June evermore is near:
He breathes her rose amid the snows,
   And still he seems to hear
The lark from wintry fields arise
Into the blue of summer skies.

Both April and December
   Time doth to mortals bring,
But in the seed, for future need,
   Eternal waits the Spring;
And there be stars that never set,
For him who knows not to forget.

January 29

GIFTS

ONE, in her service, patient wrought,
    Striving a duteous faith to prove;
But at the last, her eyes still sought
    The face of one who gave but love

Grateful, from one she daily drew
    Strength to sustain her failing breath;
But at the last, her spirit knew
    That love is more than life—than death!

January 30

MA BELLE

THE world is full of charm, ma belle,
    And blithe as you are young;
It echoes with a silver note
    The lispings of your tongue;
It lays upon your fairy hand
    A touch as light as down;
It smiles approval, and, ma belle,
    You have not felt its frown.

The world is very rich, ma belle,
    And all its gifts are yours.
It bows before you, little one,
    And while the mood endures,
With roses, freshly garlanded,
    Your pathway bright adorns;
But roses fade, ma belle, ma belle—
    And there are left the thorns!

To snare your feet, the world, ma belle,

    Has spread a shining net,
What wonder then, believing child,
    If you awhile forget,
Midst suitors who to-night adore,
    And may to-morrow range,
A love that has been always yours—
    A love that cannot change!

What wonder!—still they whisper praise,
    And I have oft reproved;
Of love they speak with eloquence,
    And I have only loved.
Sometimes, alas, I envy them,
    Yet in the days to be,
You may forget them all, ma belle—
    But will remember me!

                                                January 31

THE NEST

GLAD is the grove with light,
    And the glen is song-caressed,
But longing comes ere night
    For the one, dear nest!

Far fields may seem more fair,
    And distant hills more blue,—
Still claims that nest my care
    In the dawn—in the dew;

For though the wild may woo
    My wing to many a quest,
Sweet in the dawn and the dew
    Are home and rest!

February 1

L'AMOUR FAIT PEUR

A COWARD is man, yet a hero
    Whose will overmasters his fear,
Till peril no longer appals him,
    And danger itself groweth dear.
Poised and strong, asking no intervention,
    He hazards the rock and the shoal;
One only thing halts his pretension,—
    Love frightens the soul.

Self-disciplined, slowly but surely,
    Disaster accustomed to brave,
He makes a companion of sorrow,
    Nor falters at threat of the grave;
Nay, often would hold it at nearer
    Approach, a beneficent goal—
But, ah! with the thought of one dearer,
    Love frightens the soul!

February 2

TOO LATE

THE words of love I never said to thee
    I whisper now,
The tenderness I might have given thee
    I offer now,
As at thy feet, who hopeless knelt to me,
    I, hopeless, bow.

The wintry bush in yonder hedgerow growing,
    A rose adorns,
And near and far are snowy clusters blowing,
    Where late were thorns;

But still my heart, nor bud nor blossom knowing,
    Unpitied mourns.

I see the bird that to his mate is winging—
    His mate so dear,
The very heart within his breast is singing
    As he draws near,
And I, O love, too late my love am bringing—
    Thou dost not hear!

                                        February 3

BESIDE A PLEASANT SHORE

I LAY upon my narrow bed,
    And dreamed life's happy moments o'er;
I thought that love my footsteps led
    Beside a pleasant shore.

Care for a moment loosed its grasp,
    And breathing deep the fragrant brine,—
My hand locked in my lover's clasp,—
    I felt his pulses throb with mine;

And dear contentment seemed my right,—
    There roaming from the world apart;
I saw his eyes, I felt their light
    Beam through the shadows, in my heart;
And waves, and trees—all nature—sang
    A pæan by that pleasant shore.
Then I awoke, and with a pang
    Remembered that we loved no more.

February 4

NO MORE, DEAR HEART

NO more, dear heart—no more I moan
The loss of happiness, your gift alone,
For quiet thoughts I keep,
And in the lengthening, grief-subduing years,
Have lost the trick and sweet distress of tears.
I smile again—again, ah me! I sleep,
And half believe my heart grown cold,
Till other happy lovers I behold.

February 5

THE HOUSE OF PAIN

UNTO the Prison House of Pain none willingly repair;
    The bravest who an entrance gain
Reluctant linger there,
For Pleasure, passing by that door, stays not to cheer the sight,
And Sympathy but muffles sound and banishes the light.

Yet in the Prison House of Pain things full of beauty blow,—
    Like Christmas-roses, which attain
Perfection 'mid the snow;
Love, entering, in his mild warmth the darkest shadows melt,
And often, where the hush is deep, the waft of wings is felt.

Ah, me! the Prison House of Pain!—what lessons there are
    bought!—
    Lessons of a sublimer strain
Than any elsewhere taught;
Amid its loneliness and gloom, grave meanings grow more clear,
For to no earthly dwelling-place seems God so strangely near.

February 6

TO ENGLAND

WE are not twain, but one: though seas divide us—
    The children of the English-speaking race—
This nothing now can change: whate'er betide us,
    This is our *birthright* grace.

The tongue that holds our earliest recollection,
    Whose accents moved us like a fond caress—
The tongue in which we lisped our first affection,
    Attaches and doth bless.

America and England knit together—
    Offspring of one great Mother, Sister Lands—
Need fear nor frowning fate nor boding weather,
    While close are joined their hands.

Beneath the ocean-billow sways the cable
    That gives them instant knowledge, each of each,
And were it sunk, their hearts would still be able
    To find a way of speech.

America, who virgin prairies planted
    To bless the alien,—Teuton, Latin, Gaul,—
Welcomes the poorest, as to realms enchanted,
    And makes them English, all!

And still, the elder, in the hour of danger,
    The bond of kinship never quite forgot,
Speaks with commanding accent to the stranger:
    "Be heedful; touch her not!"

Oh, we have felt—have felt with one another,
    Sharing each other's hope, each other's dread;
And we have wept, as children of one mother,

Mourning our cherished dead.

Is 't for ourselves this friendship hath caressed us—
    That Heaven hath strengthened so the English speech?
Nay; God forbid! the mercy that hath blessed us
    Hath a diviner reach!

If with new strength there come not larger kindness,
    Men's banners, proudly borne, were better furled;
If we no longer see, for selfish blindness,
    Beyond our realms, the world,—

Then poor, indeed, though vast our rule supernal,
    Who magnify the ill we might redeem;
Missing the glory of the hope eternal—
    The godlike, human dream!

To solace life, there blooms on earth a flower
    Whose deathless name is Love. Of its increase
Are born compassion, freedom, beauty, power;
    And of its gift is peace.

O Sister Lands, thrice blest! though wisdom guide us,
    Yet in our hearts may love perfected lie—
Deep as the ocean that cannot divide us,
    Kind as the arching sky!

                                          February 7

ADONIS

LOVE is dying; lay him low;
Pile the blossoms for his bed:
    Here, where languid poppies blow,
Pillow soft his beauteous head!
Let their dream-breath float around him,
Even as my arms enwound him—

In the summer, long ago!

Say not it was yesterday!
Hours have been as years since then!
   And shall rapture, fled away,
Never more return again?
Love, with throbbing heart of fire,—
   Love, with thrilling voice and low,—
Hast thou quenchèd fond desire
   In this breast of snow?

   Then, O Death! I cry to you
From my grief immortal:
   Goddess kind—of all most true—
Ope to me your portal!
In your calm my senses steep;
   Close mine eyes, from tears grown dim;
Give me sleep—I ask but sleep—
   In the grave, with him.

   Can it be that flowers will spring
Where all lifeless love shall lie?
   Can it be that birds will sing,
Though Adonis die?

   Never earthly bloom, I wis,
With his beauty could compare;
   Never voice was sweet as his
Who lieth there;
And, thou blue Idalian sky,
   Thou didst smile upon our lot,
And I knew my love must die,—
   But believed it not!

   Whither now to take my way?
If I seek on mountains bare,
   Or in caverns hid from day,—

Shall I find him there?
Will the rivers give him back,
    Or the woods of Adon tell?
    Will the hounds that loved him well
Follow in his track?
Ah, the distance matters not,
    Nor the way I, mournful, tread:
Every path leads *from* the spot
    Where my love lies dead!

                                  February 8

DIDST THOU REJOICE?

DIDST thou rejoice because the day was fair,—
    Because, in Orient splendor newly dressed,
    On flowering glebe and bloomless mountain-crest
The sun complacent smiled? Ah! didst thou dare
The careless rapture of that bird to share
    Which, soaring toward the dawn from dewy nest,
    Hailed it with song? From Ocean's treacherous breast
Didst borrow the repose mild-mirrored there?

Thou foolish heart! Behold! the light is spent;
    Rude thunders shake the crags; songs timorous cease;
Lo! with what moan and mutinous lament
    Ocean his pent-up passions doth release!
O thou who seekest sure and fixed content,
    Search in thy soul: there find some source of peace.

                                  February 9

THE HEART OF LOVE

I KNOW a place warm-sheltered from the world—
    A place secure, in mild conditions blest,
Where fainting Toil, the homespun banner furled,

May pause awhile and rest:
I know a place where fires burn late,
And Mercy, waiting at the gate,
    Still welcomes the oppressed!

I know a shrine more rich than Plutus' fane.
    An altar fragrant with celestial dew,
Where wavering souls their virgin faiths regain
    And energies renew.
I know a garden fair and free,
Where life yet wears, unfadingly,
    Lost Eden's roseate hue!

February 10

THE UNFINISHED SYMPHONY

To Carl Pohlig

The inspired Leader of the Philadelphia Orchestra, on listening to the great Schubert.

O MUSIC of divine imagining!
    Does he not hear you in his dreams to-night?
Can you no wonder to his spirit bring—
    And no delight?

His love created you; his hopes, his fears,
    Are poignant in these tones, surmounting death—
These melodies that dim the eyes with tears,
    And snatch the breath! . . .

And can he longer sleep, nor note this strain
    Whose magic enters now, with lovelier art
That like a benediction thrills the brain
    And fills the heart?

Ah, not to one shall all earth's joys belong!
    So have the gods ordained, whom we obey,
Lest mortal men should deem themselves as strong,
    As blest as they.

On Schubert, out of love, the ecstasy
    That wrote this godlike music they conferred:
To us they gave to *hear* the symphony
    He never heard.

February 11

WINTER THE NURSERY FOR SPRING FLOWERS

DEATH wished to borrow something of thy grace;
    And now that thou art lying 'neath the snow,
The grave that holds thee seems a favored place,
    Where one might willing go.
But life is not so rich in things divine,
That it would part with such a soul as thine!
A voice of comfort breathes from sorrowing Earth
    If winter is the nursery of flowers,
If purity and loveliness have worth
    Beyond this world of ours,
If there is pity for the tears we shed,
If any truly live—thou art not dead![2]

February 12

HIS FACE[3]

THEY tell you Lincoln was ungainly, plain?
    To some he seemed so: true.
Yet in his look was charm to gain

---

[2] Helen Bell died on this day in 1895.
[3] Abraham Lincoln was born on this day in 1809.

      E'en such as I, who knew
With how confirmed a will he tried
To overthrow a cause for which I would have died.

The sun may shine with naught to shroud
      Its beam yet show less bright
Than when from out eclipsing cloud
      It pours its radiant light;
And Lincoln seen amid the shows of war
Clothed in his sober black, was somehow felt the more

To be a centre and a soul of power,—
      An influence benign
To kindle in a faithless hour
      New trust in the divine.
Grave was his visage, but no cloud could dull
The radiance from within that made it beautiful.

A prisoner, when I saw him first—
      Wounded and sick for home—
His presence soothed my yearning's thirst
      While yet his lips were dumb;
For such compassion as his countenance wore
I had not seen nor felt in human face before.

And when, low-bending o'er his foe,
      He took in his firm hand
My wasted one, I seemed to know
      We two were of one Land;
And as my cheek flushed warm with young surprise,
God's pity looked on me from Lincoln's sorrowing eyes.

His prisoner I was from then—
      Love makes surrender sure—
And though I saw him not again,
      Some memories endure,
And I am glad my untaught worship knew

His the divinest face I ever looked into!

> February 13

LEADERS OF MEN

WHEN they are dead, we heap the laurels high
Above them where, indifferent, they lie:
    We join their deeds to unaccustomed praise,
    And crown with garlands of immortal bays
Whom, living, we but thought to crucify.

As mountains seem less glorious viewed too nigh,
So, often, do the great whom we decry
    Gigantic loom to our astonished gaze—
        When they are dead;

For, shamed by largeness, littlenesses die;
And partisan and narrow hates put by,
    We shrine our heroes for the future days;
    And to atone our ignorant delays
With fond and emulous devotion try,—
        When they are dead!

> February 14

A VALENTINE

FEAR not that I shall tell the world,
    O lady mine, how sweet thou art,
Fear not that others so shall gain
    The secret of my heart;
For though my lips should carol praise
    From night till morn, from morn till eve,
Thy loveliness, O lady mine,
    Who had not known could not believe!

To praise the rose is not to paint
    Its perfume, in the air afloat;
No words can voice the violet,
    Or trill the throstle's note;
Nor may I fondly hope in song
    Thy mystic graces to impart,—
Who hath not known thee, lady mine,
    Will never dream how sweet thou art!

                                                February 15

CUPID AND THE MUSES

"Revetior illas, mater; nam venerandae sunt, et semper quiddam commeditantur..."—Lucian.

ONCE lovely Venus to her wayward boy—
    Her wilful torment and her keen delight—
Spake chidingly:—"Why must you me annoy
    With your capricious wiles by day and night?
Perplexing child, display your arts elsewhere:
Turn you to those whom idly now you spare!
    Cold in content, and armored in their pride,
Behold the Muses!—let them claim your care!"
    To whom the laughing Cupid: "Nay, I've tried
What ways I know, to move those ladies fair;
    But, ah, my mother, they're so occupied!"

February 16

PILGRIM SONG[4]

WRITTEN FOR THE SOCIETY OF MAYFLOWER DESCENDANTS IN THE STATE OF PENNSYLVANIA.

PILGRIMS of the trackless deep,
    Leaving all, our fathers came,
Life and liberty to keep
    In Jehovah's awful name.
Neither pillared flame nor cloud
    Made the wild, for them, rejoice,
But their hearts, with sorrow bowed,
    In the darkness heard His voice.

Things above them they divined—
    Thoughts of God, forever true,
And the deathless Compact signed—
    Building better than they knew:
Building liberty not planned,
    Law that ampler life controls,
All the greatness of our land
    Lying shadowed in their souls.

In the days that shall succeed,
    Prouder boast no time shall grant
Than to be of them, indeed,
    Children of their Covenant:
Children of the promised day,
    Bound by hope and memory,
Brave, devoted, wise, as they—
    Strong with love's humility.

---

[4] Set to music in 1900, "The Pilgrims" was sung by members and guests at an annual meeting of the Society of Mayflower Descendants in the Commonwealth of Pennsylvania (SMDPgallipoliA) in Philadelphia on this day in 1900.

February 17

THE LAND OF PROMISE

ALTHOUGH the faiths to which we fearful clung
    Fall from us, or no more have might to save;
    Although the past, recalling gifts it gave,
    O'er lost delights a doleful knell have rung;
Although the present, forth from ashes sprung,
    Postpone from day to day what most we crave,
    And, promising, beguile us to the grave,—
Yet, toward the Future, we are always young!

It smiles upon us in last lingering hours,
    If with less radiance, with a light as fair,
        As tender, pure, as in our childish years:
It is the fairy realm of fadeless flowers;
    Of songs and ever-springing fountains, where
        No heart-aches come, no vain regrets, no tears!

February 18

COMPENSATION

WHEN Winter's sovereignty complete
    Has left us not a leaf to cull,
Then come the feathery snow and sleet:
    So God doth love the beautiful!

February 19

IN WINTER-TIME

HOW sweet it is 'neath apple-blooms to lie,
    And breathe their breath!
To peep through waving branches at the sky,
To feel the zephyrs as they idle by,

And question of the brooklet what it saith!

How sweet it is to roam through the green wold
    When labors cease!
To hear the tranquil tale by Nature told—
The tale that was not young, and grows not old—
    To find within the heart an answering peace!

And though apart from Nature we maintain
    An alien quest,
How sweet that we shall leave the strife and strain
Some blessèd morn, and wander back again,
    And close our eyes, and in her bosom rest!

                                              February 20

IN WINTER

IT will be long ere 'neath the sunlight dimpling,
    The mountain snows melt back to earth's still breast,
Ere swallows build, and wayward brooklets wimpling
    O'er pebbly beds, wind by the pewee's nest,
Ere swells the lily's cup, ere transport strong
Thrills in the bluebird's lay,—it will be long!

It will be long ere dews and fresh'ning showers
    Descend where latticed roses languid burn,
Ere, pale from exile, nodding wayside flowers
    And timid woodland darlings home return,
Ere vesper-sparrows chant their Delphian song,
And larks at sunrise sing,—it will be long!

But though fierce blow the winds through forests shrouded,
    Where snows, for leafy verdure, cheerless cling,
Though seas moan wild, and skies are darkly clouded,—
    Within the heart that loves 't is always spring!
There memories and hopes, fresh-budding, throng,

And faith forgets that Winter lingers long.

February 21

CONSCIENCE

THE friend I loved betrayed my trust
And bowed my spirit to the dust.
I keep the hurt he gave, yet know
He was forgiven long ago.

From him I did not merit ill,
But I would bear injustice still,
Content, could years of guiltless woe
Undo the wrong I did my foe.

February 22

SELF-CONFIDENT YOUTH

THE earth is mine and its myriad flowers,
   And the stars are mine: I shall count them all;
As I hasten on with expanding powers,
   No cloud-capped peak shall my strength appal.

I will measure my might 'gainst the might of Ocean,
   In ships of my building, its wastes will dare;
I will learn of the swallow its swift-winged motion,
   And ride as it rides, through the fields of Air! . . .

I marvel my fathers have been contented
   To live and to labor in ways time-worn:
That to Fate's denials they e'er consented,
   Solaced by trifles my soul would scorn!

For the tired old world I will write a story
   That none of her children has told before:

A tale of adventure and love, whose glory
    Shall glow in her annals forevermore.

To the depths, to the heights I am called to inherit,
    I will climb, will descend, without fear of fall,
In the perilous joy of a dauntless spirit
    That nothing shall have—if it have not All!

February 23

KEATS[5]

BY the pyramid of Caius Sestius,
    Unmarked for honour or remembrance save
    By a meek epitaph, there is a grave
For sake of which, o'er oceans perilous,
As to a shrine, uncounted pilgrims come;
    Each bringing tribute unto one who gave
    Life beauty,—the one thing man still must crave,
Though worshiping from far, with passion dumb.

The Eternal City by the Tiber holds,
    In the broad view of Buonarotti's dome,—
    With all its treasure,—naught that is more dear
Than the low mound that easefully enfolds
    The English poet who lies buried here
By the pyramid outside the walls of Rome.

February 24

SECURE

OUR single lives are circled round
    By an embracing sea;
Are joined to all that has been, bound

---

[5] John Keats died on this day in 1821.

To all that is to be;
The past and future meet and cross,
And in life's ocean is no loss.

We know there is no loss—and yet—
　　Dismayed, perplexed,—poor dupes of time—
　　We see youth stricken ere its prime,
And in our grief forget.
But pitying Nature takes our part:
Slowly she heals the breaking heart,

And Sorrow's self procures us gain;
　　For in her steps ascending higher,
We come, at last, where waits nor pain
　　Nor unfulfilled desire,—
Finding the path lit from above
That leads from love—to Love!

Nothing is premature with God:
　　His are the harvest-time and sowing,
The seedling nestled in the sod,
　　The flower in beauty blowing,
The languid ebb, the eager flow,
The pulse of spring, the brooding snow.

　　　　　　　　　　　　　　　February 25

TRANSITION

AWAKE my soul!
　　Thou shalt not creep and crawl—
　　An earth-bound creature, pitiful and small,
Whose weak ambition knows no higher goal!
O wistful soul,

When morning sings,
　　Forgetful of the night,

Bathe all thy restless being in the light;
Till 'neath the mesh that close about thee clings
Thou feel thy wings!

Then find life's door,—
    Trusting the instinct true
    That points to Heaven and the aerial blue,
A wingèd thing impelled forevermore
To soar and soar!

February 26

CONFLICT AND REST

THROUGH the long voyage we may welcome day,
    Glad when the night is gone,
So many threat'ning perils of the way
    Vanish before the dawn;

And yet a deeper darkness we may crave
    When strife indeed is past,
And we from stress of tempest and of wave
    Are nearing port at last.

February 27

HENRY WADSWORTH LONGFELLOW[6]

IF tasting Heliconian springs
    He of their waters drank not deep,
If, smiling, he beheld not things
    Revealed to eyes that weep,
If dread Dodona's Oracle
    And Delphi's voice for him were mute,
If grave Minerva in his path

---

[6] Henry Wadsworth Longfellow was born on this day in 1807.

Dropped never silver flute,—

Yet beauty wove a magic spell
    For him, and early, at his need,
Upon a bed of asphodel
    He found a tuneful reed,—
The Syrinx-reed Thessalian,
    Of plaintive, far renown,
The universal pipe of Pan,—
    Where the god laid it down.

Right reverently from the ground
    He lifted up the sacred thing,
Accepted it with awe profound,
    With faith unfaltering;
And when its music forth he drew
    Earth half forgot her ancient pain,
For Marsyas himself ne'er blew
    A purer, sweeter strain!

What though there be who self-attired
    In robes of judgment some misuse,
Protest that he was not inspired
    By the authentic Muse,—
Love, granting all his faults to these,
    Forever holds his name apart,
Who moved not senseless stones and trees,
    But the quick human heart.

"The people's poet." Did he lack
    Return? He served in his degree
The people, and they gave him back
    Their immortality!
Time careless grows of costly wit,
    Brave monuments are quickly gone,—
But that which on the heart is writ
    Lives on, and on, and on!

February 28

HENRY JAMES[7]

YOU were not of one country. To one Race,
    Rather, you gave your spirit's full devotion.
Careless a little as to bounds of space
    Set by dividing hill or severing ocean,
An exiled patriot, wherever dwelling,
    An alien on either side the sea,
You gave your loyalty, through love's compelling,
    To English speech and English liberty.

We claim you—both, drawn closer through your coming,
    England and she that nursed you at her breast.
Beauty you loved, and ne'er from truth went roaming,
    Through all the long desire, the ardent quest.
Ah, never quite at home, but ever homing,
    Passionate pilgrim, you have found your rest!

February 29

BEFORE THE HOUR

UNTIMELY blossom! poor, impatient thing,
    That starting rashly from the sheltering mould
    Bravest the peevish wind and sullen cold,
    Mistaking thine own ardors for the spring!—
Thou to my heart a memory dost bring
    Of hopes once fair like thee, like thee too bold
    To breathe their fragrance, and their flowers unfold,
    That droop'd, of wintry rigors languishing.

Nor birds, nor bees, nor waters murmuring low,

---

[7] Henry James died on this day in 1916.

    Nor breezes blown from any Arcady,
        Found they,—earth's welcome waiting to bestow;
    Yet sweet, they felt, sweeter than dreams, would be
        The summer they had sought too soon to know,—
        The summer they should never live to see!

March 1

FOR THE BIRTHDAY OF WILLIAM DEAN HOWELLS[8]

SEVENTY-FIVE glad years of blessing,
    And the hope of blessing more;
Memories the heart caressing,
    Dreams that beckoning wait, before;

Life—full life, made rich by giving:
    Life that can create, and lend
To the poor—delight in living,
    To the lonely—many a friend

Wisdom that can teach through laughter—
    Seeming but to entertain,
Or through pathos which, thereafter,
    Leaves no dull, regretful pain;

Years of blessing, years of kindness,
    And the courage that can smile
Though the eyes be dim to blindness
    With a sorrow, hid the while,—

These are thine, thou selfless schemer,
    Chanter of brave *carmina*:
These thy gifts to us, dear dreamer,—
    Traveler from Altruria.

---

[8] William Dean Howells was born on this day in 1837.

March 2

A FAREWELL

"The utmost for the highest."—*Motto of* George F. Watts.

AVE! Thou goest from us,
    Apart from us to dwell;
Through sacrifice to find thyself.
    Ave!—but not farewell.

Thou hast dreamed a dream of Leisure;
    Thou hast heard her call thy name,—
The handmaid of enduring Art,
    Who feeds the quenchless flame,—
And after the Ideal
    Thou wistfully would'st fare,
Before whose shrine 't is blest to wait,
    Though ne'er to enter there!

Go forth,—for thou hast willed it,
    Untrammelled as the sea!
To find new forms of loveliness,
    Go forth! Lo, thou art free
To hope, to learn, to listen,
    To be breathed upon, inspired,
To wait on the unhasting gods,
    With soul intent, untired;

Careless of gain or profit,
    Of markets, or applause,
To yield thy heart to Nature's heart,
    To learn her dearer laws;
To gaze beyond the present,—
    From the fleeting view of things,
To lift the vision up and up;
    To feel the growth of wings;

Through love and self-denial,
    To gain at last the goal
That hidden from the vulgar gaze
    Beckons the purer soul;
Naught asking of the moment,
    Content to strive and strive,
Knowing when lesser gods depart,
    The gods themselves arrive!
   . . . . . .

Ave! Thou goest from us,
    Apart from us to dwell;
Through sacrifice to find thyself.
    Ave!—but not farewell!

March 3

LIFE

THOU art more ancient than the oldest skies,
But youth forever glances from thine eyes;
    Time wars against thee, and consumes thy fires,
Yet, wingèd, thou from ashes dost arise!

March 4

TO-DAY

WHERE hast thou gone, my Day?
    I meant to follow,
Extracting from thine every hour its sweet;
    But thou, beguiling hope with pledges hollow,
Art flown on wingèd feet.

Hardly I greet thy morn,
    The glory dwindles;
And as I plan thy moments with delight,
    The evening-primrose in my pathway kindles

Her taper for the night.

Ah, too precipitate!
    Might I not linger
To gather a stray blossom by the way,
    But pointing onward with thy warning finger,
Thou must outstrip me, Day?

Gladly I welcomed thee,
    An eager lover
Who deemed he knew each fleeting moment's cost,
    Is there no way, no method, to recover
The treasure I have lost?

Ah, no! From Time, alas!
    One may not borrow;
Nor move him what is squandered to restore.
      The tide flows back, and there may dawn a morrow.
    Thee I shall find no more.

                                            March 5

MEMORIA

IF only in my dreams I may behold you,
    Still hath the day a goal;
If only in my dreams I may enfold you,
    Still hath the night a soul.
Leaden the hours may press upon my spirit,
    Nor one dear pledge redeem,—
I will not chide, so they at last inherit
    And crown me with the rapture of that dream.

Ten thousand blossoms earth's gay gardens cherish;
    One pale, pale rose is mine.
Of frost or blight the rest may quickly perish,—
    Not so that rose divine.

Deathless it blooms in quiet realms Elysian;
    And when toil wins me rest,
Forgetful of all else, in blissful vision
    I breathe my rose, and clasp it to my breast!

March 6

DU MAURIER[9]

TWO rocked his infant cradle as he slept,
    And crooned for him their native lullabies.
One gave her sense of beauty to his eyes,
    One taught his heart her smiles, the tears she wept.
Each made him love her as the child his home,
    And, mother-wise, reclaimed his wandering glance:
    Belovèd England and belovèd France,—
Each drew him, though, afar, he could not come.

In his imagination, fleur-de-lis
    And English daisy blossomed side by side,
And dreams were his, lost transports to renew.
Half exiled wheresoe'er he chanced to be,
    Like migrant birds his thoughts went soaring wide,
Wooed onward by the vision of the True!

March 7

DITTY: MY TRUE LOVE'S EYES

MY true-love's eyes are a surprise
    To put an end to ranging;
They vary so,—come weal, come woe,—
    One can but watch their changing!

Sometimes they shine with light divine,—

---

[9] George du Maurier was born on this day in 1834.

    Twin deeps where moonbeams hover,—
Anon they seem like stars agleam,
    With laughter brimming over.

My true-love's mouth is as the south
    In time of blossom, sunny;
A rose, in death, bequeathed it breath,
    And bees have lent it honey.

But oh, her heart is still the art,
    The magic fresh and living,
That wins the free her slaves to be
    By its own gift of giving!

March 8

AFTER THE PLAY

YOU say I'm dying! It is so, I think:
All pain has left me, and I seem to sink—
A child, content, back to the Mother's breast.
Life grew full sweet of late,—but death is best.

I wanted just this one last quiet hour
To tell you how hope grew fruition's flower,—
Giving me, in a moment, bliss to know,
Beyond what tranquil ages might bestow.

You must not weep, my friend! Consider still
How many lives go frustrate of their will;
How many spend in vain, and fruitless tire!—
I near the goal of my supreme desire.

Your tears reproach the happiness I feel,
And from this dear contentment something steal.
Smile, if you can, beloved! nor delay
What I would tell you ere I go my way.

. . . .
Love gives but as Love will: this have I proved,
Who through long wistful years have vainly loved,
Yet find my life at last on death's sheer brink—
From lethal fountains purest rapture drink.
. . . .
You know 't was not my right to dream of her,
Though I had served her long—love's pensioner—
Grateful for modest favor at her hands,
For mere acceptance, or for mild commands;

But on that night, across the theatre
I saw her come, and felt the restless stir
Of mad desires held in leash till then:
A longing to stand equal with the men

Who, for no merit, dared to keep her side,
Suspecting not the barriers that divide
Natures like hers from those of meaner birth.
I knew her throned above me, felt the worth

Of things they recked not of—her richest dower—
Yet longed that life should yield me for one hour
The right to stand before her—even as these?
Nay; but the right to fall before her knees,

To touch in worship her white garment's hem,
To win the smile so lightly given them
Because her heart with happiness o'erflowed,
Unconscious of the largess it bestowed.

Ah, me!—to think, what barren pain I felt!
Hopeless as one who in a desert dwelt,
Exiled from all that made his soul's delight,
I gazed upon her,—was it, friend, last night?

The Play—what matter? It drew near the end,

Scarce marked by me. You know the rest, my friend:
Waiting I sat there full of sad desire,
When, suddenly, it came—that cry of "Fire!"

How suddenly! I started to my feet:
But—as when two on-rushing torrents meet
And break the one the other—mad with fear,
The panic-stricken people, deaf to hear

Counsel or warning, in that burning tomb
Hurtled each other, battling to their doom.
Kind God, blot out the scene—soon past!
I to a column near me clinging fast,

Resisted the fell tide that onward bore
Its helpless prey with hideous uproar.
Twice had I lost my footing; yet I clave,
As one who struggles more than life to save,—

My every thought of her; but when at last,
Sore bruised and breathless, as one shoreward cast
After rude shipwreck, I dared raise my eyes,
Seeking in that vast Hell my Paradise,—

There, like some virgin image carved in stone,
She stood in her white radiance—alone.
Where were the men that loved her, as they said?
Ah, bitter "where"! They, all, too rashly fled,

Had entered that ignoble human strife,
Paying a shameful price for paltry life.
She read my soul, I think; and then—she smiled.
Nay, friend,—imagine not my speech grown wild!

I tell you true: in that appalling place
She smiled—the calm of Heaven in her face:
Her service had been long my soul's emprise;

Yet a new, wistful wonder lit her eyes,

And pale—ay, pale as Hades' death-crowned queen,
Across the fatal barriers between,
Her glad look seemed to say:—"At last, I know!
You, who alone have loved me, *could* not go!

"All help were vain. Stay!—let me see your face!"
So plead the look; then, with a poignant grace,
Her form bent toward me, her white arms apart,
She gave me the veiled secret of her heart.

Think you we marked the fiery sepulchre
In which we stood,—thence nevermore to stir?
A glory strange enwrapt us. Then, my friend,
I woke, and saw your face, and knew the end,—

Not that which you *suppose*—the end of strife,
Not dissolution—and not loss—but life!
. . . .
I think she felt no anguish, knew no fear,
So mercifully swift the flames drew near;

For, even as she smiled, narcotic death
Enveloped her and stifled her sweet breath;
And the fire passed her by and left her there,
Like to a sleeping child, untouched and fair.
. . . .
All—all that life withheld—is mine at last!
With love, with God,—believe me,—there's no past.
The future waits; it calls—I must not stay!
The night is over,—look! the dawn of Day!

March 9

CRUEL LOVE—ANACREONTIC

I LOOKED from out my window once
    And saw Love standing there;
No cloak had he to cover him,
    His dimpled feet were bare,
And fast and chill the snowflakes fell
    On his ambrosial hair.

He lifted up to mine a face
    Filled with celestial light;
Fond, fond with pity grew my heart
    To see his hapless plight,
And down I sped to offer him
    Warm shelter for the night:—

"Come in, come in, thou tender child,
    A wanderer from thine own!
Hath all the world abandoned thee,
    That thou art thus alone?
Come in, come in! that straightway I
    For others may atone!"

I took his icy hand in mine,—
    Why swifter throbbed each vein?
Was it the impulse of my blood
    To ease his frozen pain?—
Yet still his lips refused to smile,
    Still fell his tears like rain.

Bashful he seemed, as half inclined
    To shiver there apart:
I led him closer to the fire,
    I drew him to my heart:
Ah, cruel Love! my trustful breast

He wounded with a dart!

Ah, cruel Love! He smiled at last—
    A wondrous smile to see!
And passing from my sheltering door,
    With step alert and free,
He took my warmth, my joy with him,—
    His tears he left to me!

March 10

LOVE CONQUERS DEATH

LOVE conquers Death by night and day,
Beguiles him long of his destined prey;
    And when, at last, that seems to perish
    Which he hath striven still to cherish,
Love plucks the soul from the fallen clay.

Death is not master, but Love's slave,
He smites the timid and the brave;
    Yet as he fares, with sweet low laughter,
    Love, the sower, follows after,
Scattering seed in each new-made grave!

March 11

A DÉBUTANTE

    AT last, for weariness,
She slept, yet breathed in dreams a fragrance of success
    Sweeter to her desires than cooling showers,
    Than honey hived in flowers,
Or than those notes which ere the night is done,
Are shyly fluted forth in worship of the sun.
    The longed-for prize
    Her own, again she heard delighted plaudits rise,

    Again her conquest read in beaming eyes,
And scanned each upturned face, and missed but one!

    "O love," she, dreaming, sighed,—
In joy grown sudden sad, and lonely in her pride,—
    "O love, dost thou, of all the world, not care
    These triumphs dear to share?
Dost thou, who sued in griefs to bear a part,
Who lightened discontent, and soothed with heavenly art,
        Forbearing blame—
    Remove when all besides with praises speak my name?"
    Distinct, yet as from far, the answer came:
"Love still demands an undivided heart!"

March 12

DAPHNIS

HAIL, Solitude! hail, maiden coy and sweet!
The vesper veil descends,—hail, nymph discreet!
We would awhile forget the din and roar
Of feverous life, contending evermore,—
    Lead to thy hush'd retreat!

Where shall we find thee, who desire thee so?
Where 'midst the lengthening shadows dost thou go?
Where slumberest thou when stars the night adorn?
    Where glide thy feet at morn?

Seek they that rugged promontory
Where Athos towers lone above the sea?
Stray they where 'gainst the mountains hoary
Axenos moaning beats incessantly?
Or all the day in some shy sylvan nook,
Where cowslips pale and daffadillies blow,
Tread they the mellow turf, or weedy brook
Whose wimpling waters prattle as they flow?

Goddess with breath of balm,
What dear contentments nestle in thy calm!
The leveret and the fawn pursue
Thy paths through coverts dim, the halcyon blue,
By seas Ægean, grieved remembrance heals.
    As she thy joyance feels,
And far below the merry-twinkling waves,
Bright Thetis breathes thy praise in orient caves.

And here, in this delightful wood,
Where saucy elves and winsome fairies bide,
We, also, would draw near thee, Solitude,
    And lay our cares aside:
Draw near thee, nymph demure, and drain,
From flowery cups that know no touch profane,
The dews, delicious brimming,
    Recline where poppies, purple-hued,
Droop low in lovely lassitude,
While belted bees in amorous mood
O'er thymy beds are swimming,
Or musing 'neath some drowsy hemlock, gain
The sweet Morphæan anodyne for pain.

Long, long ago, to such seclusion—
Filled with accusing shame and grieved confusion—
Life's noontide dark, its promise dead,
The youthful Daphnis fled.
Child of the God, ill could he brook
That curious eyes should gaping look
    Upon the sightless face,
Where, deeply written, burned his deep disgrace.
Fearful of wrongs he could not see,
He brought his bruisèd heart to thee.

And thou with solemn stillness didst caress him.
Forbearing to afflict with comfort crude,
Mistimed advice or cheap solicitude,

Thou with thy mild tranquillity didst bless him.
Thou didst not proffer fond, unmeaning words;
But whisperings of leaves, and notes of birds,
And breathings of fresh flowers; things which stole
Through the unlighted chambers of his soul,
And made him—how, he knew not—less alone.
Like dreams that come where misery hath slept,
Recalling tender hopes and pleasures flown,
    He welcomed them, and wept.

Then with unsteady hand from out his breast
He drew the pipe of Pan—the reedy flute
That long neglected in inglorious rest,
Dark, like his vision, lay there cold and mute.
Up to his quivering lips he raised it slowly;
A moment paused, then blew a fainting strain:
His rigid brow relaxed, his head drooped lowly,
He felt the old, the sweet, immortal pain!
Again the mellow, melting notes he tried,—
Again meek Echo caught her breath and sighed.

Then freer, stronger, lovelier grew the lay;
Uncertain fears fled guiltily away;
The lilies, listening, paled, the breeze grew whist,
The violets flushed to deeper amethyst,
The restless Hours, departing, longed to stay.
And he forgot his melancholy state,
Fair Nomia's blissful love and fatal hate,—
In the rapt exaltation of his mind,
Forgot that he was blind;
And poured that moving music in thine ear,
Which still Sicilian shepherds in the dawn
And deepening twilight, from some balmy lawn
Or grove of Ætna, fondly think they hear.

March 13

FRITZ SCHEEL[10]

HE gave his life to Music,—gave—
    For love, not hire,—himself denying;
His body rests, o'erwearied, in the grave,
    But Music lives and gives him life undying.

In the deep silence, may he hear
    Such harmonies as he could wake,
And O, may some faint accents reach his ear
    From the great City's heart that sorrows for his sake!

March 14

BASE-BORN

MY parents had great joy, I wis,
    Of their young days of love.
In thought they were as deathless gods,
    Mere human laws above:
As deathless gods! But I?—alas!
    Of joy what can I tell?
Who am but as a broken vase
    Beside a brimming well.

My parents in each other's eyes
    Beheld the heavenly stars,
And found in one another's arms
    The bliss that heaven unbars:
They vowed when pleasure filled the cup
    None should resist its spell:
They quaffed,—and emptied me of joy,
    Beside life's brimming well!

---

[10] Fritz Scheel died on this day in 1907.

March 15

AN ADIEU

SORROW, quit me for a while!
    Wintry days are over;
Hope again, with April smile,
    Violet sows and clover.

Pleasure follows in her path,
    Love itself flies after,
And the brook a music hath
    Sweet as childhood's laughter.

Not a bird upon the bough
    Can repress its rapture,
Not a bud that blossoms now
    But doth beauty capture. . . .

Sorrow, thou art Winter's mate,
    Spring cannot regret thee;
Yet, ah, yet—my friend of late—
    I shall not forget thee!

March 16

THE CLOUDS

THE clouds give back to earth again
    The moisture they absorb;
An atom floating in the sun
    Is lasting as an orb.

We fear lest ill should fly itself,
    And wrong at last prevail:
Lest good should lack its just reward
    And light untimely fail:

We falter, and distrust the fate
    We may not understand,
Interrogate the oracle,
    When God is close at hand.

And still the clouds go drifting by,
    Or fall in fruitful rain;
High over us the stars, undimmed,
    Benignant shine again;

And from that temple, viewless, vast,
    Where failure is unknown,
The Father of existences
    Keeps watch above his own.

March 17

THE IRISH SHAMROCK IN SOUTH AFRICA

O LITTLE plant, so meek and slight,
    Tinct with the emerald of the sea
Which like a mother, day and night,
      Croons melodies to thee;
Emblem of Erin's hope and pride!
Though crushed and trampled under foot,
    Thou still art found
    The meadows round,
Up-springing from thine own sweet root!

Of sorrow thou hast been the sign
    Through weary, unforgiving years;
The dews upon thy tender vine
    Have seemed thy country's tears;
Now, now, forevermore, thou art
    Symbol of all that's brave and true—
      Blest as a smile
      Of thy sunlit isle,

In the Old World honored, and the New!

   For they lie asleep in a land of strangers,—
Far from the home their fame endears—
     The Inniskillings, the Connaught Rangers,
        The Dublin Fusiliers;
   And the little plant they loved so well—
     Better than fairest flower that blows—
       Is set apart
       In Britannia's heart
With the Scottish thistle and the rose:

Is set apart, and never again
    Shall human eyes the shamrock see
Without a thought of the heroes slain
    Whose splendid loyalty,
Stronger than ancient hate or wrong,
Sublimed them 'midst the battle's hell—
     A tidal wave
     From the souls of the brave,
That made them deathless as they fell!

                                              March 18

DIVINATION

HOW do you know the Spring is nigh,
    Heart, my heart?
Is it a something in the sky?
Is it a perfume wafted by?
Or is it your own longing's cry—
    Heart, my heart?

Oh, yes, I know you 've ways to tell,
    Heart, my heart,
When Spring released from Winter's spell
Sows amaranth and asphodel:

Ways tender and impalpable,
    Heart, my heart:

Signs that have never yet betrayed,
    Heart, my heart:—
The bluebird's note in a leafless glade,
An answering rapture, half afraid,
The dream-filled eyes of a shy, sweet maid,—
    Heart, my heart!

                                            March 19

THOMAS BAILEY ALDRICH[11]

1836-1907

WE celebrate with pomp and pride
    A Cromwell or a Wellington;
We venerate who, self-denied,
    Earth's higher victories have won;
But through the all-remembering years,
We love who give us smiles and tears.

The voice that charmed us may grow still,
    The poet cease to weave his spell:
Ascended to the skyey hill
    Remote, where the immortals dwell,—
Time to our thought but more endears
    Who gave us smiles and gave us tears.

---

[11] Thomas Bailey Aldrich died on this day in 1907.

March 20

PERSEPHONE

THE wild bird's first exultant strain
    Says,—"Winter is over—over!"
And spring returns to the world again,
    With breath as of lilac and clover.

With a certain soft, appealing grace
    (Surely some sorrow hath kissed her!)
She gives to our vision her girlish face,
    And we know how we've missed her—missed her!

For on a day she went away,
    Long ere the leaves were falling,
And came no more for the whitethroat's lay,
    Or the pewee's plaintive calling.

In tender tints on her broidered shoon
    Blossomed the leaves of the myrtle,
And silky buds of the darling June
    Were gathered up in her kirtle;

And fair, fair, fair, in her sunlit hair
    Were violets intertwining,
That seemed more fresh and unfading there
    Than with dewdrops on them shining!

She hid them all in her dim retreat;
    But, heart! a truce to sighing;
She's here—incomparably sweet,
    Unchanging and undying!

We see her brow, and we rejoice,
    Her cheek, as it pales and flushes,
We hear once more in her thrilling voice

The note of the woodland thrushes;

And through her lashes, tear-empearled,
   A mystic light is breaking,
And all the love of the whole wide world
   Seems in her eyes awaking!

March 21

O GIORNO FELICE!

MY store is spent; I am fain to borrow:
   Give me to drink of a vintage fine!
Pour me a draught—a draught of To-morrow,
   Brimming and fresh from a rock-cool shrine:
Nectar of earth,
For the longing and dearth
Of a heart still young,
That waiteth and waiteth a song unsung!

Glad be the strain!
In the cup pour no pain:
Leave at the brim not a taste of sorrow!
   Spring would I sing! For the bird flies free,
   The sap is astir in the oldest tree,
And the Maiden weaves,
Mid a laughter of leaves,
   The bud and the blossom of joys to be! . . .

Ay, Winter took all;
But I heard the Spring call,
And my heart, denied,
With a rapturous shiver—
Like that that makes eager the pulse of the river
   When something at last tells it Winter is past—
Awoke at the sound of her voice, and replied.
   A libation to Spring!—ah, quickly! pour fast!

She is there! She is here!—in the sky—on the sea—
In the Morning-Land waiting my heart and me!

March 22

THE RETURN OF PROSERPINE

TO welcome her the Mother wakes
    The myriad music of her rills,
And trims the border of her lakes
    With sun-lit daffodils:
Softly she counterpanes the leas,
    With primrose-bloom bedecks the vales,
    While answering her wooing gales
Come ruby-pied anemones;
And as her wintry doubts depart,
    And brightening hopes foretell the morrow,
Such happiness o'erflows her heart
    There's left no room for sorrow!

March 23

CORA

I

    WHEN through thy arching aisles,
      O Nature, I perceive
What brooding stillness fills the lonesome choirs
Where, heaven'd late, thy sweet musicians sung;

    What rude benumbing touch
    Strips from reluctant boughs
The languid leaves and bares to common view
The sacred nest,—the mute, expressive nest,

    Whose state defenseless tells

      Of fledgeling treasures flown,—
Then, like the prudent birds, my thoughts take flight,
Winging o'er wintry fields to find the spring.

II

      Somewhere on Earth's cold breast
        The dauntless crocus glows,
And fair Narcissus hangs his head and dreams.
There,—laughing, blushing, like a happy bride,

      With tears in her sweet eyes
        To kiss away—shyly
The Maiden comes, and, as she moves along,
The woods and waking wolds intone her praise.

      I, too, where all things tell
        Of Autumn chill and blight,—
I, too, will praise her, ay, with transport hymn
The unforgotten sweetness of the spring.

III

      How desolate were Man
        If, robbed of dear delight,
He might not with remembrance fond pursue
And find his happiness, and lead it back!

      The mournful Stygian shades
        Were less forlorn than he;
For they have memory, and cannot lose
Bright visions once in conscious bliss possessed!

      Through Hades' wailful halls,
        Bereft of Proserpine,

They pensive glide, yet feel the far, sweet spring,
And seem to breathe lost Enna's distant flowers.

March 24

ON A POET TOO EARLY DEAD

WHEN to the undesired home
    Where you are queen, Persephone,
The Dreamer had untimely come,
Surely, I think for one brief hour
A brightness must have touched your gloom,
And that your yearning must have caught,
From something that his presence brought,
A breath of Enna bloom.

About your throne, so wintry lone,
    O sorrow-veiled Persephone!
I think bright visions, once your own,
Must pale have blossomed into flower:
That there, your home-sick heart to greet,
Narcissus, wraith-like, must have sprung
While memory gave plaintive tongue
To song Sicilian sweet.

If he, who plucked the asphodel,
    Brought you one breath, Persephone,
Of the fair meads you loved so well
And dream of, pensive, hour by hour,—
Oh, tell him, who with shades must live,
Vexed by forlorn regrettings vain,
How mortals, mid earth's greater pain,
May, loving, all forgive!

March 25

I KNOW NOT HOW TO FIND THE SPRING

I KNOW not how to find the Spring,
    Though violets are here,
And in the boughs high over me
    The birds are fluting clear;
The magic and the melody,
    The rapture—all are fled,
And could they wake, they would but break
    My heart, now you are dead.

March 26

BEETHOVEN[12]

HE cursed the day that he was born:
    And deaf and desolate,
Resolved, in bitterness forlorn,
    To end his hapless fate.

But as the deeper silence grew,—
    An exile from the throng,
His yearning spirit voices drew
    From *inner* founts of song;

And he who called unfriendly death
    To calm rebellious strife,
Won from his own despair the breath
    Of an immortal life.

---

[12] Ludwig van Beethoven died on this day in 1827.

March 27

EURYDICE

I HEAR thy voice!—
   Ah, love, I hear thy voice!
Faint as the sound of distant waters falling,
I hear thy voice above me calling, calling,—
And my imprisoned heart,
Long held from thee apart,
   Responsive thrills, half-tempted to rejoice.

   In Hades though I be,
Where the unnumbered dead abide
In uneventful, sunless eventide,
   I yet live on,—for thou rememberest me!
And like to far-off waters falling,
I hear thee, from the distance, calling,—
   Eurydice! Beloved Eurydice!

   In thy bright world I know,
   The firstlings of the Spring begin to blow:
Moss-violet and saffron daffodil
Their perfumes new distil,
And through the veiled elysian hours,—
Sweeter for wafted scent of citron-flowers,—
   Voices of nightingales soft come and go.

   The halcyon again
   Contented broods beside the quiet main;
The ringdove tells her wound
With throbbing breast, and undulating sound
Which still, thy passion wronging,
Awakes in thee the wilder, lonelier longing.
   And still my buried heart reflects thy pain!

   Of yore I had a dream:

I thought—the awful sentinel asleep—
   Thou, with that lyre divine, supreme,
Which first drew Argo downward to the deep,
    Entering here, where chains are never riven,
    Had with thy golden strain, Apollo given,
Taught Dis, the pitiless, himself, to weep:

   I had a dream of yore:
I thought Love, mightier than Death,
   Wide opened the inexorable door,
And offered me pure draughts of sun-warmed breath.
I saw thy form; trembling, I seemed to follow,—
When, sudden, to these rayless caverns hollow
   Fate caught me back—thee to behold no more!

   .   .   .   .

   Yet still I wait for thee!
   And thou wilt come!—wilt come—wilt come to me!
The hours delay; I make no moan,—
Apart from thee,—yet not alone,—
Sweeter than far-off music sighing,
I hear thy voice forever crying:—
   "Eurydice!—lost, lost Eurydice!"

                                        March 28

SAINT THERESA[13]

WEARY and long the winding way;
   Yet as I fare, to comfort me,
Still o'er and o'er I tell the beads
   Of love's perfected rosary.

The fire that once hath pierced the heart,
   If from above, must upward flame,

---

[13] Teresa of Ávila was born on this day in 1515.

Nor falter till it find at last
    The burning fountain whence it came.

O fire of love within my breast—
    O pain that pleads for no surcease—
Fill me with fervor!—more and more,
    Give me thy passion and thy peace!

O love, that mounts to paths of day
    Untraversed by the soaring lark,
O love, through all the silent night
    A lamp to light the boundless dark,

O love, whose dearest pangs I bear,
    This heart—this wounded heart—transform!
That all who seek its shelter may
    There find a refuge safe and warm.

Were there no heaven of high reward,
    Man's service here to crown and bless,
Were there no hell,—I, for love's sake,
    Would toil with ardent willingness.

And if—O Thou that pitiest
    The fallen, lone, and tempest-tost!—
If, Love Divine, Thou wilt but save
    Whom *I* do love, none shall be lost!

                                                            March 29

TO BRITANNIA

On seeing a picture of the cairn and cross under which lie Captain Scott[14] and his men

---

[14] Robert Falcon Scott died on this day in 1912.

BRITANNIA, they who perished here have crowned thee—
  Have proved the dauntless temper of thy soul;
Great memories of the past, through them have found thee
  Intrepid as of old, untouched and whole.

Triumphant Mother! Make an end to sighing
  For these, thrice happy!—with sonorous breath
Let bugles sing their requiem who are lying
  In all the full magnificence of death!

They knew not failure: dream and aspiration
  They knew, indeed, and love, and noble joy;
And at the last faith brought them the elation
  That Destiny is powerless to destroy.

The utmost summit of desire attaining,
  What further is there left deserving strife?
Ah, there is still the peerless hope remaining,—
  In death to prove one's worthiness of life!

Sublime thy grief, Britannia! sons have crowned thee—
  With hard-won laurels have enwreathed thy name:
Have shown the world the bulwark set around thee,
  Adding new consecration to thy fame.

Nor have they blessed thee, only: Fate defying,
  Others in lands remote shall fear contemn,
And find it easier, themselves denying,
  To die like heroes, too,—remembering them.

They do not lie in lonely graves forsaken,
  Who for high ends can so supremely dare;
From human hearts they can no more be taken,
  And Immortality is with them there.

March 30

PSYCHE

SOFTLY, with palpitating heart,
She came to where he lay concealed apart.
The lamp she held intensified the gloom
And in the dusk wrought shadowy shapes of doom.

   Her starry eyes
O'er-brimmed with troubled tears,
Her pulses throbbing wildly in her ears,
   She stood beside him where he lay,
Hushed in the deep
Of sweet, unconscious sleep.
   But as she stifled back her sighs
And tried to look upon that cherished form,
Remembrance shook her purpose warm,
   And, chiding, seemed to say,—
"Why seek to solve, why, curious, thus destroy
The mystery of joy?
   What doubt unblest, what faithless fear is this
That tempts to paths none may retrace,
That moves thee, fond one! to unveil the face
   Of bliss?
Is 't not enough to feel it thine?
Like Semele, wouldst gaze on the Divine?
Secret the soul of Rapture dwells;
Love gives, yet jealous tests repels,
Nor will of force be known,
And bashful Beauty viewed too near—is gone."

March 31

IN PATHETIC REMEMBRANCE

E. N. W.[15]

Author of "David Harum"

A DYING man, so say you, wrote this book?
    Life is abundant here: from every page—
    Cheerful, courageous, philosophic, sage,
With no repining and no backward look—
It flows, as healthful as the mountain brook,
    That gathering scent of grape and saxifrage,
    Makes joyous pastime of its pilgrimage,
Fresh'ning each pebbly bend, each mossy crook.

The story journeys to forgetfulness?
    Truly: yet he who wrote, with failing breath,
    Ennobled human nature; for since he
    Who died in far Samoa by the sea,
There scarce hath come, through failure and success,
    A braver spirit to the gates of death!

April 1

IN APRIL

WHEN beeches bud and lilacs blow,
    And Earth puts on her magic green;
When dogwoods bear their vernal snow
    And skies grow deep the stars between,—
Then, O ye birds! awake and sing
The gladness at the heart of Spring!

---

[15] Edward Noyes Westcott died on this day in 1898.

When flowers blossom for the poor,
    And Nature heals the hurt of years,
When wondering Love resists the cure,
    Yet hopes again, and smiles through tears,—
Then, O ye birds! awake and sing
The gladness at the heart of Spring!

April 2

APRIL

SWELLING bud and fond suggestion,
    Wafting of perfume,
Tearful rapture, thrilling question
    Of restraint or bloom,
Life all dreamlessly asleeping,
    As in death, but now,
Upward to the sunlight creeping,—
    April, that is thou!

Mystery's authentic dwelling,
    Faith's expanding wing,
Maiden loveliness foretelling
    Fuller blossoming,
Prophet of the new creation,
    Priestess of the bough,
Month of the imagination,—
    April, that is thou!

April 3

POOR ICARUS[16]

POOR Icarus!—to soar so high,
Then fall! For you 't was vain to try

---

[16] Calbraith Rodgers died on this day in 1912.

    By cunning craft, on faithless wings,
      To capture empyrean things,
That still to men the Fates deny!

Yet, even knowing Death so nigh,
Had you reluctant been to fly
    Beyond earth's sure, safe harborings,—
      Poor Icarus?

I think not so. All, all must die!
But you the pathways of the sky
    Found first, and tasted heavenly springs,
    Unfettered as the lark that sings,
And knew strange raptures,—though we sigh:
      "Poor Icarus!"

April 4

WOULDST THOU LEARN

WOULDST thou learn what coldness is,
    Seek it not where Hebrus flows,
Shuddering, to the abyss;
    Nor where Hermon's gleaming snows,
    On its frozen heights, repose;
But on such a morn as this,
    When no blade of grass is dumb,
When the birds, low-twittering, build,
And Earth's heart is passion-thrill'd,—
    Come to Love's deserted home!

April 5

KINDRED

TENDER grass in April springing,
    Scent of lilacs wet with rain,

Bluebird jubilantly singing
    Snatches of a loved refrain,

Falcon soaring high above me,
    Light of stars in deeps divine,
Creeping earth-bound things that move me
    To compassion, ye are mine!

Wind in varied cadence playing
    Mystic runes on harps unseen,
Blossom hardily delaying
    Where lost summer late hath been,

Shadow drifting o'er the mountain,
    Mist blown inward from the sea,
Hidden spring and bubbling fountain,—
    Ye are mine and parts of me!

What am I? The stars have made me,
    And the dust to which I cleave,
Rivers, and the hills that aid me,
    Past and future, morn and eve,

Nightshade lightly plucked unknowing,
    Roses fondly twined with rue,
Harvestings of mine own sowing,
    And from fields I never knew!

I have gained mid loss and capture
    Strength not found in vanquishing,
Sharing oft the mounting rapture,
    Trailing oft the broken wing;

Kindred with the sunlight streaming
    Where nor dew nor rain-drop gleams,
With the parchèd desert dreaming
    Incommunicable dreams,

Laid in cavern-bed at even,
    Throned on rose-flushed Apennine—
Multitudinous earth and heaven,
    Naught ye hold that is not mine!

                                        April 6

IMMORTAL[17]

HOW living are the dead!
Enshrined, but not apart,
How safe within the heart
We hold them still—our dead,
Whatever else be fled!

Our constancy is deep
Toward those who lie asleep,
Forgetful of the strain and mortal strife
That are so large a part of this our earthly life.

They are our very own:
From them—from them alone,
Nothing can us estrange—
Nor blight autumnal, no; nor wintry change!

The midnight moments keep
A place for them; and though we wake to weep,
They are beside us: still, in joy, in pain—
In every crucial hour, they come again,
Angelic from above—
Bearing the gifts of blessing and of love—
Until the shadowy path they lonely trod
Becomes for us a bridge that upward leads to God.

---

[17] Florence Earle Coates died on this day in 1927. This poem was read at her funeral service.

April 7

BREATHLESS WE STRIVE

BREATHLESS we strive, contending for success,
    According to the standards of our day.
    What is success? Is it to find a way
Wealth out of all proportion to possess?
Is it to care for simple pleasures less
    (While grasping at a more extended sway),
    And sacrificing to our gods of clay,
Submerge the soul, at last, in worldliness?

By Grasmere stands a cottage small and poor:[18]
    The *Dove* was once its emblem, and the sign
That marked it as a wayside inn obscure;
But, frugal, dwelt high consecration here,
    And gratitude still guards it as a shrine,
Hallowed by that success which time but makes more dear!

April 8

WITH BREATH OF SPRING

    THE air is full of balm, I know;
The winter vanished long ago.
In sheltered plots along the street
Crocus and tiny snowdrop meet,
And children skip about and play—
Rejoicing in the glad noonday—
Or loiter 'neath some budding bough
Where bird-notes will be warbled now—
    Outside the prison wall.

The brook, by winter long enchained,

---

[18] William Wordsworth was born on this day in 1770.

Flows through the meadow unrestrained;
The violet will blossom soon,
The moth will break from the cocoon;
And where the happy children sing,
The fledgling bird will try his wing,—
But, O my heart! the sunshine there!—
The grateful shade!—the boon, free air—
    Outside the prison wall!

April 9

AT BREAK OF DAY

I THOUGHT that past the gates of doom,
    Where Orpheus played a strain divine
    Of love importunate as mine,
Unto the dwellings of the dead I came through paths of gloom.

Around me, looming dark through cloud,
    Vast walls arose whence mournful fell
    The shadow and the hush of hell;
And silence, brooding, palpable, enwrapped me like a shroud.

Naught blossomed there; in that chill place
    Where longing dwells divorced from hope,
    Naught to a joyless horoscope
Lent prophecies of future grace, but—I beheld thy face!

And I awoke,—songs trembling near,—
    Awoke and saw day's chariot pass
    Bright gleaming o'er the meadow-grass,
And knew this glad earth without thee, than realms of Death more
    drear!

April 10

LONGING

THE lilacs blossom at the door,
    The early rose
Whispers a promise to her buds,
    And they unclose.

There is a perfume everywhere,
    A breath of song,
A sense of some divine return
    For waiting long.

Who knows but some imprisoned joy
    From bondage breaks,—
Some exiled and enchanted hope
    From dreams awakes?

Who knows but you are coming back
    To comfort me
For all the languor and the pain,
    Persephone?

O come! For one brief spring return,
    Love's tryst to keep;
Then let me share the Stygian fruit,
    The wintry sleep!

April 11

NATURE

TO see thee, hear thee, wistful watch I keep—
    Mother, who in Immensity dost dwell—
A child who listens for the boundless deep,
    Her ear against a shell:

And vainly though I seek thy face to scan,
    Lost in the vasty temple where thou art,
Faint breathings of thy voice æolian
    Vibrate against my heart.

April 12

SURVIVAL

THE knell that dooms the voiceless and obscure
    Stills Memnon's music with its ghostly chime;
    Strength is as weakness in the clasp of Time,
And for the things that were there is no cure.
The vineyard with its fair investiture,
    The mountain summit with its hoary rime,
    The throne of Cæsar, Cheops' tomb sublime,
Alike decay, and only dreams endure.

Dreams for Assyria her worship won,
    And India is hallowed by her dreams;
The Sphinx with deathless visage views the race
    That like the lotus of a summer seems;
And, rudderless, immortally sails on
The wingèd Victory of Samothrace.

April 13

INDIA

SILENT amidst unbroken silence deep
    Of dateless years, in loneliness supreme,
    She pondered patiently one mighty theme,
    And let the hours, uncounted, by her creep.
The motionless Himalayas, the broad sweep
    Of glacial cataracts, great Ganges' stream—
    All these to her were but as things that seem,
Doomed all to pass, like phantoms viewed in sleep.

Her history? She has none—scarce a name.
    The life she lived is lost in the profound
        Of time, which she despised; but nothing mars
The memory that, single, gives her fame—
    She dreamed eternal dreams, and from the ground
        Still raised her yearning vision to the stars.

                                    April 14

THE BAND OF THE TITANIC[19]

"These are the immortal,—the fearless"—Upanishads

UP, lads! they say we've struck a berg, though there's no danger yet,—
    Our noble liner was not built to wreck!—
But women may have felt a shock they're needing to forget,
    And when there's trouble, men should be on deck.

Come!—now's the time! They're wanting us to brighten them a bit;
    Play up, my lads—as lively as you can!
Give them a merry English air! they want no counterfeit
    Like that down-hearted tune you just began!...

I think the Captain's worried, lads: maybe the thing's gone wrong;
    Well, we will show them all is right with us!
Of Drake and the Armadas now we'll play them such a song
    Shall make them of the hero emulous.

When boats are being lowered, lads, your place and mine are here,—
    Oh, we were never needed more than now!
When others go, it is for us those left behind to cheer,
    And I am glad, my lads, that we know how!

---

[19] The RMS Titanic hit an iceberg on this day in 1912 and sank in the early morning hours the following day.

If it is Death that's calling us, we'll make a brave response;
    Play up, play up!—ye may not play again;
The prize that Nelson won at last, the chance that comes but once,
    Is ours, my lads!—the chance to die like men!

THE "TITANIC"—AFTERMATH

O NATURE! overmastered by thy power,
Man is a hero still
And knighthood is in flower!
All save his tameless will
Thou can'st subdue by thine appalling might;
But failest utterly to quench his spirit's light.

Yea, though he seem, in conflict with thy strength,
A pygmy of the dust,
Heroic man, at length
Greater than thou, through trust,
Sovereign through something thou can'st not enslave,
Finds once again, in death, the life he scorned to save!

April 15

A HERO[20]

HE sang of joy; whate'er he knew of sadness
    He kept for his own heart's peculiar share:
So well he sang, the world imagined gladness
    To be sole tenant there.

For dreams were his, and in the dawn's fair shining,
    His spirit soared beyond the mounting lark;
But from his lips no accent of repining
    Fell when the days grew dark;

---

[20] Abraham Lincoln died on this day in 1865.

And though contending long dread Fate to master,
    He failed at last her enmity to cheat,
He turned with such a smile to face disaster
    That he sublimed defeat.

April 16

THROUGH THE RUSHES

THROUGH the rushes by the river
    Runs a drowsy tremor sweet,
And the waters stir and shiver
    In the darkness at their feet;
From the sombre east up-stealing,
Gradual, with slow revealing,
Comes the dawn, and with a sigh
      Night goes by.

Here and there, to mildest wooing,
    Folded buds are open-blown;
And the drops their leaves bedewing,
    Like to seed-pearls thickly sown,
Sinking, with the blessing olden,
Deep into each calyx golden,
A supreme behest obey,
      Then melt away.

And while robes of splendor trailing,
    Fitly deck the glowing morn,
And a fragrance, fresh exhaling,
    Greets her loveliness new-born,
Midst divine melodic voicings,
Midst delicious mute rejoicings,
Strong as when the worlds began,
      Awakens Pan!

April 17

BENJAMIN FRANKLIN[21]

"Eripuit cœlo fulmen, sceptrumque tyrannis."[22]

FRANKLIN! our Franklin! America's loved son!—
    Loved in his day, and now, as few indeed:
Franklin! whose mighty genius allies won,
    To aid her in great need!

Franklin! with noble charm that fear allays,
    Tact, judgment, insight, humor naught could dim!—
"Antiquity," said Mirabeau, "would raise
    Altars to honor him!"

How should one country claim him, or one hour?
    Bound to no narrow circuit, and no time,
He is the World's—part of her lasting dower,
    One with her hope sublime.

His kindred are the equable and kind
    Whose constant thought is to uplift and bless;
The witty, and the wise, the large of mind,
    Who ignorance redress:

His kindred are the bold who, undismayed,
    Believe that good is ever within reach;
All who move onward—howsoe'er delayed—
    Who learn, that they may teach;

Who overcoming pain and weariness,

---

[21] Benjamin Franklin died on this day in 1790.
[22] "Eripuit coelo fulmen, sceptrumque tyrannis": A line in Latin that Marquis Turgot had inscribed under a portrait of Franklin. An English translation by James Elphinston (pre-1817): "He snatcht the bolt from Heaven's avenging hand, / Disarm'd and drove the tyrant from the land."

In life's long battle bear a noble part;
All who, like him,—greatest of gifts!—possess
  The genius of the heart!

How should we praise whose deeds belittle praise,
  Whose monument perpetual is our land
Saved by his wisdom, in disastrous days,
  From tyranny's strong hand?—

How praise whose Titan-thought, beyond Earth's ken
  Aspiring, tamed the lightnings in revolt,
Subduing to the will of mortal men
  The awful thunderbolt?

Our debt looms larger than our love can pay:
  We know not with what homage him to grace
Whose name outlasts the monument's decay,—
  A glory to our race!

April 18

THEY TOLD ME

THEY told me: "Pan is dead—Nature is dead:
There is no God." I read
The words of Socrates, and then I read
Of Jesus; and I said:—
"*Divinity* 's not dead!"

Good can nor poisoned be
Nor slain upon a tree:
The soul of good, escaping, still is free,
And in its ministry
Lives God eternally.

April 19

LOVE AND THE CHILD

LOVE came into the world and said:
"With the tender infant on this bed
   Shall be my home; I will impart
   The winning graces to its heart
That blessing in life's pathway spread."

So—for Love crooned its lullabies—
His own smile dawned within its eyes,
   And into its small being stole
   The laughing radiance of his soul,
And all its eager sympathies.

Unconscious as the flowers that bless—
A tiny flame of lovingness—
   To any palm it gave at once
   A dimpled hand, in quick response,
Nor what "a stranger" meant might guess.

That to distrust is often well,
It heard with smile ineffable.
   Then, on a morn, Love came to say:
   "Thou child of mine, come, come away!
In Paradise to dwell!"

April 20

AB HUMO

THE seedling hidden in the sod
   Were ill content immured to stay;
   Slowly it upward makes its way
And finds the light at last, thank God!

The most despised of mortal things—
    The worm devoid of hope or bliss,
    Discovers in the chrysalis
Too narrow space for urgent wings.

These are my kindred of the clay;
    But as I struggle from the ground
    Such weakness in my strength is found,
I seem less fortunate than they;

Yet though my progress be but slow,
    And failure oft obscure the past,
    I, too, victorious at last,
Shall reach the longed-for light, I know!

April 21

IN A COLLEGE SETTLEMENT

THE sights and sounds of the wretched street
Oppressed me, and I said: "We cheat
    Our hearts with hope. Man sunken lies
In vice, and naught that's fair or sweet
    Finds further favor in his eyes.

"Vainly we strive, in sanguine mood,
To elevate a savage brood
    That, from the cradle, sordid, dull,
No longer has a wish for good,
    Or craving for the beautiful."

I said; but chiding my despair,
My wiser friend just pointed where,
    By some indifferent passer thrown
Upon a heap of ashes bare,
    The loose leaves of a rose were sown.

And I, 'twixt tenderness and doubt,
Beheld, while pity grew devout,
   A squalid and uneager child,
With careful fingers picking out
   The scentless petals, dust-defiled.

And straight I seemed to see a close,
With hawthorn hedged and brier-rose;
   And, bending down, I whispered, "Dear,
Come, let us fly, while no one knows,
   To the country—far away from here!"

Upon the little world-worn face
There dawned a look of wistful grace,
   Then came the question that for hours
Still followed me from place to place:
   "Real country, where you can catch flowers?"

                                      April 22

NEAR AND FAR

THE air is full of perfume and the promise of the spring,
   From wintry mould the dainty blossoms come;
There's not a bird in all the boughs but's eager now to sing,
   And from afar a ship is sailing home!

The cherry-blooms, all lightly blown about the verdant sward,
   With silver fleck the dandelion's gold;
The jasmine and arbutus breathe the fragrance they have stored;
   The crumpled ferns, like faery tents, unfold.

And low the rills are laughing, and the rivers in the sun
   Are gliding on, impatient for the sea;
The wintry days are past and gone, the summer is begun,
   And love from far is sailing home to me!

Ah, blessed spring!—how far more sweet than any spring of yore!
   No note of all thy harmonies is dumb;
With thee my heart awakes to hope and happiness once more,—
   And from afar a ship is sailing home!

April 23

SHAKESPEARE[23]

O'ER-TOPPING all—upon how lone a height!—
   A demiurge beneficent, a seer
   Like his own Prospero, he doth appear,
'Mid clouds that half conceal him from our sight,
A being god-like in creative might:
   He who so very human was! so near
   To Nature that her voice through him we hear—
Her voice of truth and beauty infinite.

Shakespeare! With love and awe we breathe his name
Who needs not mortal praise! Deathless in fame,
   Far from our dull activities he seems;
But let us turn, a-wearied, from the strife,
To share with him the high adventure,—life,
   Straightway we feel the stirrings of Great Dreams!

I TOO HAVE LOVED

I, TOO, have loved the Greeks, the Hero-sprung,
   The glad, spoiled children of Posterity:
   Have closed my eyes, more near their shrines to be,
Have hushed my heart, to hear their epics sung.
Upon their golden accents I have hung,
   With Thyrsis wooed to vales of Sicily,
   And Homer, blind, has given me to see

---

[23] William Shakespeare died on this day in 1616.

Olympus, where the deathless Gods were young.

But still, that one remembering with awe
Whose vision deeper than all others saw,
   I feel the dearer debt my spirit owes
To him, who towers, peerless and sublime,
The noblest, largest intellect of Time,
   Born where the English Avon softly flows.

April 24

INHERITOR

SAY not the gods are cruel,
   Since man himself is kind—
Man, who could give no tenderness
   If, impotent and blind,
He stretched appealing hands on high
   No tenderness to find,—

Who, wakened to compassion,
   No longer stands apart,
Careless of others' suffering,
   But, rather, shares the smart,
Because of pity drawn from out
   The Universal Heart,—

Who feels within him glowing
   A spark that dares aspire,
Flame-like, unto supernal things,
   With never-quenched desire,
And knows that Heaven bestowed on him
   A spark of its own fire!

April 25

MASEFIELD

On re-reading *Gallipoli*[24] and the *Sonnets*

I THOUGHT on England in her tragic hour
    Of sacrifice supreme for human right;
    Beheld her bleeding, broken in the fight
With a massed tyranny's stupendous power;
And musing on far graves where lie her flower
    Of manhood, memory so dimmed my sight
    That I forgot the dawn that crowned her night—
The victory that was her valor's dower.

Then, even as I grieved, I saw once more
    How genius can atone and re-create:
How, by its own high gift, it can restore
    The Land that gives it birth to sovereign State,
Rekindling glories that it knew before,
    And deepening its life to life as great!

April 26

SONG

HER cheek is like a tinted rose
    That June hath fondly cherished,
Her heart is like a star that glows
    When day hath darkling perished,
Her voice is as a songbird's sweet,
    The drowsy wolds awaking—
But, ah, her love is past compare,
    And keeps my heart from breaking!

---

[24] The battle of Gallipoli began on this day in 1915.

Lost sunbeams light her tresses free,
    Along their shadows gleaming!
Her smiles entangle memory
    And set the soul a-dreaming,
Her thoughts, like seraphs, upward soar,
    Earth's narrow bounds forsaking—
But, ah, her love abides with me
    And keeps my heart from breaking!

April 27

INTERCHANGE

THE oriole sang in the apple tree;
    The sick girl lay on her bed, and heard
    The tremulous note of the glad wild bird;
And, "Ah!" she sighed, "to share with thee
    Life's rapture exquisite and strong:
Its hope, its eager energy,
    Its fragrance and its song!"

The oriole swayed in the apple tree,
    And he sang: "I will build, with my love, a nest,
    Fine as e'er welcomed a birdling guest:
Like a pendant blossom, secure yet free,
    It shall hang from the bough above me there,
Bright, bright with the gold that is combed for me
    From the sick girl's auburn hair!"

So he built the nest in the apple tree;
    And, burnished over, a ball of light,
    It gleamed and shone in the sick girl's sight,
And she gazed upon it wonderingly:
    But when the bird had forever flown,
They brought the nest from the apple tree
    To the bed where she lay alone.

"O builder of this mystery!"—
    The wide and wistful eyes grew dim,
    And the soul of the sick girl followed him—
"Dear bird! I have had part, through thee,
    In the life for which I long and long:
Have shared its hope, its energy,
    Its rapture and its song!"

April 28

FOR JOY

FOR each and every joyful thing,
For twilight swallows on the wing,
For all that nest and all that sing,—

For fountains cool that laugh and leap,
For rivers running to the deep,
For happy, care-forgetting sleep,—

For stars that pierce the sombre dark,
For Morn, awaking with the lark,
For life new-stirring 'neath the bark,—

For sunshine and the blessèd rain,
For budding grove and blossomy lane,
For the sweet silence of the plain,—

For bounty springing from the sod,
For every step by beauty trod,—
For each dear gift of joy, thank God!

April 29

SONG

THE new-born leaves unfolding fast
    Make nests of green on every bough;
The pilgrim birds, their wanderings past,
With joy return,—but thou, my love,
    Oh, where, my love, art thou?

Soft tumults fill the balmy air,
    Faint breathings of the flowers to be;
Life glows and gladdens everywhere,—
But I am lone for thee, my love,
    Oh, lone, my love, for thee!

Give me the voice of moaning pines,
    The frozen wold, the desert space;
Give me the winter Earth resigns,—
But let me see thy face, my love,
    Oh, let me see thy face!

April 30

VITA NUOVA

    WHAT miracle is here—
    What vision of forgotten things and dear?
The grass—how green it lies in coverts deep!
The pussy-willows—sentinels of the wood—
How slim, how fair, each 'neath its downy snood,
    They stand, new-waked from sleep!

    And the enchantment cold
    That seemed as death? Could it no longer hold
Against the glow that warmed the breast of Earth?
Hearken! what myriad little lives once more

Come knocking, knocking at the Mother's door,
   Importunate for birth!

   The trees, that look so bare,
      Are conscious that the tender leaves are there—
Folded, yet faintly stirring in the bud;
And upward from each buried rootlet runs,
The golden ichor, gift of vernal suns,
      On-swelling to the flood.

   And, oh! thrice loved of yore—
      Whence comes that note? It was not here before!
The white-throat! By what blest magician's art—
Flung out of silence, comes that clear appeal,
To make the jaded and insensate feel
      New yearnings of the heart?

   A something in the song
      Shall hardly to a later strain belong—
A tremulous and naïve ecstasy
That moves the soul; which, eager then to live,
Petitions life: "Ah, stay awhile, and give
      A little heed to me!

   "I, also, feel the Spring!
      I, also, long to spread my wings and sing,
Unvexed by cares that canker and consume:
To hope, to dream,—ere winter come, to capture
The fleeting thrill, the fragrance and the rapture
      Of beauty in its bloom!"

May 1

UNBIDDEN

AS shakes the breast of giant Kaf
   When Allah's thunders near resound,

So nations quail before my wrath,
And shudder at its sound.

   The broad Euphrates bears my name
To Oman's waves triumphantly;
The lordly Indus sings my fame
To the wondering Indian sea.

   For me Khorasan tempers steel,
The Turkoman rears matchless steeds;
Azerbijan grows me her wine,
And luscious fruit for summer needs;
My peacock throne burns like a gem,
And stars blaze in my diadem.

   The mighty vie to honor me:
Kings at my table humbly sit,
And tributary satraps fret
When banished over-long from it.

   What then have I to do with thoughts
That blanch the cheek and chill the blood?
Some wretched slave may quake and start,
Who hast'ning through Ghilan's lone wood,
Hears ravening jackals distant howl,—
But I? Nay, who doth not revere
The brazen doors my guards defend?
Who dares, unsummoned, enter here?

   Shall baseless terrors mock my peace,
And chide desired Sleep away?
Forbidding her to close mine eyes,
Tormenting me when I would pray?
The years are long; yet time hath sped,
And Earth forgets what once she knew,
For hidden far beneath her view,
The grasses wave above my dread.

The guests attend me. Wake, my will!
Put off this garb of sullen gloom!
The dead may neither wound nor blight;
And vengeance slumbers in the tomb.
Be thou but firm, and all's secure:
Match well thy purpose to the hour,
Nor babble what is voiceless still,—
Not Eblis shall abase thy power!

   . . . .

   Heard you a knocking then, my lords?
No?—and the wind, you think, sounds so?
To me 't was as a stroke of doom,
Reverberate from some long ago.

   Well, since 't was nothing, speed the cheer!
Nor sit like phantoms dull and mute,
For something which ye did not hear.

   Ye thought me weary? So: and then?
Am I not mortal like the rest?
May I not falter in my mirth,
Nor palsy every guest? . . .

   That knocking!—Ah! you note it now.
It vexed me men should disallow
A sound more dread than frenzy's shriek,—
And prate of a wind-blown bough!

   . . . .

   Thine errand, sirrah! Who's without
That may not be denied?
A stranger? And thou darest bring
His hests unbidden before thy king?

A stranger? Though his need be stout,
And stubborn as his pride,
Is 't here that he should seek our face?
Command him to the appointed place,
And those who should provide!

  Ha! answerest thou? Not be denied?—
Grows life so worthless then?—
Go drive him hence, thou tiresome knave!
... Friends, to our feast again!
  This imbecile hath broke the cheer;
But day is distant yet,
And ere her joyless flags appear,
We'll pay mad pleasure's debt.

  Drink to all revels—foes to thought!
Drink, drink to poppy-trances deep!
And since from some sleep holds aloof,
To oblivion drink!—the dreamless sleep.

  Again that sound affronts the air!
Ill-omened wretch, proclaim thy care—
My soul thy pallor hates!
What hounds thee back? Whence, whence this din?
The stranger? He hath passed the gates—
And waiteth there—within?

  And waiteth there? ... Admit him then:
Who hunts the panther to his den
Flies not the panther's rage.
... Fool! fool! Thou deem'st it wise to beard
Our fury? ... Gods! the face I feared!

  At height of bloom, so cometh blight.
Avaunt! avaunt, thou withering sight!
Eternal pains begin:
I swoon to Hell's abysmal night,—

Ah, horror!—Back, my Sin!

                                                  May 2

RHAPSODY

AS the mother-bird to the waiting nest
    As the regnant moon to the sea,
As joy to the heart that hath first been blest—
    So is my love to me!

Sweet as the song of the lark that soars
    From the net of the fowler free,
Sweet as the morning that song adores—
    So is my love to me!

As the rose that blossoms in matchless grace
    Where the canker may not be,
As the well that springs in a desert place—
    So is my love to me!

                                                  May 3

EVERY HEART

WHEN wintry wells are water-filled,
And killing Death itself is killed,
Then wingèd things begin to build;
And maids and men with happy birds do sing,
For every heart's a lover in the spring!

When brooklets ripple into song,
And strivings faint of life grow strong,
Then all things 'gin to dream and long;
And maids and men with wistful birds do sing,
For every heart's a poet in the spring!

May 4

IMMORTAL

LIFE is like a beauteous flower,
    Closing to the world at even,—
Closing for a dreamless hour,
    To unfold, with dawn, on heaven.

Life is like a bird that nests
    Close to earth, no shelter scorning,
Yet, upmounting from her breast,
    Fills the skies with song at morning.

May 5

SHE WILL NOT HEAR

SHE will not hear you if you sing,
Bluebird and whitethroat of the Spring!
Why did you stay away so long,
She wearying for your song?

She will not notice if you pass,
Sweet airs that woo the meadow grass!
Why could you not have spread, more fleet,
Soft carpet for her feet?

She will not see the crocus rise,
Nor smile into the violet's eyes;
Pale dogwood bloom from Winter snow
My darling will not know.

You come too late! too late, too late,
O longed-for Spring! She tried to wait,
Wistful your breathing joys to share.
Come now,—she will not care!

May 6

BROOK SONG: TO THE SPRING

O BEAUTY! vision of forgotten gladness!
    Fulfillment of a dream that ne'er betrays!
O miracle of hope, and balm of sadness!
    Creative ecstasy and fount of praise!

. . . .

I lay upon the ground and gave no token,
    I hid my face mid sodden leaves and sere,
My languid pulses chill, my spirit broken,—
    I knew not, O divine one! you were near;

For snows and frosts of winter, new-departed,
    Still held my will in thrall and weighed me down;
And I forgot—forlorn and heavy-hearted—
    Your promise, goddess of the violet crown!

But soft as music in remembrance sighing,
    You fanned me with your wooing breath, and I
Who shed no tears when lone I seemed and dying
    Wept at your touch, and knew I should not die.

Now by my banks are tender blossoms blowing:
    In fragrant loveliness they smile on me,—
But I must hasten to the river, knowing
    The river will lead onward to the sea.

High over me the budding branches quiver
    With songs that swell in happy harmony;
But sweeter is the murmur of the river,—
    The river that leads onward to the sea!

May 7

IN THE OFFING

THE Ship of the Spring in the offing at last!
    Oh, rude blew the hindering gales,
But perfumes entrancing, the danger o'erpast,
    Are wafted afar, from her sails!

The bearer of treasure more fragrant than myrrh—
    More precious than jewels of Inde,
The stars in their courses keep watch over her,
    The gods for her temper the wind.

She comes as a maid whom life's vision elates,
    Out-spreading her draperies white;
She comes as a bride whom a lover awaits
    With proud and impatient delight.

A queen, as she glides to the goal of her dreams
    With movement majestic and slow,
So still is her beauty, half-conscious she seems,—
    But the heart in her breast is aglow;

For she hears the far murmur of myriad things
    That shall at her coming have birth.
O sails in the offing! ye are as the wings
    Of angels that bring her to Earth!

May 8

ONCE IN A STILL, SEQUESTERED PLACE

ONCE in a still, sequestered place
    Where fell a shade, as of approaching death,
A lily drooped upon its wounded stem.
    But, ah, how sweet its breath!

The shadow deepened into night,
    Life flows no longer in the lily's veins;
But there where for a fragrant hour it bloomed,
    A perfume still remains!

May 9

THE MORNING GLORY

WAS it worth while to paint so fair
    Thy every leaf—to vein with faultless art
Each petal, taking the boon light and air
    Of summer so to heart?

To bring thy beauty unto perfect flower,
    Then, like a passing fragrance or a smile,
Vanish away, beyond recovery's power—
    Was it, frail bloom, worth while?

Thy silence answers: "Life was mine!
    And I, who pass without regret or grief,
Have cared the more to make my moment fine,
    Because it was so brief.

"In its first radiance I have seen
    The sun!—why tarry then till comes the night?
I go my way, content that I have been
    Part of the morning light!"

May 10

IN MEMORY OF HENRY LA BARRE JAYNE[25]

HE was of those who knew that love is giving;
    So, though he sleeps, his mortal service done,

---

[25] Henry La Barre Jayne died on this day in 1920.

In countless human hearts he still is living,
    Because of the great love he gave—and won!

Though day by day, with happy touch caressing,
    Earth's simple joys returned to him again,
And high poetic thoughts renewed their blessing,
    His *care* was always for his fellow-men.

He held them dear, whate'er their place or station—
    Dearer, perhaps, as greater was their need,
And gave, with the idealist's elation,
    His best to make their lives more worthy, indeed.

So, though he left us when his day was ended,
    And, like all lovely things, lay down to rest,
His dreams, forever with our visions blended,
    Live in our lives—a memory dear and blest!

May 11

THE CHILD AND THE HEART BEREFT

MY garden, long time desolate,
    Were still of pleasure reft and bare
But for one single, lonely bloom
    That would insist on flowering there.

A fragile thing, in that chill place
    It grew where other joys were not,
Waxing a lovelier hope each day,—
    Albeit half tended, half forgot,—

Until with wild, resistless charm
    That sorrow's very self doth cheat,
It maketh of my desert drear
    A sunlit garden, fresh and sweet.

May 12

YOUTH AND AGE

FOND Youth and Age met face to face,
    And each the other doubted sore.
Age mourned: "Your follies grow apace
    More dangerous than of yore.

"Old standards trampled in the dust,
    Where you are wending who can tell?"
Youth, wondering, smiled, at his distrust,
    And answered: "Nay; all's well!—

"Your day gone by, why fear that I
    Shall lack the strength for mine own hour?
Each new demand of destiny
    Brings with it a new power.

"For you the past: for me the *Now*—
    The wonder-working Now divine!
A weight too heavy for your brow
    The Fates transfer to mine."

Age, out of heart, impatient, sighed:—
    "I ask what will the *Future* be?"
Youth laughed contentedly, and cried:—
    "The future leave to me!"

May 13

HONOR

DIVINE abstraction, shadowy image, dream
    More vital than substantial shapes made strong
    By all the tireless energies of wrong,—
Who should deny thy being would blaspheme

The power that made thy loveliness supreme,
    Lending thee accents of auroral song
    To comfort those who unto thee belong,
Though they go down to dark Cocytus' stream.

Patient as Time art thou, eternal one!
    Yet who may change thy judgments—or destroy?
The conqueror whom wily Egypt won
Found with life's honeyed draught a bitter blent;
    And Hector, fallen by the walls of Troy,
Looked up, and saw thy face, and was content.

May 14

PHILISTIA

SHE waits for man, and leads him artfully—
    In seeming freedom that beguiles his will—
    Unto the great wheels grinding in her mill;
And with a voice of suasive melody,
Entreats him: "Lo! all gifts I proffer thee—
    All joys that adolescent hopes fulfill,
    All riches that the old may covet still—
So thou wilt bow thee down and worship me!"

But list'ning her, the spirit that would live
    Must hear, from far, a nobler message sent:
        Distrustful most where most she seeks to please,
        Unsoftened by her luxury and ease,
    Must hope through higher things to find content,—
Toiling for triumphs which she cannot give!

May 15

THE SONG THAT IS FORGOT

TIME, like to sand from out the glass, unceasing flows away;
Then wherefore deem to-morrow more worth than yesterday?
The fairest rose the future knows Time darkling will entomb
With the rose that breathed in Persia, long since, its rare perfume.

If sands of time, effacing, flow, then what—ah, what of fame?
Nothing is lost that blesses the hour to which it came;
Nay, questioning heart, which gave it most the world itself knows
 not—
The song that is remembered, the song that is forgot.

May 16

SONG

FOR me the jasmine buds unfold
 And silver daisies star the lea,
The crocus hoards the sunset gold,
 And the wild rose breathes for me.
I feel the sap through the bough returning,
 I share the skylark's transport fine,
I know the fountain's wayward yearning,
 I love, and the world is mine!

I love, and thoughts that sometime grieved,
 Still well remembered, grieve not me;
From all that darkened and deceived
 Upsoars my spirit free.
For soft the hours repeat one story,
 Sings the sea one strain divine;
My clouds arise all flushed with glory,—
 I love, and the world is mine!

May 17

FAIRER THAN VIOLETS ARE

FAIRER than violets are
    That blossom in the virgin Spring,
More sweet than the song of birds
    When first of love they sing,
A gift of pure and perfect worth,
She came to this our darkened earth
    A smile of God to bring:

She came that we might lay
    Our griefs, submissive, 'neath the sod;
She came that light might beam
    From every path she trod;
She came that memory might confer
Blessing and hope, for, knowing her,
    We know the love of God.

May 18

HYLAS

UNTO the woodland spring he came
For water welling fresh and sweet;
An eager purpose winged his feet
And set his heart aflame.
But musing on Alcmene's son—
Reviewing, emulous, each prize
By the godlike hero won,
A-sudden, with surprise,
He heard soft voices call upon his name:

"Hylas, Hylas, stay and listen!
Though but a moment, bright dreamer, delay!
    Pleasure greets thee,

    Youth entreats thee,—
From their enchantments, ah, turn not away!
    Where the eddies dimpling glisten,
    To the love-lorn naiads listen!

"Let not carping care destroy
Life's jocund prime with counsels cold!—
From happy youth the gods withhold
The sordid gifts that they employ
    To plague the old.
Let not fruitless toil destroy
Days fresh as blossoms newly sprung!
Ere sages spoke, ere poets sung,
Youth was the gala-time of joy,—
    And thou art young!

"Glory?—ah, 't is labor double!
Wealth?—alas! 't is costly trouble!
Foolish Hylas! Wouldst thou follow
Glistering shows and phantoms hollow,
Vague intents and dreams ideal?
Here are pleasures sweet as real:
    Still delights
    Of summer nights,
Rest—which e'en ambition misses—
    Soft repose
    On beds of rose
In murmurous grots, and waking blisses.
Hither comes no word of duty;
Life is love, and love is beauty.
Hither comes no note of strife;
Life is love, and love is life.
Raptures bubbling to the brink,
Would not a wise man stoop and drink?

"Though Heracles sit in his tent
And boast to warlike Telamon

Of monsters tamed and labors done;
Though he recount in lofty strain
How dread Nemea's plague was slain,
And loudly vaunt, grown eloquent,
The rattling heaven-descended spell,
And Cerberus upborne from Hell,—
Yet, even as he tells the story,
And boasts a world-renownèd glory,
Telamon applauding—then,
Ay, even then, let him recall
Shy Megara's face—he'd give it all,
All, Hylas, to be young again!

The wondering boy beheld the gleam
Of tresses mirrored in the spring:
Naught else; yet soft as in a dream,
Those voices sweetly ravishing
Fell on his ear.
He bent more near,
Trembling, amazed,
And wistful gazed—
Grown eager more to hear—
Far down below the cool reflection
And wavy sheen of auburn hair.
But, Eros blest!—what marvel rare,
What more than mortal beauty there,
What coy, what wooing-sweet perfection
Entrancèd held him, bound as in a snare?

No need to urge him now to stay! . . .
Alas! he could not turn away,
But on the Naiad's nearing charms
Gazed amorous:—on locks of brown,
On melting eyes, and rubied lips,
Slim throats and dewy finger-tips.
He stooped; they caught him in their arms,
And held him fast, and drew him down.

    Down, down, down, down,
Through the liquid deeps of the soundless well:
    Down, down, down, down,—
How many fathom, ah! who can tell?
Away from the day and the starlit hours,
Away from the shadows, the birds, and the flowers;
Away from the fell and the spicy dell,
From the fountain's smile and the mountain's frown;
    Down, down, down, down!
He tried to ascend, but the lithe arms enwound him;
He sought to escape, but the wily weeds bound him.
By pleasure's softening touches thrill'd—
The dainty marvels at his side—
He missed not tasks left unfulfill'd,
Nor heard despisèd honor chide;
And sinking slowly to the watery goal,
His visage shrank to match his ebbing soul.
  . . . .

Late in the purple twilight of the day
Alcides came with heavy tread that way,
Crushing the fragile reeds and shrinking ferns,
Searching now here, now there—by doubtful turns—
And calling loudly on the boy,
    His dear annoy.
Long, long he stayed, still hoping to rejoice,
While babbling Echo, with her far-off voice,
Railed at his care. Then, sad and slow, he passed—
Reluctant to resign the quest at last,
Nor dreamed, beholding a poor frog emerge
From that enchanted fountain's plashy verge,
That Hylas, once so ready to aspire,
There harshly croaked, contented in the mire!

May 19

GREATNESS[26]

MIDST noble monuments, alone at eve
I wandered, reading records of the dead,—
In spite of praise forgotten past recall;
And near, so sheltered one might scarce perceive,
I found a lowly headstone, and I read
The word upon it: HAWTHORNE—that was all.

May 20

THE CHRYSANTHEMUM

A ROSE-TREE, all ablush with opening flowers,
    Just nodded to the heliotrope and pink,
    Greeted the lilies by the fountain's brink
    And curtseyed toward the jasmine's star-wreathed bowers.
She then perceived a plant which, in the hours
    Since May-time blossoms blew and bobolink
    Sang blithely, constant grew, yet seemed to drink
    No beauty from spring sun or summer showers.
Scornful, she tossed her head, but soothingly
    Dame Nature to the plant dishonored said: "Time conquereth
    The proud. Yon rose her petaled pomps shall see
Torn rudely by the Frost-King's icy breath,
    When life luxuriant shall throb in thee,
    And blossom in the very midst of death!"

---

[26] Nathaniel Hawthorne died on this day in 1864.

May 21

OLD ST. DAVID'S[27]

"What an image of peace and rest."—Longfellow

IN Radnor Valley, from the world apart,
    The little Church stands peaceful as of old,
    Guarding her memories yet half untold,
Deep in the silent places of her heart.

Life comes, and passes by her, as it wills;
    But musing on loved things evanishèd,
    She keeps the generations of the dead,—
Herself unchanged amid her beauteous hills:

Unchanged, though full of change her days have been,
    Since builded here, ere Washington was born,
    She seemed the *home* of exiled hearts forlorn—
The open portal to hope's fair demesne.

Close as the ivy that adorns her walls,
    So grateful thoughts have twined themselves and clung
    About this lowly sanctuary, sprung
From that necessity which ever calls

The soul of man to seek for something higher—
    Anhungered for a more celestial bread
    Than that wherewith his earthly life is fed—
And faith was kindled here, and patriot fire!

Yea; from this sacred pile, in days gone by,
    Brave men, to duty nobly dedicate,
    Went forth to strive against despotic fate—

---

[27] Written by request of the Pennsylvania Society of Colonial Dames of America and read on this day in 1904 at Old St. David's. [original footnote]

Content for liberty to live—or die.

Some came not back; but some returned, victorious,—
    Needing nor badge nor ribbon on the breast,—
    To find here by the little Church their rest:
Heroes and martyrs lowly—yet how glorious! . . .

Healed of all hurt, emparadised afar
    Though they abide, yet to our reverent sight,
    About their graves there lingers still a light
Which is not as the light of moon or star;

And very peaceful after stormy days,
    And sturdy as the antique oaks remain,
    Which sentinelled the burial of Wayne,—
Illustrious beyond the need of praise,—

Old Radnor Church bestows her benison,
    Calling to us who from the past yet borrow,
    To love the right and, living for the morrow,
Fulfil the hopes of heroes that are gone.

So, through whate'er of change the future brings,
    Shall she our memories and faiths defend,—
    A temple of the highest to the end,
Immortal through the love of deathless things!

May 22

THE FROGS

A CONCERT IN THE MARSH

THE perfect eloquence of silence; then,
    Amid the softened afterglow,
From each bay-bordered island fen
    On either hand, distinct but low—

Was it the twang of strings?...
 O'erhead there is a whirr of homing wings,
And silence falls again.

But now—ah, timely,—the choragus! Hark!
 Leader of choric minstrels grim,
Grave his solemnity: and mark
 What eerie voices follow him
 As strophe and antistrophe
 Swell to the roar of a far-sounding sea,
Out of the marshy dark!

Can these, indeed, be voices, that so greet
 The twilight still? I seem to hear
Oboe and cymbal in a rhythmic beat
 With bass-drum and bassoon; their drear
 And droll crescendo louder growing,
 Then falling back, like waters ebbing, flowing,—
Back to the silence sweet!

May 23

ROUEN: IN THE PRISON OF JOAN OF ARC[28]

SHE laid her head upon the straw,
 She who had crowned a king of France,
And angel shapes, whom no man saw,
 For her deliverance,
Knelt at her feet—less pure, less sweet—
 A blessing in each glance.

She laid her head upon the straw,
 She who gave France her liberty,
And angel shapes, whom no man saw—
 Ah me! how could men see?—

---

[28] Joan of Arc was captured at Compiègne on this day in 1430.

Watched till the day, then bore away
    Something the flames set free.

                                                            May 24

THOUGH THOU HAST CLIMBED

THOUGH thou hast climbed, by patient effort slow,
    O'er barriers that thy course denied,
And from proud summits gazest down below—
        Self-satisfied;

Though thou hast felt the clouds beneath thy feet,
    And to past triumphs fond returning,
Wakest no more, sublimer heights to greet
        With upward yearning,—

Better for thee hadst thou been taught to bow,
    Through lengthening years of blest probation,
Looking to something loftier than thou,
        In adoration:

Better for thee had thine unconquered will,
    So scornful of restraining bars—
Been held earth's captive thrall, thy strivings still
        Unto the Stars!

                                                            May 25

TO R. R.

ON REREADING THE "DE PROFUNDIS" OF OSCAR WILDE[29]

HE stood alone, despairing and forsaken:

---

[29] Oscar Wilde was convicted and sentenced to two years in prison on this day in 1895.

Alone he stood, in desolation bare;
From him avenging powers e'en hope had taken:
  He looked,—and thou wast there!

Why hadst thou come? Not profit, no: nor pleasure,
    Nor any faint desire of selfish gain,
Had moved thee, giving of thy heart's pure treasure,
    To share a culprit's pain.

In that drear place, as thou hadst lonely waited
    To greet with noble friendship one who came
Handcuffed from prison, pointed at, and hated,
    Bowed low in mortal shame,

No thought hadst thou of any special merit,
    So simple, natural, seemed that action fine
Which kept alive, in a despairing spirit,
    The spark of the divine,

And taught a dying soul that love is deathless,
    Even as when its holiest accents fell
Upon a woman's heart who listened, breathless,
    By a Samarian well.

May 26

THE MOURNER

"'TIS over—all over!" the mourner said.
"My love, in the grave of my love, lies dead:
Barren of bloom as yon wintry tree,
Lifeless and chill, is the heart of me!

"I shall smile no more: a tale that is told
Is the rapture of being. Now would I were old,
Who wearying years would no longer see
Stretching away unendingly!

"What value has Time? The last to-morrow
For me will hold but the one, one sorrow
Which, lone, I still shall endure, forlorn
As the bird that, above me, its mate doth mourn."
 . . . . . .

Full wearily wasted the months; and still
Guarding his grief with a constant will,
It chanced that the mourner, one halcyon day,
Wandering sadly the self-same way,

Beheld, half doubting, the wintry tree
A bower of blossom—a thing to see!—
And heard with emotion the sad bird sing:—
"O beauty! O love! O delight!—It is Spring!"

              May 27

MEMORY

IF it be true, as some aver,
 With wisdom naught endears,
That portioned to each human lot
 Are fewer smiles than tears,—

Then, merciful Mnemosyne,
 How great to thee our debt,
That we remember all our joys,
 Our sufferings forget!

              May 28

WATER LILIES

I GATHERED them—the lilies pure and pale,
 The golden-hearted lilies, virgin fair,
 And in a vase of crystal, placed them where
Their perfumes might unceasingly exhale.

High in my lonely tent above the swale,
    Above the shimmering mere and blossoms there,
    I solaced with their sweetness my despair,
And fed with dews their beauteous petals frail.

But when the aspens felt the evening breeze,
    And shadows 'gan across the lake to creep,
When hermit-thrushes to the Oreades
    Sang vesper orisons, from cloisters deep,—
My lilies, lulled by native sympathies,
    Upfolded their white leaves and fell asleep.

                                               May 29

REVEILLE

WHAT frolic zephyr through the young leaves plays,
    Scattering fragrance delicate and sweet?
    What impulse new moves Robin to repeat
    To pale Anemone his roundelays?
What winning wonder fills the world with praise
    In this mysterious time? Lo, all things greet
    A loved one, new redeemed from death's defeat—
    A youth whose languid head fair nymphs upraise!

For him the crocus dons his bravery,—
    And violets for him their censers swing;
    For him the shy arbutus, blushfully,
Peeps through the mosses that about her cling;
    Adonis wakes! Awake, earth's minstrelsy!
    In swelling diapason hymn the Spring!

May 30

JOAN OF ARC[30]

HER spirit is to France a living spring
    From which to draw deep draughts of life. To-day,—
    As when a peasant girl she led the way
Victorious to Rheims and crowned the King,—
High and heroic thoughts about her cling,
    And sacrificial faiths as pure as they,
    Moving the land she loved, with gentle sway,
To be, for love of her, a better thing!

Was she unhappy? No: her radiant youth
    Burned, like a meteor, on to swift eclipse;
    But where it passed, there lingers still a light.
She waited, wistful, for the word of truth
    That breathed in blessing from immortal lips
    When earthly comfort failed, and all around was night.

"BLESSÈD"

BLESSÈD: so have they named her. With just pride,
Deliberate care, and cautious circumstance,
The Holy Council have beatified
The Maid of Orleans, martyred child of France,
Who, at Domrémy's village altar kneeling,—
    Ignored by friend and foe,
Through all her young unsullied spirit feeling
The tears of a despairing people flow,—
Implored relief; and following the word
    Which none save she had heard,
Delivered France, and crowned her—long ago.
Rejoice, Domrémy, 'midst thy bowery green!

---

[30] Joan of Arc was burned at the stake on this day in 1431.

She was thine own, whom all, at last, would claim—
The greatest miracle that Earth hath seen
Since out of Nazareth a Saviour came.
Lowly as thou (though sheathed in armor bright),
    Her soul was as the snow—
Yea, as the lilies of her banner, white.
The Church hath blessed her; but man's heart, less slow,
Remembering her service and the price
    Of her dear sacrifice,
Gave her the name of blessèd—long ago.

                                    May 31

BY THE CONEMAUGH

(MAY 31, 1889)

FOREBODING sudden of untoward change,
    A tight'ning clasp on everything held dear,
A moan of waters wild and strange,
    A whelming horror near;
And midst the thund'rous din a voice of doom,—
"Make way for me, O Life, for Death make room!

"I come like the whirlwind rude,
    'Gainst all thou hast cherished warring;
I come like the flaming flood
    From a crater's mouth outpouring;
I come like the avalanche gliding free—
And the Power that sent thee forth, sends me!

"Where thou hast builded with strength secure
    My hand shall spread disaster;
Where thou hast barr'd me, with forethought sure,
    Shall ruin flow the faster;
I come to gather where thou hast sowed,—
But I claim of thee nothing thou hast not owed!

"O Life, from the fire-swept mould
    Arise new forms of beauty;
Out of the waters cold
    Diviner thoughts of duty;
The sunlight gleams where hath swept the tide,
And flowers blossom as flames subside!

"On my mission of mercy forth I go
    Where the Lord of Being sends me;
His will is the only will I know,
    And my strength is the strength He lends me;
Thy loved ones I hide 'neath my waters dim,—
But *I cannot take them away from Him!*"

                                                                               June 1

AT DUSK

EARTH, mother dear, I turn at last,
    A homesick child, to thee!
The twilight glow is fading fast,
    And soon I shall be free
To seek the dwelling, dim and vast,
    Where thou awaitest me.

I am so weary, mother dear!
    Thy child, of dual race,
Who gazing past the star-beams clear,
    Sought the Undying's face!
Now I but ask to know thee near,
    To feel thy large embrace!

Tranquil to lie against thy breast—
    Deep source of noiseless springs,
Where hearts are healed, and wounds are dressed,
    And naught or sobs or sings:
Against thy breast to lie at rest—

A life that folds its wings.

Sometime I may—for who can tell?—
    Awake, no longer tired,
And see the fields of asphodel,
    The dreamed-of, the desired,
And find the heights where He doth dwell,
    To whom my heart aspired!

And then— But peace awaiteth me—
    Thy peace: I feel it near;
The hush, the voiceless mystery,
    The languor without fear!
Enfold me—close; I want but thee!
    But thee, Earth-mother dear!

June 2

ACHILLES

WHEN, with a mortal mother's helpless tears,
    Thetis, the silver-footed, to her son
    Revealed the choice in death he might not shun;
The goddess-born, longing for lengthened years
In his own land, with all that life endears—
    Renounced Earth's breathing pleasures new begun,
    And chose to die in youth, each conflict won,
Leaving a fame no blight autumnal sears.

The Argives sleep, the Trojan hosts are dumb,
    And no man knows where Homer's ashes be;
Yet, echoing down the list'ning ages, come—
    E'en to this distant nineteenth century—
The hero's words by warlike Ilium,
    And strengthen others, in their need, and me!

June 3

LIMITATION

AS when the imperial bird, wide-circling, soars
    From his lonely eyrie, towered above the seas
    That wash the wild and rugged Hebrides,
    A force which he unconsciously adores
Bounds the majestic flight that heaven explores,
    And droops his haughty wing; as when the breeze
    Tempts to o'erleap their changeless boundaries
    The waves that tumble foaming to those shores;

So thou, my soul! impatient of restriction,
    With deathless hopes and longings all aglow,
    Aspirest still, and still the stern prediction
Stays thee, as them,—"No further shalt thou go!"
    But, ah! the eagle feels not thine affliction,
    Nor can the broken waves thy disappointment know.

June 4

A DESCANT

WHEN Spring comes tripping o'er the lea
    And grasses start to meet her,
        The bluebird sings
        With quivering wings
    Brief rhapsodies to greet her,
And deems—fond minstrel!—none may be,
The wide world over, blithe as he.

And where the brooklet tinkles by,
    And the yellow-snowdrop dances,
        And windflowers frail
        And bloodroots pale
    Lift up appealing glances,

The flute-voiced meadow-lark on high
Sings, "None on earth is glad as I!"

Laughs Corydon, "Your hearts are bold,
   Yet little ye can measure,
      Poor, silly birds,
      Spring's sweetest words,
   Or guess at my proud pleasure,
When Phyllis comes, and all the wold,
For sudden joy, buds into gold!"

                                                                        June 5

A LOWLY PARABLE

AT first the birds—so runs the gentle story
   The priest of Buddha to the people told,
     With only feet to bear them o'er the mould,
Hopped to and fro, nor marked the varied glory

Of days and seasons in their wondrous passing;
   Saw not the wintry branches overhead
     By vernal airs revived, engarlanded,
Saw not the clouds, their forms in rivers glassing,

Dreamed not of birch-tree-haunts on lovely islands
   Where sunsets tarry late, as loth to go,—
     Nor ever knew what winds delicious blow
From piny mountain-peaks o'er verdurous highlands.

Now here, now there, absorbed in one endeavor—
   One single aim—poor birds!—the search for food,
     They looked on all which aided that as good,—
Toward any larger goal aspiring never.

But came a morning, strange and unforeboded,
   When from their tiny shoulders started things,

    Feathered atip, which presently were wings,—
Full irksome to the birds, and heavy-loaded.

Impatient of the undesired burden,
    They huddled on the ground, disconsolate,
    While some complained reproachfully:—"Does Fate
Lay on us this new care in lieu of guerdon

"For all that we have done and borne so bravely?
    Is't not enough that oft, through blight and snow,
    We starve—we who from toil no respite know?"
They drooped, they pined; but said the bluebird gravely,

His pretty head with gallant air uplifting:
    "This is indeed a burden which we bear—
    An added burden; yet—O why despair?"—
Then, from one foot to t' other his weight shifting,

He hopped about, in valor growing bolder,
    Till—for new effort new ambition brings—
    He found at last that he could stretch his wings! . . .
Straightway the birds forgot the day grown colder—

Forgot the future's care, the past's privation;
    And when, their fond desires fixed on high,
    They knew—O happy birds!—that they could fly,—
The burden had become their exaltation!

                                                            June 6

AN OPTIMIST

"O AGED man, pray, if you know,
    Now answer me the truth!—
Which of the gifts that gods bestow
    Is the greatest gift of youth?

"O aged man, I have far to fare
    By the divers paths of Earth,
Which of the gifts I with me bear
    Is the gift of the greatest worth?

"Is it the might of the good right arm,
    Whereby I shall make my way
Where dangers threaten and evils harm,
    Holding them still at bay?

"Is it the strength wherewith I shall climb
    Where few before have trod—
To the mountain-tops, the peaks sublime
    That glow in the smile of the god?

"Is it the never-failing will,
    Invincible in might,
Which armed against oppression still
    Shall vanquish for the right?

"Or is it the heart, thou aged man!—
    The heart, impassioned, strong,
Which shall be blest, as naught else can,
    In perfect love ere long?"

The old man smiled: a listening breeze
    Grew whist on the sun-lit slope;
The old man sighed: "Ah, none of these!
    Youth's greatest gift is its hope."

June 7

ART

SHE stood a vision vestureless and fair,
    Glowing the canvas with her orient grace:
    A goddess grave she stood, with such a face

As in Elysium the immortals wear.
But some, unworthy, as they pondered there,
Cold to the marvel of her look divine—
Saw but a form undraped, in Beauty's shrine.

Then she, it seemed, rebuked them: "Old and young
    Have worshiped at the temple where I breathe,
    And deathless laurels, for my sake, enwreathe
The brows of him from whose pure thought I sprung:
Lips consecrate as yours his praise have sung,—
Who neither sued for praise nor courted ease,
But reverently wrought, as from his knees.

"No raiment can the base or mean reclaim,
    And that which sacred is must sacred be,
    Clothed but in rags or robed in modesty.
In the endeavor still is felt the aim:
The workman may by skill exalt his name,
But, toiling fault and failure to redeem,
Cannot create what's loftier than his dream!

"For chaste must be the soul that chastely sees,
    The thought enlightened, and the insight sure
    That separates the pure from the impure;
And who Earth's humblest faith from error frees,
Awakening ideal sympathies,
Uplifts the savage from his kindred sod;
Who shows him beauty speaks to him of God!"

                                                                     June 8

HOW WONDERFUL IS LOVE

HOW wonderful is love!
More wonderful, I wis,
Than cherry-blossoms are when spring's first kiss
Warms the chill breast of earth,

And gives new birth
To beauty! High above
All miracles—the miracle of love,
Which by its own glad and triumphant power
Brings life to flower.
Oh, love is wonderful!
    More wonderful than is the dew-fed rose
    Whose petals half unclose,
        In welcome of the light,
When first the Dawn comes robed in vesture cool
        Of fragrant, shimmering white!—
More wonderful and strange
Than moonrise, which doth change
Dulness to glory—
Yea, with a touch transforms the mountains hoary,
        And fills the darkling rills with living silver bright!

Not music when it wings
From the far azure where the skylark sings
    Is wonderful as love!—
Not music when it wells
From the enchanted fairy-haunted dells
Where, shrined mid thorn and vine—
    An ecstasy apart,
    Drawn from the life-blood of a breaking heart—
    The nightingale pours forth forever
    The rapture and the pain that naught can sever,
Of love which mortal is, yet knows itself divine!

                                                                June 9

TRUE LOVE

TRUE love is not a conquest won,
    But a perpetual winning;
A tireless service bravely done
    And ever new-beginning;

Gold will not buy it for to-day
    Nor keep it for to-morrow,
From Pleasure's path it turns away,
    To make its bed with Sorrow.

White, Aphrodite, are thy doves,
    But 'neath their snows are burning,
Undying flames, and he who loves
    Aspires with flame-like yearning:

Aspires unto a far-off bliss
    Whose vision makes him younger,
And moved to rapture by thy kiss,
    Still for thy soul doth hunger!

                                                                June 10

YOU

IF you no more should love me?—you?
    It takes my breath, a thought so strange
As that aught earthly could your spirit woo
        To change!
Remote from doubt, I dwell secure
    In faith all minor faiths above,
So do I trust, so live, in your
    Incomparable love!

I laugh for joy to think how much
    A question would your nature wrong,
Whom Heaven created, with a noble touch,
        So strong!
Nay; doubt, for me, new born were over.
    You will remain unchanged and true—
Not, not that I am I, my lover,
    But just that you are *you!*

June 11

WINGS

THAT Love has wings the poets say;
White wings where lights and shadows play,
    Swift wings, that sail from shore to shore,
    From sea to sea, or lightly soar
To happy Edens far away.

Where'er they gleam the world grows gay,
December smiles, and rosy May
    With fluttering transport feels once more
        That Love has wings.

But Youth is fond, and hearts are clay,
And faults deceive, and doubts betray,
    And some forget the winning lore
    That drew the blessing to their door,
And learn too late—ah, well-a-day!—
        That Love has wings.

June 12

SONG

SWEET is the birth of love, and the awaking,
    The bashful dream, the faltering desire,
The vision fair—of all fair things partaking—
    The wonder, the communicable fire:
Sweet is the need to give and to obtain,—
    And sweet love's pain!

June 13

TO WILLIAM BUTLER YEATS[31]

TELL us of beauty! Touch thy silver lyre
    And bid thy Muse unfold her shining wings!
    Tell us of joy—of those unaging things
Which wither not, nor are consumed by fire,
Things unto which the souls of all aspire!
    Sing us the mystic song thine Erin sings,
    Her poignant dreams, her weird imaginings,
With magic of thy "Land of Heart's Desire!"

Let others hate!—from lips not thine be hurled
Reproaches; since all hate at last must prove
    Abortive, though it triumph for a while.
The gospels that indeed have won the world
Laid their foundations in the strength of love.
    Sing thou, a lover, of thy wave-washed Isle!

June 14

THROUGH THE WINDOW

THROUGH the window Love looked in
    For an instant only,
And behold!—a little maid
    In the silence lonely.

At his glance, her lily cheek
    Took the tint of roses,
And her lips soft parted, like
    A bud that half uncloses.

Gentle tremors filled her breast,

---

[31] William Butler Yeats was born on this day in 1865.

    And her eyes grew tender
With a something wistful that
        His presence seemed to lend her.

Ah, 't was strange! Love there looked in
        For an instant only,
Yet the lass, so lone before,
        Seemed, methought, less lonely.

June 15

FREDERICK[32]

"RESPECT the Future, *which belongs to me!*"
    So speak thy yearning and imperious will,
    Making the Present distant faiths fulfil,
And raised from falling kingdoms—Germany.

No idle name, no doubtful dream to thee
    That Future: actual, its clasp grown chill,
    It led thee, and thy soul sublimed it still,—
Heir of a more than earthly dynasty!

O didst thou think, untimely called to rest,
    The preparation of a life o'erthrown—
To lose what thou so bravely didst resign?

Forevermore the Fatherland shall own
    Her nobler liberties thy dear bequest:
    The future thy great spirit saw—was thine!

---

[32] Frederick III of Germany died on this day in 1888.

June 16

AN IDLE DITTY

'TIS I have been waiting to know, dear,
    The day that ye'r ship would come in,
For if I'm to love ye at all, dear,
    I'm thinking it's time to begin.

The mavis is singing hard by, dear,
    The hedges are white wi' the may,
And there's never a cloud i' the sky, dear,
    To hinder a ship on its way.

Ye've told me o' castles a many,
    And though they're but castles in Spain,
I surely were better in any
    Wi' you, than alone wi' my pain!

The mavis that's close to her mate, dear,
    For no castle would part wi' her nest,
And the ship that brings you, though it's late, dear,
    Brings me what is worth all the rest!

June 17

AN IDLER

SHE cannot wind the distaff,
    She can nor bake nor brew;
Her hands are indeed too dainty
    Such labors to pursue.

She cares not to follow the harvest,
    She neither can sew nor glean,
But waits for the weary reapers
    With cheerful calm serene.

Commanding all to serve her,
    From service she is free;
But, ah, my babe so helpless
    Is health and wealth to me!

                                                  June 18

CRADLE SONG

THY heart and mine are one, my dear,
    At dawn and set of sun;
When skies are bright, when days are drear,
    Thy heart and mine are one!

About us move the hapless folk
    Whom paltry things estrange;
The friends that feel their bond a yoke,
    The loves that lightly change;

But thou and I, my bonny child,
    Their dangers blithely shun,
Nor can by folly be beguiled,—
    For thou and I are one!

                                                  June 19

BEREFT

DEATH took away from me my heart's desire,—
    Full suddenly, without a word of warning;
Froze with benumbing touch her body's fire,
    And darkened her young morning.

Death hid her then where she is safe, men say,—
    Imprisoned in a deep-digged grave and hollow,
Where grief and pain may never find a way,
    Nor any torment follow.

Safe!—and because of fear, they deem 't was best
    For her, perchance,—this thing which they call dying,
But cold she could not be against my breast
    As there where she is lying!

Sometimes I dream, with sudden, wild delight,
    That she escapes the cruel bonds that bind her,
And fond I seek through all the throbbing night,
    But never, never find her!

Sometimes—But have the dead then no regrets?—
    Ah, me! I think, though she hath so bereft me,
My loved one cannot be where she forgets
    How *lonely* she hath left me!

                                          June 20

IN MEMORY

ELIZA SPROAT TURNER[33]

HOW should we think of her as dead
Whose words to many are as daily bread?
How should we deem her gone
Whose help is not, and cannot be, withdrawn?
We do not mourn the orb as set
Whose shining beams are all about us yet!

Ah, no! They live indeed—the dead
By whose example we are upward led;
Nor was her service vain
Who gave herself—again and yet again—
And when her spirit was most sad,
Healed her deep hurt by making others glad.

---

[33] Eliza Sproat Turner died on this day in 1903.

She lived to bless: her generous mind
Despaired not of the humblest of her kind
For in her heart was born
Love for the poor, unfriended, and forlorn,
Which, after love's perfected way,
Judged not itself of greater worth than they.

She lived to bless: love made her strong
To widen good, to limit hate and wrong,
To ease the path of woe;
And choosing in the Christ-like way to go,
The future held for her no fear,
Who, self-forgetting, made her heaven—here!

June 21

THE SUMMER-TIME IS IN THE ROSE

THE summer-time is in the rose;
    'T is but to breathe once more
The perfume that its leaves enclose
    The summer to restore.
But how should summer bloom for him
    Who must its rose resign?
A winter, changeless in his heart,
    Repeats:—"Not mine!—not mine!"

Ah, sorrowful to give in vain—
    To love when hope is not!
To cover with a smile the pain
    That will not be forgot!
To journey to a living spring
    Of water, welling sweet,—
To long as with a desert thirst,
    Yet turn away the feet!

June 22

ODE ON THE CORONATION[34] OF KING GEORGE V[35]

"I have vowed to God to lead a right life in all things, to rule justly and piously my realms and subjects, and to administer just judgment to all. If heretofore I have done aught beyond what was just, through headiness or negligence of youth, I am ready with God's help to amend it utterly."—King Canute's letter to his English subjects.

    WHEN Nature takes away the things we prize,
With all a mother's patient tenderness
She soothes us, and from treasure limitless
Brings forth new joys to gladden our grieved eyes.

Before the leaves fall fluttering to the ground
Affrighted at the very breath and sound
Of the wind's passion, she from blight and storm
Garners the seeds of Summer, safe and warm.

She knows, though glad and sweet the wild bird sing,
How soon the trillium of the wood shall fade,—
Nor longer with its stars illume the shade,—
She knows, and harvests for a future Spring;

And though about her winds of Autumn sigh,
And though the rose—the rose, itself, must die,
And though the lordly pine that scorns to bend
Must fall at last,—she knows there is no end.

Sure of her birthright—elemental, vast,—
Calmly she waits; but man, to whom is given
Earth in its fullness and the dream of heaven,

---

[34] The coronation of King George V. was held on this day in 1911.
[35] Published as "Henry V" in *Poems* (1916) Volume II omitting stanzas II through IV along with the quotation from King Canute's letter to his English subjects.

Still looks with fond regret unto a past

Whose colors fade not in the distant light,
But rather to his worship grow more bright,
And careless as to that the future saith,
Pays tribute to the nothingness of death.

I

    When the fourth Henry, in that chamber called
Jerusalem, lay dying, with what fear,
Knowing the Angel-of-the-Shadow near,
Must he have viewed the future and, appalled,
Beheld succeeding to his perilous throne—
To reign and rule alone—
One who to Folly turned a laughing face,
Dallied with Fortune, and out-dared Disgrace.

More grievous, as the fatal hour drew nigh,
More dreadful than the death he might not fly,
More poignant than regret or mortal pain
Or memories of woeful Richard slain,—
More tragic than all else to him the thought
That his own offspring, in but little while,
Consorting with the worthless and the vile,
Should bring his dearly purchased good to naught.

Fainting, the King saw sorrows multiply,
And out of weakness dared to prophesy
Evil of Harry Monmouth! nor might guess
How idle his distress
For one whose future Honour should secure
In human hearts and in heroic story,—
The King new found, new crowned, at Agincourt,—
Great England's darling and her future glory!

II

But how should doubt not add to care its pain
When, after Mary Tudor's baleful reign,
Forth came from prison drear
Another Queen? Yet 't was her spirit, fired
By grave ambition, nobly men inspired
To victories thrice dear,—
Giving her Age to breathe immortal breath,
Illustrious in the name Elizabeth!

III

Still with misgiving crowns are laid
Upon the brow of kings.
Yet oft have fairest plantings been repaid
With poorest harvestings,
While following vain auguries of ill
To man have come, beneficently born,
Such reigns as his whose tact and generous will
The Nations of the earth late joined to mourn.

But no misgiving clouds the Future now!
In all the ages rarely hath there been
Such light of hope upon the forehead seen
As that which haloes her auroral brow,
Whose puissance shall uplift the poor and weak,
Whose love shall teach, to such as wisdom seek,
That they are blest who give, they only free
Who in the strength of Law find liberty!

IV

England, it is thy coronation hour!
Doubt is of high and ancient lineage,

But faith is more than plenitude of power,
And now—distrust were treason. Turn in pride,

O England, to thy happy heritage!
And as the bridegroom forth to meet the bride
Fares smiling, so, from cloudy griefs of night,
Turn thou where lovely dawns the day's new light,

And with wise trust, the fruit of loyalty,
To his great father's throne
Make doubly welcome Alexandra's son—
Thy son, O England!—worthy thine to be!

Far from thy beauteous isle, across the Sea,
A Sister-Land prays heaven for him and thee—
Prays that the coming ages still may sing
The blessings of his reign. God save the King!

June 23

IN MEMORY OF CAROLINE FURNESS JAYNE[36]

COULDST thou—thou, also, die, whom life so cherished?
    Couldst thou go from us, in thy beauteous June,
Leaving a sense of joy untimely perished,
    Of music stilled too soon?

We had not dreamed, fair child, that thou before us
    Shouldst find the meadows of the asphodel—
Shouldst hear, ere we, "the high imagined chorus,"—
    But, ah, for thee, 't is well!

Not thine to creep reluctant to death's portal:
    Thy spirit from the mirk of transient things
Rose radiant to the light of the immortal,

---

[36] Caroline Furness Jayne died on this day in 1909.

With eager, outstretched wings!
For the grave gods, bestowing every blessing
　　　Upon a child of Earth, ere grief should come,
Crowned thee, in youth, with the mild touch caressing
　　　That calls their loved ones home!

June 24

DREAM THE GREAT DREAM

DREAM the Great Dream, though you should dream—you, only,
　　　And friendless follow in the lofty quest.
Though the dream lead you to a desert lonely,
　　　Or drive you, like the tempest, without rest,
Yet, toiling upward to the highest altar,
　　　There lay before the gods your gift supreme,—
A human heart whose courage did not falter
　　　Though distant as Arcturus shone the Gleam.

The Gleam?—Ah, question not if others see it,
　　　Who nor the yearning nor the passion share;
Grieve not if children of the earth decree it—
　　　The earth, itself,—their goddess, only fair!
The soul has need of prophet and redeemer:
　　　Her outstretched wings against her prisoning bars,
She waits for truth; and truth is with the dreamer,—
　　　Persistent as the myriad light of stars!

June 25

THE POETRY OF EARTH

"The poetry of earth is never dead."—Keats.

THERE is always room for beauty: memory
　　　A myriad lovely blossoms may enclose,
But, whatsoe'er hath been, there still must be

    Room for another rose.

Though skylark, throstle, whitethroat, whip-poor-will,
    And nightingale earth's echoing chantries throng,
When comes another singer, there will be
    Room for another song.

                                               June 26

ON RE-READING "THE SICK KING IN BOKHARA"

AS one grows weary dragging at the chain
Of circumstance which, unrelentingly,
Binds him to futile, joyless drudgery,
Far from the skyey paths youth thought to gain;
Though mocked by hope and teased by self-disdain,
Forgets his griefs in wingéd sympathy
When one more blest and worthier to be free
Triumphant rises from earth's sordid plain;
So, to this fragrant oriental story—
Bright, in the midst of old-world wretchedness,
With love's benignant and eternal glory—
We turn who fevered and athirst have dwelt
In desert places and with tears confess
How deeply he who wrote has thought for man—and felt.

                                               June 27

TO HELEN KELLER[37]

LIFE has its limitations manifold:
    All life; not only that which throbs in thee,
    And strains its fetters, eager to be free.
The faultless eye may not thy vision hold—
Maiden, whose brow with thought is aureoled—

---

[37] Helen Keller was born on this day in 1880.

And they who hear may lack the ministry,
   The august influence, of Silence, she
Who brooded o'er the void in ages old.

Prisoner of the dark inaudible,
    Light, which the night itself could not eclipse,
      Thou shinest forth Man's being to reveal.
   We learn with awe from thine apocalypse,
That nothing can the human spirit quell,
      And know him lord of all things, *who can feel!*

HELEN KELLER WITH A ROSE

OTHERS may see thee; I behold thee not;
   Yet most I think thee, beauteous blossom, mine:
   For I, who walk in shade, like Proserpine—
Things once too briefly looked on, long forgot—
   Seem by some tender miracle divine,
When breathing thee, apart,
To hold the rapturous summer warm within my heart.
We understand each other, thou and I!
   Thy velvet petals laid against my cheek,
   Thou feelest all the voiceless things I speak,
And to my yearning makest mute reply:
   Yet a more special good of thee I seek,
For God who made—oh, kind!—
Beauty for one and all, gave fragrance for the blind!

AGAINST THE GATE OF LIFE

TO HELEN KELLER

AS mute against the gate of life you sit,
   Longing to open it,
Full oft you must behold, in thought, a maid

With banner white, whose lilies do not fade,
    And armor glory lit.

Across the years, darkling, you still must see,
    In the hush of memory,
Her whom no wrong of Fate could make afraid—
Of all the maidens of the world, *The Maid!*—
    In her brave purity.

For she, like you, was singly set apart,
    O high and lonely heart!—
And hearkened Voices, silent save to her,
And looked on visions she might not transfer
    By any loving art,—

Knew the dread chill of isolation, when
    Life darkened to her ken;
Yet could not know, as round her closed the night,
How radiant and far would shine her light,—
    A miracle to men!

                                                                         June 28

BETROTHAL

BOTH your hands? . . . What mean they, dear?
I, unworthy,—dare I claim you?
Then, against the world, I hold you:
Mine—forever mine!

Men have waked from dreams of joy:
Teach me to believe this rapture!
Lift your eyes! O my beloved,
Let me read your heart!

Is it true? . . . Ah, me! those eyes!
How divinely kind!—how tender!

Doubt itself could not distrust them,
Or resist their light!

Dear, without you, I have been
Poorer than the humblest beggar
Who against your door at nightfall
Kneeling, asked for bread:

I have gazed upon your face
And have felt such fear oppress me
That I trembled. From this moment,
Nothing fear I more!

For whatever perils come,
Nothing henceforth can divide us;
Neither follies nor ambitions—
Neither joys nor tears:

Never can you go so far
That my love shall fail to find you;
Seeking ever to deserve you,
Upward striving still;

And though seas should lie between,
I shall feel that you are near me:
In the twilight and night-season
I shall hear your voice.

June 29

THE YOUNG WIFE SPEAKS

HAPPINESS is everywhere!—
On the earth and in the air,
With the bloom and with the bee,
With the bird that wingeth free!
Happiness is everywhere!—

And it binds my heart to thee.

"Everywhere are pain and woe"?
Ay, belovéd, that I know:
None from grief is wholly free,—
It doth even visit me!
Yet to grief I something owe,
For it closer binds to thee!

Laughter have we shared and tears,—
Knowest thou which more endears?
Tell me truly! I would be
Wise indeed to choose, nor flee
Aught in all the gift of years
That would bind my heart to thee!

June 30

THE YOUNG WIFE

SHE leaned above the river's sedgy brink—
The little wife—half-minded there to drink
Forgetfulness of all the grief and pride
That overwhelmed her spirit like a tide.

She had so blindly trusted! Yet doubt grew—
Whence it had sprung, alas! she hardly knew,—
A hydra-headed monster that devoured
Her happiness ere fully it had flowered.

He who had been her truth!—could he betray?
"Ah, let me die," she cried, "or quickly stay,
Thou who bestowed, unasked, this gift of breath,
Imaginings more terrible than death!"

Lone and forespent, she leaned her heavily
Against a willow; when she seemed to see—

Doubting if that indeed she saw or dreamed,
So full of mystery the vision seemed—

A form unknown, ineffable in grace,
With look compassionate bent on her face.
"Thy tears have moved the Heart Omnipotent,
Wherefore I come, to thee in pity sent,—"

So, as she thought, the wondrous vision spake,—
"To serve thee, if I may, e'en though I make
Confession, grievous unto me, who know
My folly was forgiven long ago. . . .

"A youth was I who fondly pleasure sought,
Careless to ask how dearly it was bought;
Who passed my days in idleness, nor guessed
How close the coils of evil round me pressed,

"Till, like some swimmer boastful of his strength
Who dares too far, I faced the truth at length—
Perceived the awful distance I had come,
And, battling back, despaired of reaching home.

"Then I had perished in my utter need,
Had no one trusted me beyond my meed;
But—I reached port at last, my fate withstood,
Because one woman still believed me good."

Softly the vision faded, and was gone.
The young wife by the river stood alone;
Musing, she lingered there a little while,
And to her pensive lips there came a smile.

July 1

JOHN HAY

AMID ferns and mosses brown,
From the little mountain-town,
    Through the driving rain they bore him,
Kearsarge frowning down:

Onward bore him, wrapped from sight
Under palms and blossoms white,—
    While the grieving hearts of thousands
Followed through the night

To that grave, love-sanctified,
Where, in the full summer-tide,
    Low they laid him, who had cherished
Sympathies world-wide.

Honored grave! Yet Azrael's dart
Only slays the mortal part,
    And they die not who have written
On the human heart.

Sad Roumania, far Peking,
East with West, his praise to sing
    Who deemed justice more than power,
Hither tribute bring;

And the mother-land who bore—
She whom most he labored for—
    Bows her head in sorrow, knowing
He returns no more.

Fame has crowned her own again,
Writing with illumined pen,—
    Lincoln's friend, who loved and truly

Served his fellow-men.

July 2

TO THE MUSE

ONE spot of green, watered by hidden streams,
Makes summer in the desert where it gleams;
   And mortals, gazing on thy heavenly face,
Forget the woes of earth, and share thy dreams!

July 3

AFFINITY

ALL are not strangers whom we so misname:
Man's free-born spirit, which no rule can tame,
   Careless of time, o'er vasty distance led,
Still finds its own where alien altars flame,
   Still greets its own, amongst the deathless dead!

July 4

LINES FOR A FIFTIETH ANNIVERSARY

GOLDEN their days have been, for love is golden—
   Golden as sunshine warm with life, not cold;
Lighting earth's pathway with the blessing olden
   That never groweth old.

It owns no *Past;* a help divine in sorrow,
   A strength to overmaster each annoy,
Love holds the faithful promise of a morrow,
   Immortal in its joy!

July 5

A LITTLE SONG

ROSES are but for a day,
    Amaranths endure for ever;
Joys there be that fade away,
    Dreams that perish never;
But, whate'er the future's holding,—
Crown of all, all else enfolding,—
    Love lives on!

Well they know, who with content
    Hear his oft-repeated story,
How to earthly glooms are lent
    Reflexes of glory!
Rapture's first and final giver,
Star of Charon's rayless river,—
    Love lives on!

July 6

ADIEU

ADIEU! I know that I no more
    Shall behold you,
Your future lies beyond her door
    Who consoled you;

The world has promised to redeem
    Each new sorrow,
It beckons, and you lightly dream
    Of a morrow.

I weep not, nor shall futile sighs
    Hold you longer,
The pity in your loveless eyes

Makes me stronger,

For terrible, past loss of mine,
    Hath arisen
The dread to know what was your shrine—
    But your prison.

I listen while your lips protest,
    Heavy hearted,
For by your wishes unexpressed—
    We are parted:

I listen, and hope's fickle glow
    Fades away.
Why mock my grief? If you can go—
    Wherefore stay?

In all the past we still were true,
    You and I, love;
Few words suffice to bid adieu,
    Few to die, love;

The loneliest stand face to face,
    Disunited,
And thoughts of love that strain through space
    Are requited!

                                            July 7

STANZA: "THE VOICES OF ALL WATERS"

THE voices of all waters that make moan—
Loudly upbraiding the impassive sky,
Have not the meaning of one human groan,
Have not the pathos of one human sigh;
And neither that blithe strain whereby
The brook doth wintry doubts destroy,

Nor that pure rhapsody the woodland sings,
When Summer to its heart contentment brings,—
Breathes unto Heaven such praise as human joy!

                                                July 8

A ROSE

A SINGLE rose in yonder ruined bed
Makes beauty where all beauty else had fled;
Like love, which, careless or of time or death,
    About earth's shattered hopes its tendrils wreathing,
    Blooms in the wilderness, divinely breathing,
Till all around grows fragrant with its breath.

                                                July 9

POETRY

CONTEMPLATIVE and fair, with look divine,
    Her wistful vision fixed on the unseen,—
    The future hers, as the long past has been,—
She waits apart. Who disregard her shrine,
Who pour to her libations of red wine,
    Who heal their griefs at her loved Hippocrene,
    She noteth not—enwrapt in thought serene,
And pondering grave meanings, line by line.

She has envisaged the veiled heart of things—
    Has passed through Purgatory, and her way,
        Darkling, unravelled through the deeps of Hell;
        And thence arising where the blessèd dwell,
Has touched the stars with her aspiring wings,
    And knows that she is deathless as are they!

July 10

ROMANCE

HOW fair you are, wondrous maiden,
As from the aisle I behold you
In the old English cathedral,
Standing so rapt and apart!

Glintings of gold from the stained glass
Brighten the coils of your dark hair
Waving away from a forehead
Pure with the freshness of youth,

And your face flower-like lifted,
With the blue eyes full of worship,
Fairer you seem than the angels
Carved near the altar, in stone.

What though I know not your name, dear,—
Though I to-day first behold you—
You who must pass as a vision
Nobly enthralling and glad?

Does he who, lone in the forest,
Finds there an exquisite blossom,
Joy in it less that its beauty
Blooms not to fade on his breast?

Nay: nor does one who at nightfall
Harkens the voice of the mavis
Feel less delight that the singer
Blesses him, high out of reach.

So, though you pass—and for ever,
Yet I, afar, shall remember
That the world holds such a maiden,

And, you remembering, love!

> July 11

TO THE AUTHOR[38] OF "MADAME BUTTERFLY"

ON SEEING THE OPERA

POET, it was your soul created her:
    Yours was the vision lovely and supreme,
    Yours the appealing, high-imagined theme,
That like a breath of attar-rose or myrrh,
Piercing the sense, made Art her worshiper—
    Made heavenly Music long to be, and seem,
    A part of the impassionating dream,
An added accent, beauty to confer.

And Music to that service, as desired,
Brought lofty harmonies—so love inspired—
    And melodies as pure as they are sweet;
Yet 't is the soul of Cio-Cio-San alone,
Untouched by any genius but your own,
    That makes the charm so lasting, so complete.

> July 12

TO ONE IN HOSPITAL PENT

LITTLE sister, everywhere
There is sorrow: here—where men
Greet the day-beam often when
They the lagging moments measure
By the suffering they bear—
    Just as there!

---

[38] John Luther Long.

Earth-born children all are due
At one goal, and none is free:
Nay; not I, who seem to be
Privileged at large to wander
Where no walls obstruct the blue,
    More than you!

But where tears have wet the sod,
Beautiful may flowers spring,
And in cages birds may sing;
For there's love, too, little sister,
Everywhere that grief hath trod;
    And there's God!

July 13

NOTHING THAT CAN DIE

NOTHING that we deem can die
    Has any thought of death:
The mortal thing, without a sigh—
Without reproachful plaint or cry—
    Yields scarcely conscious breath;
The coming sleep to it the same
As that from which it all-unknowing came.

But spirit cannot so resign
    A hope that o'er the depths of sorrow
Like to a star remains: a sign
That strengthens, by its beam divine,
    To-day with promise of To-morrow!
Nay; longing, vital, and foreseeing,
Itself becomes a pledge of deathless being.

July 14

CIVILIZATION

OLD as the race of man,
    Young as the child new-born,
From glooms Plutonian
    I mount to paths of morn;
And as I move o'er vale and hill,
    Before me flees the night,
For on into the darkness still
    I bear my light.

The desert stayed me long
    Its fancied worth to tell;
The savage, subtle and strong,
    Opposed me, and he fell:
But the savage learned from conflict past
    To battle and succeed,
And the foolish desert came at last
    To bloom indeed.

I halt not for the maimed,
    I wait not for the blind;
My foot is never lamed,
    Whoe'er may lag behind:
I hasten on, like the wind of God,
    To the conquest He ordains:
Parting the human from the clod,
    Undoing chains.

The thing that hindereth
    My progress as I pass,
Is withered in my breath
    Like parchèd summer grass.
I hasten on, like the wind of God,
    That must unfettered blow,

Wooing the blossom from the sod
    Where'er I go.

I taught the Hindoo throng
    To worship: I awoke
The Pyrrhic phalanx strong,
    To break the Persian yoke:
I set great Pharaoh's captives free,
    The Tarquin's pride down-hurled,
And in a child of Galilee,
    O'ercame the world!

July 15

THE IDEAL

"Not the treasures is it that have awakened in me so-unspeakable a desire, but the *Blue Flower* is what I long to behold."—Novalis.

SOMETHING I may not win attracts me ever,—
    Something elusive, yet supremely fair,
Thrills me with gladness, but contents me never,
    Fills me with sadness, yet forbids despair.

It blossoms just beyond the paths I follow,
    It shines beyond the farthest stars I see,
It echoes faint from ocean caverns hollow,
    And from the land of dreams it beckons me.

It calls, and all my best, with joyful feeling,
    Essays to reach it as I make reply;
I feel its sweetness o'er my spirit stealing,
    Yet know ere I attain it I must die!

July 16

THE WHITE-THROATED SPARROW

"When the whitethroat builds, and all the swallows."

WOULD you feel the witching spell
    Of the whitethroat, listen!
There are secrets he can tell
Of the marsh, and of the dell
    Where the dewdrops glisten.

Poet of the brooding pine
    And the feathery larches,
Dawn-lit summits seem to shine,
Lucent in each throbbing line,
    Under azure arches.

All his soul a floating song,—
    Sweet, too sweet for sadness,—
At his bidding, hither throng
Memories that make us long
    With a plaintive gladness.

Ah, were all the woodland bare,
    Should those notes but quiver,
Straight I'd see it budding fair!—
And the lilies would be there,
    Floating on the river!

July 17

JAMES McNEILL WHISTLER[39]

GREATEST of modern painters, he is dead!—

---

[39] James McNeill Whistler died on this day in 1903.

Whistler, in whom death seemed to have no part:
   He of the nimble wit and jocund heart,
Who sipped youth's nectar at the fountain-head,
And felt its wine through all his veins run red:
   Who worshiped the ideal—not the mart,
   And blessed the world with an imperial Art,
Whereby who longs for beauty may be fed!

When things men deem momentous are forgot,
Laurels will bloom for him that wither not;
   And Death's inverted torch shall fail to smother
The light of genius, tender and sublime,
Which with austere restraint, and for all time,
   Painted the gentle portrait of the "Mother"!

July 18

ON THE DEATH OF LADY CURZON[40]

JULY 17, 1906[41]

INTO the light where beauty doth not pale,
Into the glory that can never fail,
   Beyond our yearning care, she passed from view.
Two nations loved and claimed her,—English flower,—
One gave her birth, one gave a regal dower,
But both—ah, both forgot how Heaven must love her too!

---

[40] Mary Curzon, Baroness Curzon of Kedleston died on this day in 1906.
[41] Date likely incorrect in originalt.

July 19

EAGLES[42]

GIBERT'S[43] BATTLE FOR THE AIR

IT rose, and swam into the sky—
    The man-made bird;
And the great Eagle saw it fly—
    Saw it, and heard
The whirring of its plumeless wings,—
The bird that mounts and soars, but never sings!

The falcon-eyes that face the sun
    Blinked on the flight
Of the dread creature that had won
    The unwelcome right
To leave its native earth, and dare
Intrude upon the monarch of the Air!
As moved the monoplane, the man,
    Strange soul of it,
Sailing the sea cerulean,
    The whole of it
Seemed his; ay, subject to his sway.
Then he beheld—an Eagle in his way!

Awed, each upon the other gazed
    A moment's space,
When sudden-swooping talons grazed
    The pale man face,
As the fierce earn, there, mid the skies
Struck with blind fury at his rival's eyes.

---

[42] Eugène Gilbert was born on this day in 1889.
[43] Sic. [Gilbert's]. The original spelling has been preserved as it appeared in the original editions.

Up-fluttering, the feathered king
    Plunged down again.
His rushing anger seemed to bring
    Fate nearer; then
The man-bird knew the moment's strife
Not for supremacy alone, but life!

With nerve that grows in peril great,
    He toward him drew
A thing to strengthen him with Fate,
    Whence instant flew
A wingèd death, and far behind
Headlong the Eagle fell, the abyss to find.

. . . .

Thy fight was over, glorious bird!—
    Thy scornful strength
Which the sky's sovereignty conferred,
    Subdued at length,—
An autumn leaf against the wind,
In conflict with a greater power—called Mind!

                                          July 20

UNREST

WE trekked our way to the desert,
    My soul and I, alone:
We passed beyond the world of men,
    And all men call their own,
And came where never yet were laws
    On parchment writ or stone.

Mid vast and barren stretches
    Where Age speaks not to Age,
Where ne'er doth spring a living thing
    Save the everlasting sage,
I felt as the savage coyote, free—

With a freedom naught could cage.

No milestones mark the desert:
    Though seasons come and go,
Where the arid sands unmeasured lie
    None through the hour-glass flow;
The desert has no memory—
    Nor can of promise know.

Unfettered mid the silence,
    Escaped from rule and law,
The desert, like a sea-floor vast,
    Exultantly I saw;
Yet distant heights that pierced the blue,
    Still troubled me with awe;

And when, turned from the mountains,
    I passed beyond the brush
Where a sea-floor without weed or shell
    Burns breathless in the hush,
There came mirage my sense to mock
    With grasses sweet and lush.

Thirst, not as that for water,—
    A thirst ne'er felt before,—
Parched gradual in the soul of me
    Till I could bear no more;
Earth seemed to cry: "Now whither fly
    From the dearth you struggled for?"
    . . . .
Reluctant, slow returning
    The common lot to share,
With a new and strange emotion—
    Half longing, half despair,
I said: "For man is no escape:
    Here bides the Law, as there!"

July 21

DEMETER

THOU, thou hast seen the child I seek!
The vale is thine and the cloudy peak,
    Divine Apollo
    Whose eye doth follow
Each secret course! Ah, speak!

I have sued to the other gods in vain:
Thou wilt not disregard my pain;
    But by thy power
    Win back my flower
To gladden earth again!

Fair as the poppy mid the wheat,—
Her breath as the breath of the wild grape, sweet
    In the twilight tender,—
    She loved thy splendor
Of perfect day to greet.

And it is thou—of gods most dear!—
Thou, sun-god! who hast led me here:
    Whose smile caressing,
    My wrong redressing,
Tells me the Maid is near!

Blessèd, O blessèd, be thy light!
She comes from the shadows—blissful sight!—
    To the breast that bore her
    To the yearning for her,
That fills me, day and night!

July 22

ODE TO SILENCE

O THOU, sublime, who on the throne
Of eyeless Night sat, awful and alone,
    Before the birth of Cronos—brooding deep
    Upon the voiceless waters which asleep
Held all things circled in their gelid zone:
O Silence! how approach thy shrine
    Nor falter in the listening void to raise
    A mortal voice in praise,
Nor wrong with words such eloquence as thine?

Amid the fragrant forest hush,
The nightingale or solitary-thrush
May, on thy quiet breaking, give no wound;
    For they such beauty bring as all redeems,
    Nor fear to interrupt thy dreams
Or trouble thy Nirvana with a sound!

And though more fitting worship seem the breath
    Of violets in the sequestered wood,
The zephyr that low whispereth
    To the heart of Solitude,
The first unfolding of the bashful rose
That noiseless by the wayside buds and blows:

More fitting worship the far drift of clouds
    O'er azure floating with a swan-like motion,
The Siren-lays faint heard amid the shrouds,
    The voiceless swell of the unfathomed ocean,
The silver Dian pours on the calm stream
Where pale the lotus-blossoms lie adream,—

Yet, mother of all high imaginings,
    In whom is neither barrenness nor dearth,

Wise guardian of the sacred springs
    Whose fresh primordial waters heal the earth,—
O soul of muted fire,
Of whom is born the passionate desire
    That gives to beauty birth,—

All music that hath been, howe'er divine,
All possibilities of sound are thine!
    The syrinx-reed, the flute Apollo owns,
    Symphonic chords, and lyric overtones,
First draw their inspiration at thy shrine.
    There come heart-broken mortal things;
    There once again they find their wings;
There garner dreams benign,—
O nurse of genius! unto whom belong
Beethoven's harmonies and Homer's deathless song!

July 23

NATURA BENIGNA

I WEAVE the beginning, I fashion the end;
Life is my fellow, and Death is my friend;
    Time cannot stay me,
    Nor evil betray me,—
They that would harm me, unknowing, defend.

I ravel asunder, I knit every flaw;
Blossoms I scatter, with tempests I awe;
    Birthplace of duty,
    And shrine of all beauty,—
Firmly I govern, and love is my law!

July 24

HOMEWARD

WHEN I come to my Father's house he will hear me:
        I shall not need
        With words implore
Compassion at my Father's door:
With yearning mute my heart will plead,
    And my Father's heart will hear me.

One thought all the weary day hath caressed me:
        Though cloud-o'ercast
        Is the way I go,
Though steep is the hill I must climb, yet, oh,
When evening falls and the light is past,
    At my Father's house I will rest me.

For thither,—whatsoe'er betide me;
        Howe'er I stray,
        Beset by fears,
Wearied by effort, or blinded by tears,—
Ah, surely I shall find my way,
    Though none there be to guide me!

July 25

EARTH'S BLOSSOMS

EARTH has her blossoms, and the sea his shells
    Wrought with as fine a workmanship, and fair
    As they had been some god's peculiar care;
And in the heart of each a spirit dwells
Whose voice, in flowers,—for they to earth belong—
    Is but a perfume, evanescent, sweet,
    While in the sea-born shell, as seemeth meet,
It is an echo faint of an unending song!

July 26

SONG

IF love were but a little thing,
    Strange love, which, more than all, is great—
One might not such devotion bring,
    Early to serve and late.

If love were but a passing breath—
    Wild love—which, as God knows, is sweet—
One might not make of life and death
    A pillow for love's feet.

July 27

ISRAFEL[44]

A DREAMER midst the stars doth dwell,
Known to the gods as Israfel.
    His heart-strings are a lute;
And when, the magic notes outpouring,
He parts his lips, the gods, adoring,
    Listen in transport mute,
Subdued and softened by the spell
Of the dreamer, Israfel!

And mortals, as they toil apart,
Listen with awe, and call him—Art,
    And fain his gift to gain,
Essay to imitate the fashion
Of his rare song, and breathe its passion,—
    But, ah, they strive in vain;

---

[44] "The angel Israfel, whose heart-strings are a lute, and who has the sweetest voice of all God's creatures."—Koran. See Edgar Allan Poe. [original footnote]

For his song is more than art,
Whose lute-strings are his heart!

And others, unto whom he wings
The sweetest melodies he sings,
    In worship, name him—Love;
Yet longing the pure strain to capture,
When at the very height of rapture,
    A sadness oft approve,
And fancy, strangely, that he wrings
The music from their own heart-strings!

                                                                                     July 28

LOVE NEVER IS TOO LATE

LOVE never is too late; it sums,
    Within itself, all that is lasting gain,
And, or at morn or midnight, comes
    With blessings in its train.

We tarry, slow to give, alas!
    But though delayed, love never is too late—
Love that has power beyond the grave to pass
    And enter Heaven's gate!

                                                                                     July 29

CHILD-FANCIES

I

ASPHODEL

THE children played at naming, every one
    Her favorite blossom, in the mild June even;
When, at the last, the others having done,

A little maid—her years but numbered seven—

Stood shyly forth and answered in her turn:
   "Pale violets I love,—and love full well
Red poppies, which the elves for torches burn,—
   But for my own I choose—the asphodel."

Indignant stared the children; then they cried—
   Amid their pastime ready still for strife—
"The asphodel! You only choose through pride
   A flower you never saw in all your life!"

Abashed, the culprit hung her pretty head,
   As she accusèd of a crime had been;
Then, bravely, with conviction sweet she said:—
   "But I love best the flower I have not seen!"

Ah, wistful child! Such lonely dreams as thine
   Others have cherished in their hearts, I ween,—
And, grateful for *all* good, with thee incline
   To love the best the flower they have not seen!

II

GATHERED WILD-FLOWERS

I've brought you some flowers, mother!
   Please look at them, mother, look!
See this one!—and here's another
   I found beside the brook!

They're very warm, for I held them tight;
   You'll want them, I know, to keep,
When they wake again and you see them right,—
   But now they're all asleep.

July 30

BEFORE THE DAWN

I LOOKED on beauteous forms, as I lay dreaming,
   But on no form as beautiful as thine,
Who here, amid the moonbeams white and holy,
   Standest in silence by this bed of mine.

I looked on faces fair, as I lay sleeping,
   But on no face that seemed as nobly sweet
As that which in the pallid light above me
   My wondering, half-awakened sense doth greet.

Who and what art thou? Have I kept thee waiting?
   My sleep was as a river deep and calm;
Bring'st thou perchance some word of import for me?
   Hast thou, for broken hearts, like mine, some balm?

Who and what art thou? In my tranquil vision
   I gazed through rifted clouds on azure skies,—
I seemed to gaze beyond them,—but naught moved me
   Like the deep pity in thy brooding eyes.
Why art thou here to-night? I have been lonely—
   Have waited, prayed, for such an one as thou,
To still with presence kind my pulse's throbbing,
   To lay a cooling touch upon my brow.

Tell me thy name! Then, pain and fear forgotten,
   I straightway will arise and follow thee,
Who, so I think, art hither come to guide me
   To larger hope and opportunity.

Tell me thy name! I long, I need, to hear it!
   Thy name!—I may not plead, for failing breath,—
With look compassionate, the august stranger
   Made answer very softly: "I am Death."

July 31

FIRST AND LAST

HOPE smiles a welcome, if no other smiles,
    Upon our entrance to this world of pain;
    And on each purpose of our youth again,
    With an inspiring sympathy, she smiles.
She leads us forth to battle, and beguiles
    Our anguish when the long fight proves in vain;
    Till, pierced by countless wounds, amongst the slain
    We leave her, while the victor foe reviles.
But even as we touch at ruin's verge,
    And hear the voices of despair that urge
    The fatal plunge to chaos, Hope alone,—
How healèd and how ransomed none may guess,—
    Rising again in pallid loveliness,
    Resumes her sway, a thousand times o'erthrown.

August 1

"ASK WHAT YOU WILL"

ASK what you will, I must obey your hest!
Thus much, my lady-bird, seems manifest
    To you and me, who well each other know.
    What you, small tyrant, beg, I must bestow.
Come; falter not, but proffer your request!

Is it the flower I wear here on my breast?
My favorite nag? The book I love the best?
    Some dainty gown? Some brooch or necklace? No?
      Ask what you will!

See how the sun, down-sinking to his rest,
Gilds with his glory all the roseate west!
    I linger on, in life's chill afterglow.

Nay; smile, beloved!—like your mother—so!
Stay but a moment! Now—my own! my blest!
    Ask what you will!

August 2

WHO WALKS THE WORLD WITH SOUL AWAKE

WHO walks the world with soul awake
    Finds beauty everywhere;
Though labor be his portion,
    Though sorrow be his share,
He looks beyond obscuring clouds,
    Sure that the light is there!

And if, the ills of mortal life
    Grown heavier to bear,
Doubt come with its perplexities
    And whisper of despair,
He turns with love to suffering men—
    And, lo! God, too, is there.

August 3

CENDRILLON

    I AM a dream,
      A fairy gleam
    Of rose and amethyst;
A creature of the moonlight and the mist,
Woven of stars that, meeting, silent kissed.
    Think of me as a dream!

I am a note of melody that woke
Within your breast, and to your longing spoke:
    A lonely strain
      Of ecstasy and pain;

A hope that, glimpsed, must fade;
A form, illusion made,
That, vanishing, shall come no more again!

Regret me not that I
Must like to music die!
The virgin rose,
In blossoming, hastes to its fragrant close,
And whatsoe'er this magic hour I seem,
I am enchantment, only, and a dream,—
Love always is a dream!

August 4

HEIMWEH

THE birds returning seem so glad
As from the South they come,
They teach my heart, forlorn and sad,
How distant is my home:
O'er land and sea wild roaming free,
They little understand—
Glad nomads—that there is for me
One home—one only Land!

And yonder dancing rivulet
That merrily on doth go,
Humming a tune I 'd fain forget,
Adds something to my woe:
Ah, had it but a thought for me
'T would either now be dumb,
Or it would croon a melody
Less dear to me at home!

Fond memories of days of yore!—
My heart so hungereth,
The smell of upland clover or

The dew-wet violet's breath
Might quickly fill it with delight;
　　But exiled here I roam,
And dread, beyond all else, to-night,
　　The scents that speak of home!

August 5

THERE'S A SPOT IN THE MOUNTAINS

THERE'S a spot in the mountains, where the dew, dear,
　　Is laden with the odours of the pine,
Where the heavens seem unbounded, and their blue, dear,
　　Is deepest where it mirrored seems to shine.

There, at morn and eve, with rapture old and new, dear,
　　The thrushes sing their double song divine,
And the melody their voices breathe, of you, dear,
　　Speaks ever to this happy heart of mine.
There's a cabin in the mountains, where the fare, dear,
　　Is frugal as the cheer of Arden blest;
But contentment sweet and fellowship are there, dear,
　　And Love, that makes the feast he honors—best!

There's a lake upon the mountains, where our boat, dear,
　　Moves gayly up the stream or down the tide,
Where, amid the scented lily-buds afloat, dear,
　　We dream the dream of Eden as we glide!

August 6

EROS

I, WHO am Love, come clothed in mystery,
As rose my beauteous mother from the Sea,
　　Veiling my luminous wings from mortal sight—
　　Whether at noon or in the star-strewn night—

That I may pass unrecognized and free.

Ignoring them that idly seek for me,
Unto mine own, from all eternity
    I come with heart aflame and torch alight—
        I who am Love!

What bring I them? Ah, draughts that sweeter be
Than welling waters of Callirrhoe!
    What give I them? Life!—even in Death's despite;
    And upward still I lead them to the height
Of an immortal passion's purity!—
        I who am Love.

                                    August 7

THE CHOSEN

DEATH pitying stood before one bent and old,
    And said:—"Forbear your griefs, and go with me:
The tale of your misfortunes—all is told,
    And I am come at last to set you free."

But, lo! the man fell trembling to his knees,
    Affrighted, and entreating in sad plight:—
"Though poverty and pain deny me ease,
    Yet spare me!—but a day—a single night!"

Then Death, disdaining misery so base,
    Turned, silently, and sought whom life held dear.
He found you, my belovèd! in the place
    You glorified, and touched you with his spear;

And as one startled wakes from a fair dream
    He fain would dream again, if that might be,
You looked on Death clothed in his might supreme,
    And gave yourself to him,—forgetting me.

All beauteous in the blossom-time of youth,
    Ere yet a cloud your radiance could dim,—
You knew him for God's messenger, in truth,
    And like an angel, went away with him.

                                                              August 8

TIME

WHAT thought can measure Time?—
Tell its beginning, name
    The void from which it first, faint-pulsing, came?—
    Follow its onward going,—
    A restless river without tumult flowing,—
Or with sure footing climb
Unto its unlit altitudes sublime?

What thought can trace the wonders it hath seen—
Time, the creator of all that hath been,
    Giver of bounty where was dearth,
    Bringer of miracles to birth:
Time, through whose office is the seedling sown,
The fruit up-gathered, the ripe harvest mown,
    And beauty made to glorify the earth?

Before the land took shape and rose
    Black and chaotic from the old, old sea,
Before the stars their courses chose,
    Before the moon's most ancient memory,
Time to Earth's vision, veiled in night, appears
Back of the viewless cycles of the years.

The Hours, his little children, run
    Lightly upon his errands ever;
By sure and swift relays is done
    His will, disputed never;

The while these transient Hours infirm
Measure of mortal things the destined term.

Ah, me, the days! the heavy-weighted years,
    Each with its Spring and Winter, dusk and dawn!
The centuries, with all their joys, and tears,
    That came, and now—so utterly are gone!
Gone whither? Whither vanished so?
Does broad Orion, or does Hesper know?

There comes no answer. Are we dupes, indeed,—
    Offspring of Time, by Time relentless slain,
    Our purest aspirations dreamed in vain?
    Ah, no: man's soul indignant doth disdain
Ignoble vassalage to such a creed,
Well-knowing it is free,—
    Aye, free!—for present, past, and future blend,
    The segments of a circle without end,
Losing themselves in one, unbourned eternity!

                                            August 9

CORONATION—TO KING EDWARD VII[45]

IF thou be crowned, or if thou be not crowned
    With that imperial round
Thy forbears from the distant ages wore,
Sorrow and suffering for thee have earned
A guerdon fairer than thy hope discerned;
And through renunciation, thou hast found
A cirque of sovereignty not dreamed before.

If thou be crowned? Nay, thou art crowned now;
    For, lo! upon thy brow,

---

[45] Edward VII was crowned King of the United Kingdom on this day in 1902.

So lately shadowed by Death's mournful wing,
A mighty people's sympathy has laid
An aureole whose brightness shall not fade:
Whose light, more worth than chrism, or seal, or vow,
Sceptre or throne, makes thee, indeed, a King!

August 10

ON FINDING BUDDHA'S DUST

"One hundred million people will experience a thrill of religious enthusiasm at the recent discovery of a relic-casket near Peshawar, India, containing some of the bones of Gautama Buddha."

O ASHES of Gautama, once the shrine
    And outer temple of celestial mind!—
    Home of a spirit, pure and heavenly kind,
That moved by human sympathy benign,
Out-poured itself, like sacrificial wine,
    To bring a light of hope unto the blind,—
    O ashes of Gautama! earth shall find
Naught midst her buried treasure more divine!

Though, centuries gone by, an Emperor sealed
    In crystal and in bronze this royal dust,
    Time may uncover it through waste and rust;
But while man's heart to aught shall homage give,
Gautama's love, through sacrifice revealed,
    Eternal as that heart itself shall live!

August 11

PARIS

WHEN to thee, Trojan—firebrand of the night,
    Whom Hecuba, in fear, to Priam bore—
    The choice was given which should calm restore

To vexed Olympos, thou didst spurn the right
Of regal sovereignty, and the grave might
   Of godlike wisdom,—so renouncing more
   Than e'er was offered to a man before,—
In poor exchange for sensual delight.
Thy fame is an undying infamy;
   And the great city that hath fairest bloomed
Thine adolescent graces,—strangely she,
   As if a name resembling thine foredoomed,
Maintains the standards that appealed to thee,
   And by thy very vices is consumed.

                                        August 12

A REALM OF WONDER[46]

FAR off there is a realm of wonder,—
     Know you its name?
No region the wide heavens under
     Could be the same!
Dark orange groves it hath, and alleys
   With sunlit verdure covered over
High-mounting hills, great river valleys
   Enriched by crops of maize and clover:
A Land apart, from all asunder,—
     Know you its name?

Walls hath it—two. One—of the mind,—
To the outside world forever blind,
Itself within itself hath still confined;
   Wherefore its brooding and exclusive spirit
Craves but for progress in experience sown,
Noiseless as Nature's own;
   And with that reverence it doth inherit,
Hearkens obediently its sages,

---

[46] See *La Cité Chinoise* of Eugène Simon. [original footnote]

Mysteriously wise from distant ages,
    And with unconscious, tireless sacrifice
    Creates a paradise.

A paradise you say,
Stretching away—and endlessly away!—
    A garden—lovelily abloom
With rice and silk and tea,
Cotton and yam and wheat, all fair to see,
    And breathing forth an exquisite perfume
Of mingled mulberry and orange blows,
Azalea and rose:
    A garden, yet a tomb
Where myriads, sleeping, are remembered still
    By myriads more, who glad their precepts keep,
    And honor them in sleep.

What centuries of industries speak here!
What irrigating waters, silver-clear,
Skirting the uplands, rise, tier above tier!
    What thronged canals, through the Delta plain extending
Hundreds of miles!
    What junks, what bankside villages unending,
What cottages with brown and green roof-tiles!
What fanes! what wildwood temples without cease!
What unperturbed tranquillity! what peace!

Far off there is a realm of wonder,—
    Know you its name?
No region the wide heavens under
    Could be the same!—
    So calm, productive, full of beauty;
Unto contentment so inviting!
    A Land, through service and through duty,
The past and future so uniting
    That Death itself them may not sunder!—
    Know you its name?

Back of the centuries its birth-hour lonely
    Men vainly seek:
Of its beginnings legend only
    And myth may speak:
Ere Greece of beauty dreamed, or Rome of power,
In some mysterious, unrecorded hour,
Darkling from hushed obscurity it sprung
When the Nile gods and the Vedas yet were young.

August 13

THE LITTLE LASS

AS Douglas to his castle came,
Emotion nerved his shatter'd frame,
And soft he pondered,—"Presently
My little lass will welcome me!

"As longs the miser for his gold,
As fever longs, with thirst untold,
So yearns my heart her face to see
Who yonder waits to welcome me!"

But as he turned his steed about,
A mournful peal of bells rung out;
Whereat he cried,—"Nay, merrily!
Ring forth my bairn to welcome me!"

He entered at the castle gate;
(None marked him come, for it grew late,)
He stood within his hall at last;
(None noted him, for tears fell fast.)

Quoth Douglas: "Friends, if me ye mourn,
With drooping heads and looks forlorn,
Now for your sorrows comfort ye,—
And fetch my lass to welcome me!

"'T is true that I from out the wars
Bring back a wound and many scars,—
But life is mine, and I am free,
And my brave lass hath ransom'd me!"

Up spoke an ancient servitor:
"We mourn indeed the wrongs of war:
We bless thy loved return,— but she
No more shall rise to welcome thee!"

Sudden as falls the giant oak
When smitten by the lightning stroke,
So swoonèd Douglas to the ground,
And bled afresh his healing wound.

They strove to stay life's ebbing tide,
They chafed his hands, they swathed his side,
But Donald wailed,—"Ah, woe is me!—
Thy little lass hath welcomed thee!"

August 14

A SEEKER IN THE NIGHT

I LIFT my eyes, but I cannot see;
I stretch my arms and I cry to Thee,—
And still the darkness covers me.

Where art Thou? In the chill obscure
I wander lonely, and endure
A yearning only Thou canst cure!

Once—once, indeed, in every face
I seemed thy lineaments to trace
And looked in all to find thy grace:

I thought the thrush—sweet worshiper!—

From the minaret of the balsam-fir
Hymned forth thy praise, my soul to stir;

I thought the early roses came
To lisp in fragrant breaths thy name,
And teach my heart to do the same;

I thought the stars thy candles, Lord!—
I thought the skylark as he soared
Rose to thy throne and Thee adored!

But now a labyrinth I wind,
And needing more thy hand to find,
Grope, darkling, Lord!—for I am blind!

Ah, bridge for me the awful vast,
That I may find Thee at the last!—
Then draw me close, and hold me fast!

August 15

A ROUND

THE end of life is living,
    And 't is through love we live—
Through taking and through giving.
    Then freely take—and give!

When into life we blunder,
    Love waits to soothe our woe;
And 't is love's hand doth sunder
    Our bonds when hence we go.

Nor life nor love is mortal:
    Love holds of life the key,
And life is the veiled portal
    To love's infinity!

August 16

LEAVE-TAKING

THOUGH hence I go—though with the fading day
      I seem to fade away,
Like to a primrose which beguiling Spring,
Too early fanning with perfumèd wing,
      Tempts, only to betray:

Though soon I sleep,—yet sorrow not, nor fear
      That you shall lose me, dear!
For not one cherished memory—
One single yearning of your heart for me,
      Shall fail to bring me near!

How strange could death divide who, living, share
      All happiness and care!
Still as you gaze, bereft of your desire,
On the dull embers of your lonely fire,
      You shall behold me there,

And though through hiemal glooms you sometimes learn
      To doubt, nor hope discern,—
Yet when the timid firstling buds awake,
And birds come back and sing, your heart to break,—
      Always, I shall return!

August 17

INFLUENCE

MY friend leaned o'er the flowery brink
Of evil, bending down to drink;
But though he stooped, resolved to take
   The harmful draught despite my fears,
He yielded for my pleading's sake,

    Feeling my love and tears.

Again he stoops; again I long
To save a fellow-man from wrong.
He was my friend! Fain, in this hour,
    Would I defend him as before:
I strive—but I have lost the power,
    Who love him now no more.

August 18

MOTHERLESS

HE was so small, so very small,
    That since she ceased to care,
'T was easy just to pass him by,
    Forgetting he was there;
But though too slight a thing he seemed
    Of interest to be,—
One heart had loved him with a love
    As boundless as the sea.

He was so poor, so very poor,
    That now, since she had died,
He seemed a tiny threadbare coat
    With nothing much inside;
But, ah! a treasure he concealed,
    And asked of none relief:
His shabby little bosom hid
    A mighty, grown-up grief.

August 19

IN A TENEMENT

I THINK our alley 's darker now
    Since once I went away—

I can't exactly tell you how—
    In a strange place to play
With other children like myself,
    A whole long summer's day!

It was n't really there, I 'm sure—
    That place so strange to me,
For nobody was cold or poor:
    It just was green, and free,
And up above there seemed of blue
    A million miles to be.

The fairies live there!—little Ruth
    The lame girl told me so:
Yes; and I know it for a truth
    That there the fairies go,
And cover over all the trees
    With flowers white as snow.

The flowers made in Fairyland
    Have breath—oh, breath that 's sweet!
For once I held them in my hand—
    Far off from this dull street!—
And looked down in their hearts and saw
    The tracks of fairy feet.

I dream at night of that strange place,
    And in my dream, quite near,
They dance about before my face,—
    The fairies kind and dear;
And, oh, I want to go to them!
    You see, they can't come here.

August 20

SONG

FRIENDSHIP from its moorings strays,
    Love binds fast together;
Friendship is for balmy days,
    Love for stormy weather.

For itself the one contends,
    Fancied wrongs regretting—
Love the thing it loves defends,
    All besides forgetting.

Friendship is the morning lark
    Toward the sunrise winging,
Love the nightingale, at dark
    Most divinely singing!

August 21

THE LOST GIOCONDA[47]

THE world is poorer, Italy's fair child,
    Lacking the face
That for so long its heart beguiled;
    Nor hopeth to replace
With all its riches multiplied,
Thee, eloquent, alone, art-glorified!

But somewhere, Mona Lisa! quietly,
    With folded hands,
And in thine eye's soft mockery
    The look that understands,
Thou wearest, lost to us the while,

---

[47] The *Mona Lisa* was stolen from the Louvre on this day in 1911.

Thine own inscrutable, unaging smile!

August 22

BEAUTY'S PATH

ALL ugliness wears on its brow the brand
    Of Time and Dissolution. From of old,
Its doubtful journey through a shifting sand,
    The life in its ophidian breast is cold.
But beauty's path is one forever bright'ning
    In glory to each far horizon's rim.
Warm in the rose and golden in the lightning,
    Love's altar flame, the upward way to Him,—
Beauty, transcending all that bans and bars,
Moves as the light moves on, eternal as the stars!

Too well acquaint with passions that benumb,
    Earth is with them no more in kind accord.
'T is only by ascending we may come
    Where waits for her the new, the unexplored.
She longs—ah, how she longs!—to break asunder
    Her ancient chains, to lave in morning dew,
To stand a little space mid realms of wonder,
    To feel her nearness to the good and true:
She longs for beauty—vernal through the years—
To touch the dried-up spring and fount of happy tears!

August 23

THE CHERUBIM

TWO angels stood at Eden's gate
    And neither uttered word:
In the eyes of one, indignant hate
    Flamed like the flame of his sword.
The other's brand burned also red

With the fire that, avenging, sears,
And he waved the warning thing of dread;
But his eyes were soft with tears.

They twain had watched the Fall's disgrace,
But only one had seen
The mortal pain in the woman's face,
Where never pain had been:
Had marked the clasp of the woman's hand
On his who, Eden gone,
Seemed, through her trembling touch, new-manned,
As he drew her gently on.

Two angels turned from Eden's gate,
For Man had wandered far:
The one passed quickly, joy elate,
From star to beckoning star;
But the other angel sighed, as lone
The heavenly way he trod,
And came at last to the awful throne,
And fell at the feet of God.

Then spake God's voice:—"What earth-born grief
Dims radiance such as thine?"
The angel sighed:—"I beg relief
For woes that are not mine!—
I plead for them that exiled live.
If grace be of Thy plan,
Have mercy!—ah, have mercy! Give
Some comfort, Lord, to Man!"

The fearful angel waited: came
Long silence, then the Voice:—
"Love cannot take from wrong its blame:
Man's woes are of Man's choice;
Yet do thou bear—thy pity's price—
To them that outcast grope

This last, best gift of Paradise—
    This key whose name is Hope!"

August 24

DEATH

I AM the key that parts the gates of Fame;
I am the cloak that covers cowering Shame;
I am the final goal of every race;
I am the storm-tossed spirit's resting-place:

The messenger of sure and swift relief,
Welcomed with wailings and reproachful grief;
The friend of those that have no friend but me,
I break all chains, and set all captives free.

I am the cloud that, when Earth's day is done,
An instant veils an unextinguished sun;
I am the brooding hush that follows strife,
The waking from a dream that Man calls—Life!

August 25

DEARTH[48]

AS one who faring o'er a desert plain

---

[48] An additional first stanza is present in *The Smart Set* version (August 1908):

AS one who thirsting waits, while mocking him
    The waves o'erleap his shattered vessel's brink;
And, drifting on, life's cup but once to brim,
    Fain to sheer depths would sink—
So everywhere beholding love neglected,
Carelessly set aside, despised, rejected,
    I faint for a pure draught not mine to drink.

    Sees fountains clear in the mirage arise,
And, parchèd, longs the nectar sweet to gain
    Which still before him flies—
So, wistfully, half doubting, half-believing,
Scornful of hope—yet hopeful, self-deceiving,
    I thirst for love, which wastes before my eyes.

August 26

THEY LIVE SO LONG

THEY live so long, the Gods!
They know
What æons passed before a rose could blow;
What ages numberless, without a name,
Went out in darkness ere the saurian came,
A crawling dulness from the slime of Earth;
What further centuries with movement slow
Were borne along on Time's unebbing flow
Before the weakling man-child came to birth:
All this, and more, they know.

Our dates—how brief!
We cry:—
"Bless us to-day! to-morrow we shall die!"
Divided ever between hope and fear,
Warring with evil which we deem grows strong,
Our knowledge bounded by one little sphere,
We cannot share, for hope of good not nigh,
The peace of the unfathomable sky;
But the Gods patient be; they live so long,
And know that naught can die.

August 27

"I LONGED FOR LOVE"

I LONGED for love, and eager to discover
    Its hiding-place, I wandered far and wide;
And as forlorn I sought the lone world over,
    Unrecognized, love journeyed at my side.

I craved for peace, and priceless years expended
    In unrewarded search from shore to shore;
But home returned, the weary seeking ended,
    Peace welcomed me where dwelt my peace of yore!

August 28

SOCRATES

HE raised the hemlock to his lips,
    He drained the fatal draught,
Calmly conversing with his friends,
    As he a wine had quaffed;
And, ah! what wine so rich to bless?
    The torch of day grown dim,
Death's cup has less of bitterness
    For all, because of him!

August 29

MAN, THAT WILL NOT BE BEGUILED

MAN, that will not be beguiled
Like a fond and happy child
    From his toil or futile strife,
Feels within his bosom burning
All the deep, impassioned yearning
    Woven in the woof of life.

And though far, with weary feet,
He may wander, Man shall meet
   No content until he come—
Soon or late, his fate compelling—
To Love's domed and star-lit dwelling,
   For he has no other home.

                                        August 30

WHERE HAROLD SLEEPS

WHERE Harold sleeps the night is blest.
In the Great Mother's easeful breast
   He lies the brave and sweet among
     Who, loved by the wise gods, die young—
The goal achieved without the quest.

Though winds of Autumn from the West
May rudely rock the unsheltered nest,
   Yet shall all joys of Spring be sung
     Where Harold sleeps;

And we, our human griefs confessed,
We, too, by a dear hope caressed—
   Death's hope illimitable, sprung
     From nothing that to earth hath clung—
Shall, waiting a new dawn, find rest
     Where Harold sleeps!

                                        August 31

PROBATION

FULL slow to part with her best gifts is Fate;
The choicest fruitage comes not with the spring,
But still for summer's mellowing touch must wait,—

For storms and tears, which season'd excellence bring;
And Love doth fix his joyfullest estate
In hearts that have been hushed 'neath Sorrow's brooding wing.

Youth sues to Fame: coldly she answers, "Toil!"
He sighs for Nature's treasures: with reserve
Responds the goddess, "Woo them from the soil."
Then fervently he cries, "Thee will I serve,—
Thee only, blissful Love!" With proud recoil
The heavenly boy replies, "To serve me well, deserve!"

September 1

BE THOU MY GUIDE

BE Thou my guide, and I will walk in darkness
    As one who treads the beamy heights of day,
Feeling a gladness amid desert sadness,
    And breathing vernal fragrance all the way.

Be Thou my wealth, and, reft of all besides Thee,
    I will forget the strife for meaner things,
Blest in the sweetness of thy rare completeness,
    And opulent beyond the dream of kings.

Be Thou my strength, O lowly One and saintly!
    And, though unvisioned ills about me throng,
Though danger woo me and deceit pursue me,
    Yet in the thought of Thee I will be strong!

September 2

PER ASPERA

THANK God, a man can grow!
    He is not bound
With earthward gaze to creep along the ground:

Though his beginnings be but poor and low,
Thank God, a man can grow!
The fire upon his altars may burn dim,
    The torch he lighted may in darkness fail,
    And nothing to rekindle it avail,—
Yet high beyond his dull horizon's rim,
Arcturus and the Pleiads beckon him.

September 3

GIVE ME NOT LOVE

GIVE me not love that would enthrall
    A spirit panting to be free;
But give me love which more than all
    Would find it sweet to soar with me!
The bird that close to earth doth cling,
May, darkling, be content to sing,
But full the sunlight shines afar—
And there be heights where eagles are.

Give me not love which hour by hour,
    Like to the rose, doth pale its hue;
But love still constant as the flower
    That opens to each morn anew;
Not love which, shadowed by the tomb,
A little space doth languid bloom,
But love that draws its deeper breath
From altitudes that know not death.

September 4

JEWEL-WEED

THOU lonely, dew-wet mountain road,
    Traversed by toiling feet each day,
What rare enchantment maketh thee

Appear so gay?

Thy sentinels, on either hand
    Rise tamarack, birch, and balsam-fir,
O'er the familiar shrubs that greet
    The wayfarer;

But here's a magic cometh new—
    A joy to gladden thee, indeed:
This passionate out-flowering of
    The jewel-weed,

That now, when days are growing drear,
    As Summer dreams that she is old,
Hangs out a myriad pleasure-bells
    Of mottled gold!

Thine only, these, thou lonely road!
    Though hands that take, and naught restore,
Rob thee of other treasured things,
    Thine these are, for

A fairy, cradled in each bloom,
    To all who pass the charmèd spot
Whispers in warning: "Friend, admire,—
    But touch me not!

"Leave me to blossom where I sprung,
    A joy untarnished shall I seem;
Pluck me, and you dispel the charm
    And blur the dream!"

September 5

INDIAN-PIPE

IN the heart of the forest arising,
    Slim, ghostly, and fair,
Ethereal offspring of moisture,
    Of earth and of air;
With slender stems anchored together
    Where first they uncurl,
Each tipped with its exquisite lily
    Of mother-of-pearl;
Mid the pine-needles, closely enwoven
    Its roots to embale,—
The Indian-pipe of the woodland,
    Thrice lovely and frail!

Is this but an earth-springing fungus—
    This darling of Fate
Which out of the mouldering darkness
    Such light can create?
Or is it the spirit of Beauty,
    Here drawn by love's lure
To give to the forest a something
    Unearthy and pure:
To crystallize dewdrop and balsam
    And dryad-lisped words
And starbeam and moonrise and rapture
    And song of wild birds?

September 6

BUFFALO

SEPTEMBER 6, 1901[49]

A TRANSIENT city, marvelously fair,—
   Humane, harmonious, yet nobly free,—
   She built for pure delight and memory.
At her command, by lake and garden rare,
Pylon and tower majestic rose in air,
   And sculptured forms of grace and symmetry.
   Then came a thought of God, and, reverently,—
"Let there be Light!" she said; and Light was there.

O miracle of splendor! Who could know
   That Crime, insensate, egoist and blind,
     Destructive, causeless, caring but to smite,
   Would in its dull Cimmerian gropings find
A sudden way to fill those courts with woe,
   And swallow up that radiance in night?

September 7

THE CHRIST OF THE ANDES

FAR, far the mountain-peak from me
Where lone he stands, with look caressing;
   Yet from the valley, wistfully
   I lift my dreaming eyes, and see
His hand stretched forth in blessing.

   Never bird sings nor blossom blows
Upon that summit chill and breathless
   Where throned he waits amid the snows;

---

[49] President William McKinley was shot on this day in 1901.

   But from his presence wide outflows
Love that is warm and deathless!

   O Symbol of the great release
From war and strife!—unfailing fountain
     To which we turn for joy's increase,
     Fain would we climb to heights of Peace—
Thy peace upon the mountain!

September 8

SIBERIA

THE night-wind drives across the leaden skies,
    And fans the brooding earth with icy wings;
    Against the coast loud-booming billows flings,
And soughs through forest-deeps with moaning sighs.
Above the gorge, where snow, deep-fallen lies,
    A softness lending e'en to savage things—
    Above the gelid source of mountain springs,
A solitary eagle, circling, flies.

O pathless woods, O isolating sea,
    O steppes interminable, hopeless, cold,
O grievous distances, imagine ye,
    Imprisoned here, the human soul to hold?
Free, in a dungeon,—as yon falcon free,—
    It soars beyond your ken its loved ones to enfold!

September 9

TO THE TSAR[50] (1890)

O THOU into whose human hand is given
    A godlike might! who, for thy earthly hour,

---

[50] Alexander III of Russia.

Above reproof, self-counseled and self-shriven,
    Wieldest o'er regions vast despotic power!
        Mortal, who by a breath,
    A look, a hasty word, as soon forgot,
Commandest energies of life and death!—
Midst terrors dread, that darkly multiply,
    Wilt thou thy vision blind, and listen not
Whilst unto Heaven ascends thy people's cry?

In vain, in vain! The injuries they speak
    Down unto final depths their souls have stirr'd:
The aged plead through them, the childish-weak,
    The mad, the dying,—and they shall be heard!
        Thou wilt not hear them; but,
    Though Heaven were hedged about with walls of stone,
And though with brazen gates forever shut,
And sentried 'gainst petitions of despair,
    'T were closely guarded as thy fearful throne,
That cry of helpless wrong should enter there!

O Majesty! 'T is great to be a king,
    But greater is it yet to be a man!
The exile by far Lena perishing,
    The captive in Kara who bears thy ban,
        Ransomed at length and free,
    Shall rise from torments that make heroes strong;
Shall rise, as equal souls, to question thee;
And for defense there nothing shall endure
    Of all which to thy lofty state belong,
Save that thou hast of human, brave, and pure!

Cæsar, thou still art man, and serv'st a King
    Who wields a power more terrible than thine!
Slow, slow to anger, and long-suffering,
    He hears his children cry, and makes no sign:
        He hears them cry, but, oh!
Imagine not his tardy judgments sleep,

Or that their agonies He doth not know
Who, hidden, waste where tyrants may not see!
    Eternal watch He over them doth keep,—
Eternal watch,—and Russia shall be free!

ALEXANDER III[51]

(LIVADIA, NOVEMBER 1, 1894)

THE world in mourning for a Russian Tsar!
    A despot of the nineteenth century
      Mourned by the nations that have made men free!
    Ye captives of his rule! where'er ye be,
Whether in dungeons or in mines afar—
Wretches who mourn, yet mourn not for the Tsar,—
    Forgive the tears that seem a wrong to grief
    Barren of comfort and without relief;
The Tsar was Russia's martyr—as ye are!
He asked for peace, and she ordained him strife.
    A Slav of simple heart, disliking show,
    She bade him every lowly hope forego;
    And placing on his brow her crown of woe,
Gave him a sovereignty with perils rife,
And 'neath his sceptre hid the assassin's knife.

---

[51] Omitted from the 1916 version (as rendered above), the 1898 rendering of this poem includes the following last stanza:

Woe to the Tsar!—Livadia's cannon boom,
    Proclaiming that the Tsar from woe is free!
    Peace to the Tsar! but, Russia, woe to thee!
    Still he who rules thee shall thy victim be,
Tortured by griefs that shall his heart consume,
Till he and thou, risen as from the tomb,
    Shall see the light on Liberty's calm face,
    Shall know that tyranny must yield its place
To the great spirit that hath breathed its doom!

So, masked as Fear, she broke his nerves of steel
    Upon the circle of her racking wheel,
And set a horror at his door of life!
Humanity but sorrows for her own;
    The Autocrat she mourns not, but the man,
    Who, loving Russia, lived beneath her ban,
    Powerless to soften fate or change the plan
That called him all unwilling to a throne,
Hereditary evils to atone.
    She mourns not Cæsar, but the pathos old
    Of a quick conscience driven to uphold
A dynasty the world had long outgrown.

                                              September 10

SONG

MY love is fairer than the tasseled corn
    That matches with its gold the golden day;
My love is sweeter than the breath of morn
    Fragrant with new-mown hay.
There 's nothing dearer or more tender,
And day by day the Graces lend her
A smile, a tear, to bind the heart
    And keep it hers alway!

                                              September 11

A LITTLE MINISTER

FAR up the crag, 'twixt sea and sky,
Where winds tempestuous, blowing by,
    Leave giant boulders swept and bare:
    Where frequent lightnings fitful flare,
And petrels sound their stormy cry,—

I found a bluebell, sweet and shy,

Lifting its head complacently,
    As guarded by the tenderest care—
        Far up the crag.

And often now, when fear draws nigh,
In thought I stand 'twixt sea and sky,
    And as of old, in my despair,
    I bless the Power that set it there—
That tiny thing with courage high,
        Far up the crag!

                            September 12

KENILWORTH

TOWERING above the plain, proud in decay,—
    Her tendriled ivies, like a woman's hair,
    Veiling her hurt and hiding her despair,—
The monument of a departed day,
The shadow of a glory passed away,
    Stands Kenilworth; stripped of her pomp, and bare
    Of all that made her so supremely fair
When Power with Love contended for her sway.
In this wide ruin solemn and serene,
Where moved majestical a virgin queen,
    The peacock struts, his ominous plumes outspread;
And here, where casting an immortal spell
A sad and girlish presence seems to dwell,
    The wild bird nests, and circles overhead.

                            September 13

MEDIÆVAL

SHE said: "My babe is dead:
    Unchristened did he die.
I wake in the long, lone night

And hear his plaintive cry.

"I wonder does God hear,
    And will not let him in—
My little one who died
    All innocent of sin?
"The wicked, who repent,
    Win heaven, so men say;
And was my bonny child
    Less dear to Him than they?

"There's not a soul in bliss,
    Rejoicing in God's Son,
That's purer or more sweet
    Than was my little one!

"Lowly, at Mary's shrine
    Before the dawn of day
I kneel, for him to plead
    Who was too small to pray

"Ah, mother blessed! bring
    My babe to know the light!
Or, pitying, win for me
    With him to roam the night!"

                                            September 14

McKINLEY[52]

PEACE!—mourn no more the martyr's fate!
Death came—though by the hand of hate,
His faithful life to vindicate,
    His name to set apart.
No more assailed, misunderstood,

---

[52] President William McKinley died on this day in 1901.

He sleeps where love his grave hath strewed,
Safe sentinelled by gratitude,—
   The memory of the heart.

September 15

DREYFUS[53]

FRANCE has no dungeon in her island tomb
   So deep that she may hide injustice there;
   The cry of innocence, despite her care,—
Despite her roll of drums, her cannon's boom,
Is heard wherever human hearts have room
   For sympathy: a sob upon the air,
   Echoed and re-echoed everywhere,
It swells and swells, a prophecy of doom.
Thou latest victim of an ancient hate!
   In agony so awfully alone,
      The world forgets thee not, nor can forget.
   Such martyrdom she feels to be her own,
And sees involved in thine her larger fate;
      She questions, and thy foes shall answer yet.

September 16

DREYFUS

   IF thou art living, in that Devil's Isle
   Inquisitorial and darkly vile,
Where human hearts are pitilessly broken;
   Where treacherous hate seems stronger
Than either right or law; where grief hath spoken
Its final word and asks but to forget:
If thou art living, wretched one! live yet
     A little longer!
   Outcast, forsaken, thou art not alone,

---

[53] Alfred Dreyfus.

One bides with thee Who shall thy woes atone,
And France, entangled in her toils of hate,
   Hearkens a voice of warning.
Martyr and hope of an imperiled State,
Live yet a little! In the East is light—
A pledge to thee that long tho seem the night,
   There comes the morning!

September 17

PICQUART[54]

"FOR love of justice and for love of truth!"
   Aye, 't was for these, for these, he put aside
   Place and preferment, fortune and the pride
   Of fair renown; the friends he prized, in sooth,
All the rewards of an illustrious youth,
   And set his strength against a swollen tide,
   And gave his spirit to be crucified,—
   For love of justice and for love of truth!
Keeper of the abiding scroll of fame,
   Lo! we intrust to thee a hero's name!
   Life, like a restless river, hurrying by,
Bears us so swiftly on, we may forget
   The name to which we owe so deep a debt,—
   But guard it, thou! nor suffer it to die!

September 18

LE GRAND SALUT

THERE is a power in innocence, a might
   Which, clothed in weakness, makes injustice vain:
   A strength, o'ertopping reason to explain,
Which bears it—though deep-buried out of sight—

---

[54] Georges Picquart.

Slowly and surely upward to the light:
    A conscious certainty amidst its pain
    That, robbed of all things, it shall all regain,
Through that eternal law which guards the right.
O Dreyfus! Thy dear country has restored
    More than *thine* honour in her hour supreme.
      Noble, still noble, though she so could err,
    God spared thee to her that she might redeem
Herself, and hand thee back thy blameless sword.
      Listen! the world salutes—not only thee, but her!

                                September 19

DRYAD SONG

WHEN the wolds of Lycæus are silvery fair,
    When Mænalian forests are doubtful and dim,
When the hound strains the leash and the wolf quits his lair,
    And the startled fawn flies from the fountain's cool rim;
When with panting delight we impatiently follow
The shuddering stags over hillock and hollow,—
    A form from the shadows comes bounding out,
    And we know it is Pan by his horrid shout:

    A form from the shadows comes bounding out,
    At head of the Satyrs' impetuous rout,
    And we know it is Pan, we know it is Pan,
    We know it is Pan by his horrid shout!

When hidden with Dian in deep woodland bower,
    We loosen her quiver, her sandals unbind,
Bathe her beautiful feet in the pearl-trickling shower,
    Pellucid and pure; when we deftly enwind
The silvery fillet that clasps and caresses
The wonder and wealth of her shadowy tresses,—
    A face through the pleachèd blooms stealthily peers,
    And we know it is Pan by his furry ears:

A face through the pleachèd blooms stealthily peers,
Makes mouths to affright us, then mocks at our fears,
And we know it is Pan, we know it is Pan,
We know it is Pan by his furry ears!

When, shunning the shafts of Apollo at noon,
    To the kindly green coverts we thankfully creep,
Athirst for fresh runnels, and ready to swoon,—
    Oft, sudden we come to one fallen asleep:
Fallen asleep mid the tangle and grasses
That trip up the confident clown as he passes,
    And fearful we peep at the form supine,
    For we know it is Pan, though he makes no sign.

    And fearful we peep at the form supine,
    With the hoofs of a goat and the brow divine,
    For we know it is Pan, we know it is Pan,
    We know it is Pan, though he makes no sign!

When the shepherds are gone from the sunset hills,
    When evening is mildest in dingle and dale,
Through the hush comes a sound that enraptures and thrills,
    Light wafted along on the tremulous gale:
So passionate-sweet, so wildly out-welling,
That Ladon hears it with bosom swelling.
    We listen and sigh,—sigh and listen again,
    For we know it is Pan by that melting strain!

    We listen and sigh,—sigh and listen again,
    While the lithe reeds quiver as if in pain,—
    For we know it is Pan, we know it is Pan,
    We know it is Pan by that melting strain!

September 20

NEW YORK

A NOCTURNE

DOWN-GAZING, I behold,
    Miraculous by night,
A city all of gold.
    Here, there, and everywhere,
    In myriad fashion fair,
A mystery untold
    Of Light!

Not royal Babylon,
    Nor Tyre, nor Rome the great—
    In the all-powerful state
Her wisdom and her armèd legions won—
    Was so illuminate
As this strange world which, awed, I look upon.
With it compared, the ancient glories fail,
    And, in the glow it doth irradiate,
The planets of the firmament grow pale!

Night, birth-fellow to Chaos, never wore
A robe so gemmed before.
The splendor streams
In lines and jets and scintillating gleams
From tower and spire and campanile bright,
And palaces of light.

How beautiful is this
Unmatched Cosmopolis!—
City of wealth and want,
    Of pitiless extremes,
    Selfish ambitions, pure aspiring dreams;
Whose miseries, remembered, daunt

The bravest spirit hope hath cheered—
This city loved and hated, honored, feared:
This Titan City, bold to dare:
This wounded Might
That, dreading darkness, covers up its care
And hides its gaping hurt 'neath veils of light!

Oh, I have looked on Venice when the moon
Silvered each dark lagoon,
    And have in dreams beheld her
Clothed in resplendent pride,
The Adriatic's bride!
Naples I, too, have seen—
An even lovelier Queen—
    And thought that nothing in the world excelled her—
Nay, marvelled, as at close of day
I gazed across her opalescent bay
And saw Vesuvius burn on high
Against the soft Italian sky,
That anything on earth could wear
A charm so past compare!

But, O Manhattan! Glowing now
    Against the sombre night,
    Thine opulence and squalor hid from sight,
Never was aught more beautiful than thou
Dost in thy calm appear—
So glorified and so transfigured here—
Since the Eternal, to creation stirred,
Breathed from His awful lips the mystic word:—
    Let there be Light!

September 21

UNPARDONED

"SOME things I never would forgive!"
   So said you, dear, not knowing
That love is dead unless it live
   All charity bestowing.

O you whose heart love so could brim
In cruel need, learn this of him
   Whose all to you is owing:
The one wrong man can not forgive
   Is the wrong of his own sowing!

September 22

SAPPHO

AS a wan weaver in an attic dim,
Hopeless yet patient, so he may be fed
With scanty store of sorrow-seasoned bread,
Heareth a blithe bird carol over him;
And sees no longer walls and rafters grim,
But rural lanes where little feet are led,
Through springing flowers, fields with clover spread,
Clouds, swan-like, that o'er depths of azure swim;—

So when upon our earth-dulled ear new breaks
Some fragment, Sappho, of thy skyey song,
A noble wonder in our souls awakes;

The deathless Beautiful draws strangely nigh,
And we look up, and marvel how so long
We were content to toil for sordid joys that die.

TO SAPPHO DEAD

HOW glad you must be to lie at rest,
Forgetful of him whom you loved so,
Of him who loved you not:
To leave all the watching and waiting,
The hoping and doubting, behind you—
To know no more of the longing
That burned like a fire at your heart!

How glad you must be to lose yourself—
Utterly, utterly, Sappho,
In sleep that is sleep indeed!—
To turn from the pain and the passion,
The dreams of delight that, on waking,
But mocked you and left you more lonely—
The visions that ever betrayed!

How glad, after all—oh, how glad to forget
The golden one, dread Aphrodite!—
The laughter deceitful and sweet
Wherewith from her own glowing bosom
She gave the red rose that consumed you,
Whose fire only floods all-embracing
Could cool, as they rocked you in sleep!

Hereafter for others her emblem shall bloom:
For others shall be the delusion,
The torturing doubt, the despair;
But you, cradled deep mid the waters,
Naught heeding of ebb-tide or flowing,
Your heart pulsing not with their pulsing,—
You, Sappho, untroubled shall rest.

September 23

AUTUMN

"WE ne'er will part!" Ah me, what plaintive sounds
    Are human protests! Dear one, lift your eyes!
    Behold the solemn, widespread prophecies
Of that whose shadow all our light confounds,
Of that whose being all our knowledge bounds!
    Far from the faded fields the robin flies,
    Upon her stem the last rose droops and dies,
And through the pines a doomful blast resounds.

As dawn is portent of the day's decline,
    As joy is prelude sweet to waiting sorrow,
So ripened good is Nature's harvest sign:
    Love, only, the immortal strain doth borrow,
And, high exalted by a hope divine,
    Still whispers in the night of death,—
        To-morrow!

September 24

EXALTATION

AFTER THE FRENCH OF VICTOR HUGO

ALONE by the waves, on a starlight night,
No mist on the sea, not a cloud in sight,
    My eyes pierced further than earth's desires;
And nature—all nature, the hills, and the woods,
Seemed to question, with murmur of myriad moods,
    The waves of the sea and the heavenly fires.

And the infinite legion of golden stars
Replied in a chant of harmonious bars,
    Their scintillant crowns seeming earthward to nod;

And the waves, which no puissance can rule or arrest,
Made answer, while curbing the foam of each crest:
   —It is God! it is God! it is God!

                                                September 25

THE TOMB SAID TO THE ROSE

AFTER THE FRENCH OF VICTOR HUGO

THE tomb said to the rose:
—"With the tears thy leaves enclose,
What makest thou, love's flower?"
The rose said to the tomb:
—"Tell me of all those whom
Death gives into thy power!"

The rose said:—"Tomb, 't is strange,
But these tears of love I change
Into perfumes amber sweet."
The tomb said:—"Plaintive flower,
Of these souls, I make each hour
Angels, for heaven meet!"

                                                September 26

LAST NIGHT I DREAMED

LAST night I dreamed, mine enemy,
    That you were at my side,
As in the days ere coldness came
    Our spirits to divide.

You smiled again with cordial eyes
    And simple heart elate,
As in the happy olden time
    That nothing knew of hate,

And I forgot, in converse glad,
   The bitterness since then,
And nearer to my thought you seemed—
   Dearer—than other men;

For memory, with softened touch
   Of pity, that caressed,
Made every kindness glow more bright,—
   And blotted out the rest.

Last night from dreams, mine enemy,
   I woke in tears, and knew
The soul, apart from mortal strife,
   Has naught with hate to do.

September 27

LOVE HAS NO FOES

LOVE has no foes; where'er he goes
   Conditions full of mildness meet,
And amber honey-cells are filled,
And little birds begin to build,
   And blossoms gather at his feet,—
     Love is so sweet!

Love has no foes; the folded rose
   That answering his smile's caress
Blows into beauty,—with its heart
All bruised to fragrance by his art,
   To every breeze doth still confess
     His loveliness!

Love has no foes: who only knows
   What Love hath been when Love is fled,—
E'en he, bereft, would follow him
Unto the voiceless caverns dim

Of the wan city of the Dead,
    And share his bed!

September 28

MAN

I WAS born as free as the silvery light
    That laughs in a Southern fountain;
Free as the sea-fed bird that nests
    On a Scandinavian mountain,
Free as the wind that mocks at the sway
    And pinioning clasp of another,
Yet in the slave they scourged to-day
    I saw and knew—my brother!

Vested in purple I sat apart,
    But the cord that smote him bruised me;
I closed my ears, but the sob that broke
    From his savage breast accused me;
No phrase of reasoning judgement just
    The plaint of my soul could smother,
A creature vile, abased to the dust,
    I knew him still—my brother.

And the autumn day that had smiled so fair
    Seemed suddenly overclouded;
A gloom, more dreadful than Nature owns,
    My human mind enshrouded;
I thought of the power benign that made
    And bound men one to the other,
And I felt in my brother's fear afraid
    And ashamed in the shame of my brother.

September 29

PRIVILEGE

BLEST is the right to share
   The grief of hearts forlorn,—
With other men to bear
   What must by men be borne;
     For night bestows dawn's orient rose
   And glories of the morn;

And as its shadow-wing
   Lends to the sunlight worth,
So out of suffering
   Arise the joys of earth—
     The good and ill, united still
   And offspring of one birth.

Great is the gift of life
   To him who lives indeed,
A partner in the strife,
   The toil, the pain, that speed—
     Like hidden rills veined through the hills—
   Life's ocean-deeps to feed!

September 30

TO POVERTY

PALE priestess of a fane discredited,
   Whose votaries to-day are few or none;
   Goddess austere, whose touch the vulgar shun,
As they would shrink from a Procrustes bed,
Hieing to temples where the feast is spread,
   And life laughs loudly, and the smooth wines run;
   Wise mother!—least desired 'neath the sun,
At thy chill breasts the noblest have been fed.

Great are thy counsels for the brave and strong;
    Yet do we fear thy brooding mystery,
The griefs, the hardships, which about thee throng,
    The scanty garners where thy harvests be;
But seeing what unto the rich belong,
    We know our debt, O Poverty, to thee!

                                         October 1

OCTOBER

SWEET are the woodland notes
That gush melodious at morn from palpitating throats,
In anthems fresh as dew! Ay, they are sweet!
        But from that dim retreat
Where Evening muses through the pensive hours,
        There sometimes floats along
        A more appealing song.
So, love, thy voice breathes a diviner music in the chill
    Of autumn, when the glen is still
    And Flora's gold all tarnished on the hill,
Than in the time when merry May calls forth her bashful flowers.

                                         October 2

LIFE

BEFORE we knew thee thou wert with us; aye,
    In that far time forgotten and obscure
    When, doubtful of ourselves, of naught secure,
    We feebly uttered first our human cry.
We had not murmured hadst thou passed us by,
    And now, with all our vaunted knowledge sure,
    We know not from what source of bounty pure
    Thou camest, our dull clay to glorify.

Yet—for thou didst awake us when but dust,

    Careless of thee—one tender hope redeems
       Each loss by the dark river: more and more
We feel that we who long for thee may trust
    To wake again, as children do from dreams,
    And find thee waiting on the farther shore.

October 3

HEART-ROOM

THE heart has room for gladness,
    None for joyless things and dull;
Such a very little sadness
    Fills it over-full.
So, with boundless space for loving,
    Enmity it deems excess,
Just a little hatred proving
    Too great bitterness.

October 4

IN THE TOWN A WILD BIRD SINGING[55]

"Hear me, Theresa, Theresa, Theresa!"

HARK! Do I dream? Nay, even now I heard
    The whitethroat's music, tremulous yet clear:
The very plaint, O lonely bird,
That often midst the greening woods hath stirred
    My heart; but never here!

This is the City! High above the street,
    Before my window singing in the dawn,
By what imagination dost thou cheat
Thy hope to utter melody so sweet,

---

[55] Teresa of Ávila died on this day in 1582.

Far from thy groves withdrawn?

Thy tones transport me, wistful, to the North,
    Seeming to lay a touch upon my brow
    Cool as the balsam-laden airs that now
Through pine-woods blow: they woo my spirit forth—
    Forth of the town—forth of myself. But thou?

Dost thou an exile wander from thy home
    Or art thou hast'ning thither?
Through what beguilement dost thou friendless roam?
    And goest thou—ah, whither?

Day quickly fades, Night may refuse her star,
    Clouds may arise, and elemental strife,—
    Ah, hapless bird! what *Wanderlust* of life
Betrayed thy wings so far?

Full as my soul of tremulous desires,
    Thy voice I hear in supplication rise.
    "Theresa!" dost thou call? Unto the skies
The plaint, adoring, holily aspires:—
"Theresa!" Is it *she* keeps watch o'er thee?—
Homeless—but free?

Wise minstrel! Thou dost well to call on her;
No saint was ever lovelier.
Her heart had room for such wide tenderness
    As his who "Little Sister" called the birds,
    And pity, deeper than all words,
Taught her, like him, to bless.

Silent? Where art thou? Lo, the City wakes!
Toil's round begins, and calm the world forsakes.
Thou, too, art gone!—nor evermore shalt come
    Without my window here at dawn to sing.
    Adieu, strange guest! Theresa guide thy wing

Safe to the sweet wild woods that are thy home!

October 5

DÄI NIPPON

APART from all,
    "Child of the World's old age,"
Heedful of naught beyond the billowy wall
    That closely girt her island hermitage,
She pondered still with half-averted look,
The early lessons of the great World-book,
    Nor cared to turn the page;

For a strange dread
    Possessed her. To invoke
Aid of her gods she tried,—scarce comforted
    That countless barrier-waves about her broke;
But when with bold command, in Yeddo Bay
A squadron anchored—oh, prodigious day!—
    The Orient awoke!

Though one long blind,
    At first in fruitless quest
Must grope her course, yet, with enlarging mind,
    She quickly clearer saw; and from her breast
Sent forth brave sons—of her new hunger taught—
    Who, one by one returning, to her brought
The Wisdom of the West.

Then earth beheld,
    With awe and wonderment,
Goliath by this stripling nation felled,
    Which—rising by no tedious ascent—
Swift as the upward flight of wind-swept flame,
Leapt from obscurity to dazzling fame,—
    Star of the Orient!

And yet she won
    Sublimer victories,
Who, high enlightened all excess to shun,
    Did not exact remorseless penalties,
Nor force a brave and fallen foe to drain
Humiliation's brimming cup of pain
    Down to the poisoned lees.

In lieu of things
    Ephemeral—less worth,
She full revealed the sweep of her strong wings,
    And gained the suffrage of the grateful earth;
Choosing, as war should from her realms depart,
To give herself to the enduring Art
    That was her own at birth.

Ah, great Japan,—
    Who, staying griefs appalling,
Approved thyself magnanimous to man,—
    The World, that long had felt thy charm enthralling,
Has laid full many laurels on thy brow;
But with a new, diviner accent now
    She hears *the East a-calling!*

                                                  October 6

TENNYSON[56]

HOW beautiful to live as thou didst live!
    How beautiful to die as thou didst die,—
    In moonlight of the night, without a sigh,
At rest in all the best that love could give!

How excellent to bear into old age
    The poet's ardor and the heart of youth,—

---

[56] Alfred, Lord Tennyson died on this day in 1892.

To keep to the last sleep the vow of truth,
And leave to lands that grieve a glowing page!

How glorious to feel the spirit's power
    Unbroken by the near approach of death,
    To breath[57] blest prophecies with failing breath,
Soul-bound to beauty in that latest hour!

How sweet to greet, in final kinship owned,
    The master-spirit to thy dreams so dear,—
    At last from his immortal lips to hear
The dirge for Imogen, and thee, intoned!

How beautiful to live as thou didst live!
    How beautiful to die as thou didst die,—
    In moonlight of the night, without a sigh,
At rest in all the best that love could give!

                                        October 7

"EACH AND ALL"

I SAW a soul contended for
    By Evil and by Good;
And watching with solicitude—
    As if my yearning could
Some succor bring—I trembled
    Whiles the tempter was withstood.

Yet, soul—my soul, what meant the strife
    To thee?—what power had
Another's wrong to make thee feel
    Thyself so wronged and sad?
And when at last Good overcame,—

---

[57] Sic. [breathe]. The original spelling has been preserved as it appeared in the 1916 version of this poem.

O why wast *thou* so glad?

October 8

THE LIBERTY-BELL

(SENT FROM PHILADELPHIA TO ATLANTA, OCTOBER 4, 1895)[58]

WITH pomp attendant, and in garlands drest,
    I journey from my sacred home once more;
Not this time to the new, triumphant West,
    But to a land more dear to me of yore:
A land in memory sweet as the perfume
Of twining jasmine and magnolia bloom.

Though old and broken, for that memory's sake—
    The memory of honored things gone by,
I will forget my length of years, and make
    This pilgrimage unto her Southern sky,
So Georgia's children, too, my face may know,
And wreathe me proudly with their mistletoe.

Their fathers knew me, and in that great hour
    When in the Hall of Freedom, since my home,
They signed the Charter, born of love and power,
    That made them one, I, from the lofty dome
Above them, loudly rang the brave command,
Proclaiming Liberty throughout the land!

Men pass away, but I do not forget;
    And though, alas, I have been silent long,
The echoes of my ringing vibrate yet,
    From pole to pole, in every freeman's song;
And she who shared my May, in my December
Shall gaze upon my face, and will remember!

---

[58] The Liberty Bell reached Atlanta, GA on this day in 1895.

Georgia, to thee I come as to my own,
    Undying laurels for thy heroes bringing,
Who sacrificed themselves to right alone,
Who signed for Liberty, and set me ringing.
    The word they witnessed then, I bear to all,—
We stand, united; we, divided, fall!

O Georgia! land of Gwynnett, Walton, Hall!
    Whose star was one of the sublime Thirteen,—
A pledge of hope and happiness to all,
    A sign of victory, wherever seen,—
That vow the Fathers made, their sons fulfill,
The stars they joined shine on, united still!

October 9

THE ORCHESTRAL LEADER

ALL eyes upon him centred, motionless,
    Yet tensely watchful, vividly aware,
    He stands an instant waiting. In the air
His mystic wand, uplifted, seems to bless
The Silence, while it calls to readiness
    Forces that overwhelming Silence there,
    Shall in its stead give Sound so sweet and rare
As must its every parting pang redress.

Magician and enchanter, he doth hold
In his fine hand tones, accents, manifold,
    Interpreting the gods to mortal men:
His are the nerves that vitalize the rest;
The central heart of all beats in his breast;
    Through him the very dead revive and speak again.

October 10

NANSEN[59]

TO drift with thee, not strive against thy tide,
    All-powerful Nature! to pursue thy law,
        Attentive,—with devout and childlike awe
Hearkening unto thy voice, and none beside:
To drift with thee! With thee for friend and guide
    In fragile bark, careless of cold or thaw,
        To brave the ice-pack and the dread sea-maw!—
So are man's conquests won, so glorified.

The truest compass is the seeing soul.
    Oh, wond'ring Earth! did not thy spirit glow,
        Calling to mind the deathless Genoese,
As Nansen, pilot of the frozen Pole,
    Like a young Viking rode the icy floe,
        Wresting their secret from the Arctic Seas?

October 11

TO ALICE MEYNELL[60]

I MARVEL not that they have loved you so—
    The gifted ones who knew you;
Gazing upon your face, I know
    Why poet and why painter drew you;
Perceive the mystic thing divine
That brought their hearts to worship at your shrine!

How much the eyes are windows to the soul
    Your poet eyes have taught me,—
Those shadowed orbs that seem the goal

---

[59] Fridtjof Nansen was born on this day in 1861.
[60] Alice Meynell was born on this day in 1847.

Of all that fairest dreams have brought me,—
And, in their depths revealing you,
Win from my heart a tender homage, too.

October 12

BEATRICE BEFORE DEATH

On rereading Shelley's "Cenci"

THE day, from slumber waking, dawns most fair.
   O Helios!—thou that abhorrest night,
   Canst thou look down with radiance so bright
Upon a world woe-darkened?—look, nor care
What torments 'neath thy glorious beams prepare
   For mortals whom relentless furies blight?
   Some young, perchance, who never knew delight,
Some innocent, who long life's joys to share?

Forgive, O Heaven, if life I still desire!
   There is a thought can make stern Death my friend:
Let me remember what man was my sire—
I shall so long his part in me to fly,
   That with impatience I shall wait my end,
And find it sweet, before I live, to die!

October 13

UNITED

OUR single lives are circled round
   By an embracing sea;
Are joined to all that has been, bound
   To all that is to be:
The past and future meet and cross,
And in life's ocean is no loss.

The music of the summer dawn,
    The silence of the midnight sky,
The stars, in azure deeps withdrawn,
    Reveal a single mystery:
And blent with these, the whisperings
    Of spirit find each shy retreat,
And link the soul with viewless things,
    In union close and sweet.

Failure itself may count as gain
    In aspiration; paved with fire
May be the path that leads from pain;
    And unfulfilled desire
May kindle that pure flame above
Whose earthly name is love!

                                                    October 14

AN AMERICAN AT LINCOLN

THE vast cathedral-crown of the high hill,
    The long, low-vaulted nave, the transepts where
    The light is glory shed through windows rare
In rainbow tintings: glory deep and still,
    Gift of a past forever present there!

Beyond the lantern, the carved Gothic Choir,
    And, as interpreting the hallowed place
    Athrob with harmonies, a boyish face—
English, yet with the look of awed desire
    Which speaks America,—the younger race.

In the half-parted lips without a smile,
    In the whole rapt, impassioned gaze,
    I read the travail of the distant days,
The wistful hunger of the Long Exile—
    The yearning that survives through all delays

I read thy soul, my Country! thou dear Land
    Across the deep and all-dividing sea!
    I read thy soul and theirs who founded thee
With sacrifices few could understand—
    Renouncing and enduring silently.

And I perceived that thou hast still retained
    Their strength to toil, their courage to resist:
    That seeking ardently whate'er they missed,
Thou hast remained—in spite of all, remained—
    That which they made thee—an idealist!

And once again I felt how blest it is
    To hunger and to thirst: anew I saw
    That by eternal high-appointed law,
Sublimity and beauty most are his
    In whom they move the deepest thrill of awe!

October 15

SO YOU LOVE ME

SO you love me, have no care;
Mine will be the strength to dare
Perils that without your love
Greater than my strength might prove.
Never any knight who had
Felt your touch an accolade,
But had grown more brave, more true,
Sweetheart! sweetheart!—
    Loved by you.

In your chalice, my one rose,
All earth's fragrance you enclose;
Through your light, my one, one star,
Heaven draws me from afar.
Easy were it to lay down

All things save your love,—my crown,
And, in dying, life renew,
Sweetheart! sweetheart!—
    Loved by you.

October 16

OF LOVE

OF Love the gods require no task,
Content to grant whate'er may ask
    The boy from Venus sprung,—
For howsoever grave his mask,
    They know the lad is young:

Aye, young, indeed! Though, spite of warning,
Often at dusk, all prudence scorning,
    He daring sail unfurls,—
Yet, fragrant still, the breath of morning
    Lingers amid his curls.

What count takes he of days or years?—
E'en pain itself but more endears
    The strange, immortal boy,
Who whilst his eyes o'er-brim with tears,
    Yet keeps the heart of joy!

October 17

LOVE, DOST THOU SMILE?

LOVE, dost thou smile, believing thou shalt cheat
The triform Fates, because thou art so sweet?
Thy beauty, which delights and makes afraid,
Shall surely as the rose of autumn fade,
And pain and grief shall find thee, and slow scorn;
    And thou shalt know neglect, and friendship hollow;

And at the last, pale hope, thy light of morn,
  Shall bring thee to a goal where none will follow.

Love, dost thou weep—in all the sorrowing earth,
Thou the one only thing of perfect worth?
Midnight and morn alike to thee belong;
Poor, thou art rich; defenceless, thou art strong;
Upon thy altar burns perpetual fire
  That mounts and flames aloft to heaven's high portal;
Thou quickenest, from evil, pure desire,—
  Triumphant in defeat, in death immortal!

October 18

VAGRANT

THE love that has no memories and no hope,
  Is like the weed that blossoms for an hour;
  That putting forth its one imperfect flower,
Straightway doth languish. It can neither cope
  With the strong tempest, nor with the mild power
  Of mellow sunlight, nor with the soft shower.

It has no root in nature, and it dies,
  Leaving no fragrance and no fruit behind;
  And none lament it, nor return to find
Its bed when, beaten low, it bruisèd lies:
  Unfriended, and forsaken of its kind,
  It blows about, at mercy of the wind.

October 19

A TOMB IN TUSCANY

IN Montepulciano fair,—
Long famous for that vintage rare,
Prized by the giver of the vine

    Above all wine,—
There dwelt a man whose years had taught him
To seek, beyond what wealth had brought him,
Something to give his transient name
    A lasting fame.

"For lordly palaces," he said,
"Shall crumble; ay, and bastions dread,
And temples grave and gardens gay
    Become as they;
Each vaunted image of my power
Shall perish like a wayside flower,
And like the hawk my hand hath fed
    Lie waste and dead.

"Wherefore, ere yet my days be spent,
I will uprear a monument
That 'gainst the envious floods of Time
    Shall stand sublime;
My treasures vast shall serve and cherish
An art too heavenly to perish:
A beauty, born of passion pure,
    That shall endure!"

So spake he. . . . Now he lies asleep;
But near him forms angelic keep
Unwearied watch, and from decay
    Guard him alway:
Rare sculptured forms that blend his story
With Donatello's deathless glory,
And make mankind his debtors be
    Eternally.

For lordly castles, as he said,
Have crumbled; aye, and bastions dread,
And temples grave and gardens gay
    Are now as they:

Each vaunted image of his power
Has perished like a wayside flower,
But living in the art he fed,
   He is not dead!

October 20

MY COUNTRY

BELOVÈD thou hast triumphed everywhere!
   Thou hast outgrown, men say, that selfless Right
   Which bade thee for the weak expend thy might;
And as a giant strong, dost claim thy share
Of earth's rich conquest, and will naught forbear.
   I listen, and behold, with grievèd sight,
   Upon thy beauteous brow a baleful light,
And something sinister, new-written there.

O my belovèd! art thou changed, indeed?
   Remembering thy birth and peerless dower,
   Canst thou thine altars to Compassion find?
Ah, woe if thou deface them! set to feed
   The unappeasèd lust of wealth and power
   That leagues with the oppressors of mankind!

October 21

THE HOSPITAL

I

IN THE MATERNITY WARD

IS this the place? So still!—as with the hush
   That follows storm.
Each on her narrow bed, they quiet lie—
They who, so young, have been so near to die—

Seeming of life but effigy and form.

How fair these girlish faces with closed eyes!
    Passion and strife
Seem far from them. Are these beyond their reach?
Nay, see!—high-cradled at the foot of each,
    A tender, new-born miracle of life!

On slippered feet the nurses to and fro
    Move noiselessly.
A feeble cry!—a sigh half breathed in sleep!
But who is this that vigil here doth keep—
    What presence of august benignity?

O strangely moving vision! I behold
    The Mighty Mother!—
She who, wandering friendless and forlorn,
Sought far and near the child herself had borne,
    Finding nor help nor comfort in another.

Over the weakness here so proven strength,
    She, heavenly,
Bends down; and, lo! the room becomes a shrine
And hallowed altar for a love divine,
    Pure as her love for lost Persephone!

II

IN THE SURGICAL WARD

"He that loveth his life shall lose it"
    Last night a shape of fear
    Came in the silence drear—
        Unlooked-for and unsought—
With stealthy, ghost-like motion drawing near.

I could not see its face
In the unlighted place;
　　No sound of it I caught;
But, shuddering, I felt its creeping pace.

　A thing too dread to bear,
　I knew that it was there.
　　And, my warm blood grown cold,
An icy breathing horror stirred my hair.

　With pain-shut eyes I lay,
　Wishing yet dreading day
　　That with strange pangs untold
Should come, my frame to rack in a new way,

　And powerless to free
　Myself, despairingly,
　　"From the body of this death,"
I moaned, "Who shall deliver me?"

　Then, all my pulses stirred,
　Awed and amazed, I heard—
　　Uttered with calming breath
Distinct and clear, apart from me—a word,

　In far Judæa taught,
　That instant freedom brought,—
　　Winging my soul's escape
Through the blest miracle of heavenly thought.

　And in the dreaming dawn,
　Waiting, all fear withdrawn,
　　I knew the coward Shape
From out my life forevermore was gone.

October 22

AT THE SARAH-BERNHARDT THEATRE[61]

NOTHING that man's creative mind hath wrought
    Is wholly foreign to the mind of man:
    He looks before and after; in his span
Of life infinities of life are caught,—
Brooding, mysterious, and travail-fraught,—
    And near and distant answer, as they can,
    Enkindled at the flame Promethean
Of world-embracing, heaven-illumined Thought!

Last night a woman played in Paris here
    The rôle of *Hamlet*, each distinctive grace,
    By genius all-subduing and sublime,
    Made native in an alien land and time,—
As though she, listening with accustomed ear,
    Had learned of English Shakespeare, face to face!

October 23

LAMENT OF BRÜNHILDE

MIDST rejoicings I have wept,
And in hours when others slept,
    I have looked on Horror's face,
        In this place.
Now midst wailings I alone
    Hush the voice of mortal sorrow,
Gaze on thee, again mine own!—
    Fear no parting for the morrow.

For we meet, love, as before,

---

[61] Sarah Bernhardt was born on this day (or the next) in 1844.

By a flame-encircled shore.
  Thou once more hast stemmed the tide,
    To thy bride;
And I wake at thy command
  From my agony of dreaming,
And thy ring is on my hand,
  And I feel its clasp redeeming!

Heart to heart again responds,
Death asunder rends my bonds,
  From long exile sets me free,—
    Gives me thee!
And submissive to his will,
  With a rapture that betrays not,
Siegfried, I embrace thee still,
  And the wrath of gods dismays not!

Ah, they pitied not my pain!
Merciless, they saw thee slain,—
  Smiling though the cruel dart
    Pierced my heart,—
But with glory none shall dim
  Thou hast passed the dreaded portal,
And I bless the will of Him
  Who, in anger, made me mortal!

I shall rest, when Odin, late,
Mourns forlorn Brünhilde's fate:
  Mourns her truth, dishonor made—
    Faith betrayed;
For the Nornen ne'er forget;
  In their awful hands they hold him,
And as my spent sun shall set;
  Glooms eternal shall infold him.

Changeless guardians who keep
Watch and ward, shall give me sleep,

When hot tears—not mine—are shed
    For thee, my dead!
When thy foes in vain repent,
    Hopeless, for thy ruin languish,
When Valhalla's towers are rent
    In remembrance of my anguish!...

Godlike hero, thou and I
Loved as none should love who die!
    Dost thou call? Thy funeral pyre,
        Kindling higher,
Weds me to my destiny.
    Bridegroom! lover! last desire!
Thou who crossed the flames to me!—
    Swift to thee I mount through fire!

                          October 24

THE UNCONQUERED AIR[62]

OTHERS endure Man's rule: he therefore deems
    I shall endure it—I, the unconquered Air!
    Imagines this triumphant strength may bear
His paltry sway! yea, ignorantly dreams,
Because proud Rhea now his vassal seems,
    And Neptune him obeys in billowy lair,
    That he a more sublime assault may dare,
Where blown by tempest wild the vulture screams!

Presumptuous, he mounts: I toss his bones
    Back from the height supernal he has braved:
Ay, as his vessel nears my perilous zones,
I blow the cockle-shell away like chaff,
    And give him to the Sea he has enslaved.

---

[62] Orville Wright soared in a new glider for 9 minutes 45 seconds on this day in 1911.

He founders in its depths; and then I laugh!

II

Impregnable I held myself, secure
    Against intrusion. Who can measure Man?
    How should I guess his mortal will outran
Defeat so far that danger could allure
For its own sake?—that he would all endure,
    All sacrifice, all suffer, rather than
    Forego the daring dreams Olympian
That prophesy to him of victory sure?

Ah, tameless courage!—dominating power
That, all attempting, in a deathless hour
    Made earth-born Titans godlike, in revolt!—
Fear is the fire that melts Icarian wings:
Who fears nor Fate, nor Time, nor what Time brings,
    May drive Apollo's steeds, or wield the thunder bolt!

                                  October 25

IN THE WOOD

I WOKE in suffering, and sadly heard,
    Hard by my tent, repeated cries of pain,
    That to the wilderness, in wildest strain,
Proclaimed the trouble of a mother bird
Robbed of her young; and I, too deeply stirred,
    Thought as above me fell the ceaseless rain,
    Wherefore should one who slumbers wake again,
Since anguish is the universal word?

Then suddenly aloft the wood there rose
    The holy anthem of the hermit thrush,
    From depths of happiness toward Heaven swelling;

And o'er the forest came an awed repose,
    And griefs that chid the stormy night grew hush,
    List'ning that wondrous ecstasy upwelling!

October 26

THE LORDLY PINES

THE lordly pines like grasses wave,
    And bend before the wind,
Content to compromise with Fate,
    Security to find;
But when the storm's full wrath is spent—
    Its futile passion o'er,
The pines majestic lift their heads,
    As lordly as before!

October 27

A MEETING IN THE FOREST

LEAVING my tent once as the dawn grew fair,
    Behold! we stood at gaze, a deer and I,
    Regarding one another furtively,—
Too much surprised, too curious for a care
Beyond the miracle that each was there!
    An instant, then—as arrow swift doth fly,
    Sudden as light that darts across the sky—
Gone was he: and the wood seemed reft and bare.

What startled so the gentle, soft-eyed thing?
    'T was but my love his idle fear outran—
Love that would fain have fed him shoots of Spring,
    Balsam and cedar from the groves of Pan!
Why fled he? Ah, a voice admonishing
    Whispered the free, wild creature: "It is Man!"

October 28

A SONG OF THE RED AND THE BLUE

DEDICATED TO PROVOST CHARLES CUSTIS HARRISON, '62.

MOTHER of men, who long ago
Thy leadership had won—
Mother, whom best thy children know
When their days with thee are done;

Eager a part of our debt to pay
With thine honored sons of yore,
We follow the Red and the Blue today,
And love thee forever more.

Blue is the heav'nly hue that shows
When a cloud above us parts;
Red is the tint of the tide that flows,
The life-blood of our hearts,

Who, eager a part of our debt to pay
With thine honored sons of yore,
Still follow the Red and the Blue today,
And love thee forever more.

Pennsylvania! glorious name!
Thy brows with laurel bound
Never shall know the touch of shame,
Nor be through us discrowned,
Who, eager a part of our debt to pay
With thine honored sons of yore,
Still follow the Red and the Blue today,
And love thee forever more.

Blue for the true, we thy children who
By thy hand are upward led.

Loyal to thee, our faith renew
Till the ruby of life is fled—

And eager a part of our debt to pay
With thine honored sons of yore,
We follow the Red and the Blue today,
And love thee forever more.

                                                  October 29

UNCONQUERED

DEEM not, O Pain, that thou shalt vanquish me,
    Who know each treacherous pang, each last device,
    Whereby thou barrest the way to Paradise!
Inured to suffer constantly
    Thy joyless fellowship, I gain
    The lessons only taught by Pain,
And know, though broken, that my will
        Subdues thee still!

Man was not born the slave of things like thee
    And thy companion, Death: the livelong day
    He valiant strives, and holds ye still at bay;
And when he can no longer see
    For thickening shadows, faint and spent
    He bears his standard to his tent
And yields ye seeming victory;
    But—he is free!

                                                  October 30

DELILAH

EVERMORE I hear my name,
    Blared upon the cruel street,
    Echoed in my close retreat,

Breathing fame, and branding shame:
Evermore it mocks my dream.
    Though I wear the purple fine—
    All the pomp of Palestine—
Ravens over Gaza scream:
        "Delilah!"

And when most I should be gay
    For my triumph,—lo! my sight
    Darkens in another's night,
And accusing voices say:
"Guile may lightly vanquish odds;
    But though mortals pay the price
    And accept the sacrifice,
Treason's hateful to the gods,
        Delilah!"

Samson!—bowing reverent knee
    Unto Israel's God and thine—
    Did'st thou think I loved not mine?
Unto him I yielded thee!
Yet—O mighty in thy fall!—
    Groping still thy God to find,
    Bond and bound, bereft and blind,—
Happier thou than she they call
        Delilah!

                                              October 31

WHEN YOU CAME

DEAR, when you came the day was bright;
The moments, roseate to my sight,
    Flew by me, and my heart was glad
    Without you; but I loved you, lad—
Loved in my own despite!

As morn, I thought, so would be night,
Nor feared eclipsing cloud, nor blight—
    Nay, fancied naught to life could add,
        Dear, when you came!

And now—the good I deemed my right—
But you with love will still requite
    The follies that have made you sad!
      You smile—there—whisper! Nothing had
Illumined for me love's altar-light,
        Dear, when you came!

                                      November 1

A CATHEDRAL

ALL SAINTS' DAY IN THE GREAT NORTH WOODS

IT rises by a frozen mere,
With nave and transepts of the pines
That towering 'mid the snows appear
Majestic and sublime;
While, with a myriad fair designs
Of feathery-tufted tracery,
Their tops adorn with silver rime
The azure vault's immensity.

Rock-piled, the altar to the East
Lies argent-spread; on either hand—
Meek servers at the lonely feast—
Surpliced and tall the birches stand,
Like ghostly acolytes,
And through ice-mailèd branches pass,
Prismatic from celestial heights,
The tints of mediæval glass.

Awed, as in no cathedral raised

By human thought, alone, and still,
I muse on one who dying praised
The God of Being, here:
On him who welcomed with a will
The gift of life, the boon of death,—
The while he heard, deep-toned and near,
The solemn forest's organ-breath.[63]

November 2

TO HORACE HOWARD FURNESS[64]

WITH kind and cruel ministries
    Nature assays her metals fine,
And Heaven, bestowing joys and griefs
    With equal hand benign,
Attempers what it holds most dear—
Adds now a smile and now a tear,
    Till it creates with touch divine
    A soul like thine, a soul like thine!—
Ever to loftiest counsels moved,
By all men honoured, and by all beloved.

November 3

A SECRET

MY laddie 's a' the world to me!
    'T is to himself I owe it
That I can never more gae free;
    But, ah!—he must not know it!

When from my side he roams awa',
    I scarce believe I'm living;

---

[63] Robert Louis Stevenson at Saranac. [original footnote]
[64] Horace Howard Furness was born on this day in 1833.

But when he's here—my laddie!—ah,
    I die for want of giving!

Why must I think upon his smile?—
    His eyes o'er bright and bonny?—
His gladness that doth sae beguile
    It robs my heart of ony?

Were I a lad, and he a maid,
    I would na be sae winning;
To wound too deep I'd be afraid,
    And deem such sweetness sinning!

November 4

MORNING

I WOKE and heard the thrushes sing at dawn,—
    A strangely blissful burst of melody,
    A chant of rare, exultant certainty,
Fragrant, as springtime breaths, of wood and lawn.
Night's eastern curtains still were closely drawn;
    No roseate flush predicted pomps to be,
    Or spoke of morning loveliness to me.
But for those happy birds the night was gone!

Darkling they sang, nor guessed what care consumes
    Man's questioning spirit; heedless of decay,
They sang of joy and dew-embalmed blooms.
    My doubts grew still, doubts seemed so poor while they,
Sweet worshipers of light, from leafy glooms
    Poured forth transporting prophecies of Day.

November 5

AUTUMN

IN her arms unconscious lying,
Cytherea's love is dying.
On the hill and in the valley,
Through the grove and sun-lit alley,
Drooping flower and fading leaf
    Share her grief.
But in realms of gloom and night
Proserpine enwreathes her hair,
And a gleam of tender light
Seems to pierce the darkness there:
"Ah!" she sighs, "I long have waited
With the calm of hopeless pain,
But to me, the sorrow-fated,
Comes the lost one back again!
Lovely things that seem to die
Hither now will quickly hie,
And to-morrow, in the gloom
Of this sad and sunless tomb,
Butterflies will lightly hover,
As o'er meadows fair;" she saith,
"For Adonis brings the clover
    With his breath!"

November 6

EARTH'S MYSTERY

I LOOKED on Sorrow, tragical and dread;
    Beheld the anguish in her sunken eyes,
    Which yearned no longer upward to the skies,
As dumbly pleading to be comforted,
But bent their blinded vision on the dead:
    The dead removed—how far!—from human sighs,

  Lying majestic, as a conqueror lies,
Indifferent to tears, so costly shed.

But as I pondered, seeking, soul-oppressed,
  To read the riddle of a world like this,
    Where Nature still seems waiting to destroy,
  I saw immortal Love descend and kiss,
With timid wonder, reverent and blest,
    The quivering eyelids and the lips of Joy!

November 7

TO THE VICTOR

YOU have outstripped me in the race,
Your brow shall wear the laurel's grace;
  But though on-speeding in your might
  You pass beyond my straining sight,
My spirit shall with yours keep pace!

For I have dreamed your dream divine,
For I have worshiped at the shrine
  Whose oracles your faith have moved,
  For I have loved what you have loved—
Your victory is also mine!

Shall the grave gods pronounce their choice
And I not lift in praise my voice?
  Or shall another win the goal
  Whose vision hath illumed my soul,
And I, though distant, not rejoice?

Ah, no! Your greater gifts prevail;
But though to reach your side I fail,
  Through you triumphant in defeat,
  Even in death I will repeat,—
Hail to the victor! Hail!...

November 8

COMBATANTS

HE seemed to call me, and I shrank dismayed,
    Deeming he threatened all I held most dear;
But when at last his summons I obeyed,
    Perplexed and full of fear,
I found upon his face no angry frown, —
    Only a visor down.

Indignant that his voice, so calm and sweet,
    In my despite, unto my soul appealed,
I cried, "If thou hast courage, turn and meet
    A foeman full revealed!"
And with determined zeal that made me strong,
    Contended with him long.

But oh, the armor he so meekly bore
    Was wrought for him in other worlds than ours!
In firm defense of what he battled for,
    Were leagued eternal powers!
I fell; yet overwhelmed by my disgrace,
    At last I saw his face.

And in its matchless beauty I forgot
    The constant service to my pledges due,
And, with adoring love that sorrowed not,
    Entreated, "Tell me who
Hath so o'erthrown my will and pride of youth!"
    He answered, "I am Truth."

November 9

IN DARKNESS

    I WILL be still;
The terror drawing nigh
Shall startle from my lips no coward cry;
Nay, though the night my deadliest dread fulfil,
    I will be still.

    For, oh! I know,
Though suffering hours delay,
Yet to Eternity they pass away,
Carrying something onward as they flow,
    Outlasting woe!

    Yes, something won;
The harvest of our tears—
Something unfading, plucked from fading years,
Something to blossom on beyond the sun.
    From sorrow won.

    The agony,
So hopeless now of balm,
Shall sleep at last, in light as pure and calm
As that wherewith the stars look down on thee,
    Gethsemane!

November 10

TO HENRY MILLS ALDEN[65]

OUR days by deeds are numbered,—and by dreams,
If we dream well and nobly; for it seems
   That he who would respond

---

[65] Henry Mills Alden was born on this day in 1836.

By deed to what is loveliest and best,
Must, holding to the near and manifest,
   Find in the things beyond,
Faith, ay, and courage, duty to fulfil,—
Hearing the higher voices calling still.

Thy youth those voices heard on many a height,
In the fresh dawn and the all-fragrant night,
   For thou wast mountain-born;
And looking to the hills,—from boyhood-days
Thy comrades,—learned the wonder in their ways,
   Reglorified each morn;
Gaining, with deeper draughts of upland breath,
Large images of Life and lordly Death.

And as a man but follows his lodestar,—
For our ideals make us what we are,—
   Through self-effacing years,
Thou, toiling where the burdened city moans,
Hast lost no accent of the higher zones.
   Smiles, and the truth of tears,
And memories, and melodies unsung,
Have visited thy heart, and kept it young.

Thou hast had strength, where many failed, to glean
Good from a doubtful harvest; thou hast seen
   Light where the shade lay deep.
The future with the present praise must blend
To crown thy triumphs worthily, O friend!
   But we remembrance keep
More grateful, even, for thyself than them,
And lay upon thy brow love's anadem.

November 11

EDMUND CLARENCE STEDMAN

LIFE laid upon his forehead a caress
    And, smiling, gave him for his birthright dower,
    Humor and judgment, passion, purpose, power,
And gifts of vision, pure and limitless:
Then—for she ever tempers man's success,
    Nursing the canker in Earth's fairest flower,—
    She added pain; and taught him, hour by hour,
To know that only blessèd which doth bless!

So, following the Gleam from early youth,
    He lent a strengthening hand, and gave his heart,
    And aided feet, less sure than his, to climb:
He sacrificed not others to his art,
    But worshiped beauty with unselfish truth,
    And lives, the well-belovèd of his time!

November 12

THE "PENSEUR"

(ON SEEING THE FAMOUS STATUE)

RODIN'S[66] it was—this vital thing, this Soul,
This striving force imprisoned in clay,
This monster Shape inert, held in control
    By that it doth enshrine:
  Rodin's it was; but, ah, to-day
    It is the world's—and mine!

What mystery here is meant?
Is this Time's great event—

---

[66] Auguste Rodin was born on this day in 1840.

This creature earthward sent
    With subtle might against himself to strive—
        To struggle upward from the brutish thing
        And, ruling the blood's rioting,
    Keep the celestial spark in him alive?

What miracle is meant,
Suggested by this frame relaxed and bent?
What wonders to this Titan are revealed,
Sitting enisled and motionless as if
Lone on some cloud-invested Teneriffe?
Inward and inward still his vision sinks.
What does he here?—He thinks!

Thought is the travail that absorbs him thus;
Himself the workshop, most mysterious,
Wherein are wrought what human strengths there be.
    Detached, aloof, with eyes that seem to stare
        Beyond us and beyond apparent things,
He gazes far into futurity,
And doth with gods unbourned horizons share.
    For thoughts, upborne on never-tiring wings,
    Boldly adventure regions foul and fair:
To Hades sink, then rise to Heaven again,
    Still finding everywhere
The mystic threads whereof are joy and pain
Shaped in the penetralia of the brain!

                                            November 13

ECHO CONSOLATRIX

I SAID, "She is gone from the grieving earth—
    The Maiden, Spring; in the realms of Dis
She reigns o'er a world of tears and dearth,
    With a homesick heart that yearns for this.
Frozen the meadows, the fields lie bare,

And afar, 'mid the fragrant dusk of her hair,
The violets dream of the light, in vain.
She is gone!—ah, will she return again?"
    A voice breathed low, "Again."

I said, "In this joyless heart of me
    Is a winter chill and comfortless:
I tire of the wail of the wind-swept sea,
    My soul is afraid of its loneliness.
Is there a land, as poets tell,
Where beauty and love—as the asphodel
Unchanging—inhale an immortal air?—
And my little lad?—shall I find him there?"
    The voice made answer: "There!"

                                      November 14

MID-OCEAN

A WASTE of heaving waters to the far horizon's rim,
    And over them a vault of leaden gray;
No warmer tint or shading to relieve the aspect dim,
    Save where the riven billows break away,
Revealing as we part them to the left hand and the right,
Beneath each curling crest of foam, the marvellous green light.

Here midst the heaving billows—this unending stretch of sea
    Where scarce an ocean-bird has strength to fly,
Unnumbered leagues from any strand where habitations be,
    Alone, no comrade vessel sailing nigh,
The deep unplumbed beneath us, and, above, a frowning dome,
I do but turn my eyes on thee, and straightway it is home!

November 15

THE RETURN[67]

WHO knocks at the door so late, so late—
    Who knocks so late at the door?
Is it one who comes as a stranger comes,
    Or one who has knocked before?
Is it one who stays with intent to bless,
    Or one who stands to implore?

My days have been as the years, she said,
    And my heart, my heart is sore;
Love looked in my face for a moment's space
    One happy spring of yore—
Looked in my face with a wistful grace;
    And left me to grieve evermore!

Through all the days the door stood wide,
    For hope had breathed a vow
That love should ne'er be kept outside.
    The years were long and hope hath died;
The door at last is barred and fast—
    Why comes this knocking now?

Yet woe the waiting heart, she said,
    And the heart it waiteth for!
And woe the truth and wasted youth
    That nothing shall restore!
The faith that's fled, the hope that's dead,

---

[67] Romney, the painter, married at nineteen and had two children in 1762. He visited them only once, in 1767. When old, nearly mad, and quite utterly desolate, he found his way back to his wife in 1799, and she, after the neglect of nearly forty years, received him with forgiveness and kindness, affectionately nursing him till his death; an act, as has been said, which, even from an artistic point of view, is worth all his pictures. [original footnote] George Romney died on this day in 1802.

The dreams that come no more.

Who knocks at the gate—so late, so late?
    Thou foolish heart, be still!
What is 't to thee if love or hate
    Knocks in the midnight chill?
Art thou, poor heart, compassionate?
    Is love so hard to kill?

Ah me! the night is cold, she said;
    Would I might all forget;
But memory lives when hope is dead,
    And pity heals regret;
As light still lingers overhead
    When sun and moon are set.

                                            November 16

DAWN

IN Orient mystery
Thou veilest thee,
Pale daughter of the never-quenchèd Light,
Who from the couch of Night
By swift-ascending steeds to heaven art borne
Ere yet thy sister, Morn,
Awaking, dons her wondrous vesture bright.

Like to a handmaid lowly, day by day
Thou dost prepare her way;
But when soft-trailing saffron and warm rose
Half hide and half disclose
Her glowing beauty rare,—
When living things her sweet breath quaff,
And lift their heads for joy of her, and laugh,
Thou art no longer there.

Yet, hours there be,
Child of Hyperion, sacred to thee,
That dearer gifts confer;
When mortals lay before thy dim-lit shrine
A thankfulness of worship more divine
Than any offered her:

When, after night distressful spent—
Night sleepless and intolerably long,
Comes—unexpected, eloquent—
A tentative, faint note of song!
And the o'erwearied watcher sighs,
And lying still, with tear-wet eyes,
Hearkens the most celestial lays
Earth knows; and sees Night's curtains drawn
Slowly aside, and whispers: "Dawn!"—
Yearning beholds the tender gleam
Of Hope's pale star, where it doth beam
Eternal on thy brow,
And in its ray composed and blest,
Sinks into rest.

November 17

A BALLAD OF A DRUM

THE Austrians at Arcola[68]
   (The fight had lasted long),
The Austrians at Arcola—
   Some fifty thousand strong—
Assailed the bridge whereto the French
   (A fourth their strength) had come,
With menace dire, and murderous fire;
   Then fled before a drum!

---

[68] The battle of Arcole was fought between 15 and 17 November 1796 between French and Austrian forces.

For Estienne at Arcola—
    Heroic little lad!—
Seeing the carnage on the bridge,
    With soul grown sick and sad,
Had sworn that he, at least, would pass
    Beyond the sanguine tide,
And beat his drum, whate'er should come,
    Upon the farther side.

So Estienne at Arcola—
    No fear had he to die!—
With one brave Sergeant, swam the stream,
    His precious drum held high,
And from the river dripping rose
    Amid the battle's hum,
A French refrain, with might and main,
    To pound upon his drum.

The Austrians at Arcola
    Seemed fifty thousand strong,
But many were the raw recruits
    Among that mighty throng,
Who hearing Frenchmen in the rear,
    Listened, confused and dumb,
Then gave a shout,—"We're hemmed about!"
    And fled—before a drum!

The courage shown at Arcola
    By André Estienne—
The lesson taught at Arcola
    Is wholesome now as then.
Needs there a moral to the tale?
    Then read in this its sum:
The greatest strength may yield at length,
    When sounds a hero's drum!

November 18

SONG

IF love were not, the wilding rose
Would in its leafy heart inclose
    No chalice of perfume;

By mossy bank, in glen or grot,
No bird would build, if love were not,
    No flower complacent bloom.

The sunset clouds would lose their dyes,
The light would fade from beauty's eyes,
    The stars their fires consume;

And something missed from hall and cot
Would leave the world, if love were not,
    A wilderness of gloom.

November 19

DEATHLESS DEATH

IN MEMORY OF RICHARD WATSON GILDER[69]

WE who have seen the seed fall without sound
    Into the lifeless ground,
Through wintry days are tempted to forget
How Spring will come with the first violet
    In her dark hair,
      Fresh and more fair
Than we remembered her, a glad surprise
In the veiled azure of her shadowy eyes.

---

[69] Richard Watson Gilder died on this day in 1909.

Fear doth the heart deceive,
    And still we grieve
Where we should lift the voice
In triumph, and rejoice
    Amid our sorrow,
Because of what the past
Has given that is beauteous and shall last—
A heritage of blessing for the morrow.

Lo, in what perfect trust
Nature confides her darlings to the dust!
The rose, the crocus, the narcissus sweet,
She lays to rest, undoubting, at her feet
    Who from the meadows bright
Was snatched away to rule in the sad light
    Of Hades, and to learn
        Its lessons stern.
    For Nature's faith is deep
That, waking from the dark and dreamless sleep,
Her flowers toward the sun shall wistful yearn,
And in the fragrant breast of Proserpine return.

    Ah, lover true of men,
        Forgive, forgive us, then,
If choked by tears we falter in our praise,
Remembering that we no more again
Shall hold glad converse with your spirit brave,
Nor from your lips hear words that lift and save,
Through all the lengthening number of our days!

By the great Silence you are set apart
From all the restless travail of the heart
        That beats in us
    So passionate and strong—
Are passed beyond the evening angelus
    And Memnon's morning song.
            .   .   .   .

Man's life on earth—how brief!
Yet we with Nature hold the high belief,
   E'en when our hearts are breaking,
That death is but the vital way,
Darkness the shadow of the day,
   And sleep the door to waking!

   And shall we still with tears
Pay tribute sad to one whose soul endears
Even the dark, dark river it hath crossed?
   Shall we in grief forget
The sweetness and the glory of our debt,
And that no good, once given, can be lost?

   Distant your dwelling seems,
Poet and patriot!—but, ah, your dreams
Are living as the flame of sacrifice!
   Therefore love's roses now
We lay amidst the laurel for thy brow,
Grateful that souls like yours our earth emparadise.

November 20

REPROACH NOT DEATH

REPROACH not Death, nor charge to him, in wonder,
   The lives that he doth separate awhile,
But think how many hearts that ache, asunder,
   Death, pitying Death, doth join and reconcile!

November 21

SONG OF LIFE

MAIDEN of the laughing eyes,
   Primrose-kirtled, wingèd, free,
Virgin daughter of the skies—

Joy!—whom gods and mortals prize,
    Share thy smiles with me!

Yet—lest I, unheeding, borrow
    Pleasure that to-day endears,
And benumbs the heart to-morrow,
Turn not wholly from me, Sorrow!
    Let me share thy tears!

Give me of thy fullness, Life!
    Pulse and passion, power, breath,
Vision pure, heroic strife,—
Give me of thy fullness, Life!—
    Nor deny me death!

November 22

AMOR CREATOR

LOVE is enough: were all we fondly cherish
    To pass as visions melt at dawn of day,
Were bud and blossom, fruit and leaf, to perish,
    Love could rebuild them in his perfect way;
For he who makes the tides to ebb and flow,
Each secret of creation well doth know.

His warmth illumes the glow-worm's fickle spark,
    And beams in Aldebaran's steadfast fire:
With him there is no winter and no dark;
    The font, the burning font, of pure desire,
All forms of beauty unto him belong,—
The rose, the avalanche, the wild bird's song.

On Latmos' height pale Dian dreams about him,
    His voice low echoes in the ocean shell,
The bee could fill no honey-cup without him,
    The violet no fragrant secret tell:

Remote yet near, changeful yet still the same,
Love is creation's breath and vital flame!

November 23

NOCTURNE

THE houseless wind has gone to rest
   In some rude cavern-bed of ocean,
And Neptune smooths his foamy crest,
   At Dian's will, with meek devotion;
The shepherd, gathering his sheep,
      Has brought them safely to the fold,—
      And in my arms my world I hold!
         Sleep!

Forespent with hunting on the hill,
   My truant, in the dusk returning,
Finds the lone heart, he left at will,
   With the one worship burning.
The moonlight pales—the shade grows deep—
      The nightingale doth silence break!
      Ah, love, until the lark shall wake,
         Sleep!

No homeless wanderer art thou!
   Here, pillowed safe, thy head is lying.
The nightingale! Ah, listen now!
   What passion—death itself defying!
Peace! Stars above us vigil keep,
      While breathes for thee each mystic flower
      A-bloom to-night in Dreamland bower:
         Sleep!

November 24

EVERY NIGHT AT MARATHON

"In their plains the neighing of horses is heard nightly, and men are seen fighting; and those who purposely come as hearers or spectators into these plains suffer for their curiosity; but such as are accidentally witnesses of these prodigies are not injured by the anger of the dæmons. The Marathonians highly honor those that have fallen in battle and give them the appellation of heroes."—Pausanias.

EVERY night at Marathon
    (Shepherd boy, beware!)—
Every night at Marathon
    Sounds are in the air:
Ghostly sounds, the heart dismaying,
As of maddened horses neighing,
    Over all the plain.

Every night at Marathon
    (Boy, the vision fly!)—
Every night at Marathon,
    'Neath a darkened sky,
Form with form in shadow blending,
Warrior-shapes are seen contending
    As in conflict vain.

These are they at Marathon
    (Mark, O shepherd-lad!)
Who, for freedom, to the gods
    Offered all they had;
Who in danger, Death defying,
Triumphed over Fate in dying,
    For our gain—our gain!
Dæmons sentinel the field;
    Venture thou not near,—
Neither seek those forms to view,
    Nor those sounds to hear.

This enough for thee: they perish
Never!—whom the high gods cherish
   One with life remain.

November 25

INVIOLABLE

"And shall not Loveliness be loved for ever?"—Euripides

WHEN I hear men discoursing idle things,
   Who "beauty and corruption" would unite—
     As who should say: "Now call we darkness bright!"
My wondering soul more passionately clings
To every image, every strain that sings
   Of beauty—still, ah, still the world's delight!—
   More valuing that bloom which knows not blight,
To which no touch of Time defacement brings.

From rocky Chios, from sweet Avon's side,
   From Athens, Sicily—our earth to bless—
     From each dear Land where Joy hath dwelt with Truth,
It comes adown Time's inexhausted tide
   In myriad form, the ancient Loveliness,
   Wearing its glory of immortal youth!

November 26

TWO BROTHERS

MY brother's face is turned from me;
He sees a thing I must not see,—
Alas! what may the vision be?

His form is wasted as with pain;
A fever feeds upon his brain
Whose fire, extinguished, burns again.

Sometimes he seems to hear a cry,—
And the ravens croak on the turrets nigh,
And the echoes shudder as they die.

Sometimes a cloud o'er his sight is cast,
And something viewless, whirling past,
Is borne away on the moaning blast.

And still his face is turned from me,
To hide the thing I must not see,—
Alas! what may the vision be?
. . . .
Her lips apart, her blue eyes wide,
My mother lay in her state and pride,—
The fairest thing that yet had died!

Like a royal rose,—the story saith,—
Peerless and pale, with a rose's breath
At her parted lips, she lay in death.

Her braids were held by a jewelled dart,—
Her jewelled bodice fell apart,
A jewelled dagger pierced her heart.

To find her foe, men strove in vain;
Again they sought, and yet again,—
But no one mourned with my brother's pain.

For he had loved her from the hour
His father won her with that dower
Of beauty, rare as an aloe's flower.

And she loved him till our father died;
Then something—was it grief or pride?—
Made her as marble at his side.

They say—the vassals of our race—

She wore thenceforth a wintry grace,
Like the frozen scorn on her fair dead face;

And though my brother strove at morn
And eve to comfort her, forlorn,
She met him still with that cruel scorn.

O poor, my Mother! Soon, they say,
She hid herself with her child away,
And looked no longer on the day.

But sometimes, when our towers were white,—
Bathed in the moon's celestial light,—
Her casement opened on the night

All tremulous with mystery,
And, motionless, without a sigh,
She stood there, gazing on the sky;

And they who saw her then, declare
There was nor pride nor passion there,—
Only a tearless, mute despair.

I knew her not,—or if I knew,
Forgot her quickly, as children do,—
Alas! as little children do.

But when she died, men say that I
So plaintive wailed in the chamber nigh,
That summoned thither by the cry,

They brought my brother! In that hour,
He bore me to this lonely tower—
This fortress of our ancient power,

Where ever near me, night and day,—
And happiest with me to stay,—

He kept the vexing world away. . . .

But then, he did not seem to see
The haunting thing so constantly!—
Dear God! what may the riddle be?
. . . .
Mother! I scarce have grieved for you,—
So close to me my brother drew—
So gave me all the joys I knew,—

But I am frightened now, and cry,
Stretching my arms out to the sky.
Without my brother's love, I die!

And though I may not understand
Where lies yon far fair Heavenly Land,
I think that soon, hand locked in hand,

We two will find you where you dwell—
Will see the face he loved so well,
And, weeping, all our sorrows tell!

And then,—ah, then, through me beguiled,
You'll smile on him,—as once you smiled,—
On him—so good to your lonely child!

November 27

LOVE THAT FALTERED

    LOVE that faltered for an hour
Had not felt the awful power
Of the god whom gods adore;
    Of the god before whose portal
    Kneel the deathless and the mortal,—
Suppliant forever more.

Love that faltered had not heard
Love's divine, compelling word,
Or it instant had obeyed;
    Giving with the glad devotion
    Of the river for the ocean,—
Doubting not, and unafraid.

    For with Love alone is joy
Free from shadow of alloy;
And before his sacred shrine,
    Sorrow in her deepest sadness
    Guards a hope more blest than gladness,
And through worship grows divine!

                                           November 28

COURAGE

'TIS the front toward life that matters most—
    The tone, the point of view,
The constancy that in defeat
    Remains untouched and true;

For death in patriot fight may be
    Less gallant than a smile,
And high endeavor, to the Gods,
    Seems in itself worth while!

                                           November 29

THE EMPTY HOUSE

I SEEMED to see thy spirit leave the clay
    That was its mortal tenement of late;
    I seemed to see it falter at the gate
Of the New Life, as seeking to obey
Some inner law, yet doubtful of the way

   Provided for its passage, by that fate
      Which makes birth pain, and gives to death such state
And dignity, when soul withdraws its sway.

A tremor of the pale and noble brow,
     A tightening of the lips, and thou wast gone—
Gone?—whither? Ah, the hush of death's abyss!
All tenantless thy beauteous form lay now
     As the cicada's fragile shell outgrown,
Or as the long-forsaken, lonely chrysalis.

                                      November 30

LOVE SAILED AT MORN

LOVE sailed at morn in a fragile bark,
   With broidered pennants flying:
His skies with sudden storm grew dark,
      Yet gallant Love, with courage gay,
      Rode jocund on his conquering way,
   The winds and the waves defying.

But when, all peril overpast,
   In tranquil harbor lying,
He felt no more the billowing blast
      Oppose his sails, Love, joy-becalmed,
      Each foe subdued, each effort balmed,
   Without a wound lay dying.

                                      December 1

"GO NOT TOO FAR"

GO not too far—too far beyond my gaze,
   Thou who canst never pass beyond the yearning
Which, even as the dark for dawning stays,
   Awaits thy loved returning!

Go not too far! Howe'er thy fancies roam,
    Let them come back, wide-circling like the swallow,
Lest I, for very need, should try to come—
    And find I could not follow!

December 2

VICTORY

PEACE! for the silver bugles play,
    And the glad fifes, with shriller sound;
The drum beats fast, and, far away,
    Awakens joy profound.

From dawn unto the setting sun
    We battled, and our foes have lost;
O heart, my heart, the day is won,—
    Break thou, and pay the cost!

December 3

THE BURIAL OF ROBERT LOUIS STEVENSON AT SAMOA[70]

WHERE shall we lay you down to rest?
Where will you sleep the very best?
Mirthful and tender, dear and true—
Where shall we find a grave for you?

They thought of a spirit as brave as light
And they bore him up to a lonely height,
And they laid him there, where he loved to be,
On a mountain gazing o'er the sea!

They thought of a soul aflood with song,
And they buried him where the summer long

---

[70] Robert Louis Stevenson died on this day in 1894.

Myriad birds his requiem sing,
And the echoing woods about him ring!

They thought of a love that life redeems,
Of a heart the home of perfect dreams,
And they left him there, where the worlds aspire
In the sunrise glow and the sunset fire!

THE DIFFERENCE

HAD Henley[71] died, his course half run—
Had Henley died, and Stevenson
    Been left on earth, of him to write,
    He would have chosen to indite
His name in generous phrase—or none.

No envious humor, cold and dun,
Had marred the vesture he had spun,
    All luminous, to clothe his knight—
        Had Henley died!

Ah, well! at rest—poor Stevenson!—
Safe in our hearts his place is won.
    There love shall still his love requite,
    His faults divinely veiled from sight,
Whose tears had fallen in benison,
        Had Henley died!

---

[71] William Ernest Henley.

December 4

OMAR[72]

AN epicure in Pleasure's mart,
    Pursuing mirth, but never glad,
With melancholy songs his heart
    He soothed, and made a thousand sad.

December 5

TO HOPE

GIVER and Gift!
Immortal one whom all unite to praise:
The young, who question not that clouds will lift,
Joy treading upon joy through all their days,—
The old, who cling the more tenaciously
To thy bright promises when most unblest,
Living from hour to hour debtors to thee,
Even for their dream of rest,—

Persuasive vision, wraithlike, pale!
Man's trust adoring ever doth caress
Thy insubstantial loveliness;
For even although
None may thy viewless habitation know,
Fondly the heart still follows from afar
The soft, alluring radiance of thy star,—
The light on earth that is the last to fail!

O wise enchantress who
Regret and disappointment dost redee
And brave forecast,
Binding the future to atone the past,—

---

[72] Omar Khayyam.

Thine are the ministries whereby we live,
Inheritors of the Immortal Dream;
And though inconstant still thou seem,
Baffling and fugitive,
For *these* all thy betrayals we forgive.

                                                      December 6

I HEARD A VOICE

I HEARD a voice say: "You,
Who worship, should pursue:
The good you dream of—do.

"Arise!—perfection seek.
Surmounting what is weak,
Toil on from peak to peak!"

"Henceforth, through sun and shade,"
I answered, "unafraid,
I follow the shy maid:

"Yea, beauty to create,
Accept with heart elate
Whate'er may be my fate."

Then, in youth's ardor, strong,
I toiled my way along,
Upon my lips a song;

But as I climbed on high,
Toward the forbidding sky
Perfection seemed to fly;

And though I strove the more,
Still through some viewless door
She ever passed before.

Heart-wearied and forespent,
With body earthward bent,
I ceased from the ascent;

Then, when hope seemed too late,
Despairing,—at Death's gate
I heard a voice say: "Wait!"

December 7

"HONOR, NOT HONORS"[73]

HAST thou for honor laid ambition down?
   Honor, itself, shall be thy sure reward,
   A guard more certain than a flaming sword,—
A crown above a crown.

Since it is honor stays thy lofty quest,
   Welcome the high defeat thy spirit dares!
   Aye, wear it proudly as a victor wears
The star upon his breast!

December 8

FRIENDS TO VIRTUE

"The gods whom we all belong to are the gods we belong to whether we will or no."

INTO the theatre they came—
   "Motley's the only wear!"
Children of poverty, of shame,
   Of folly, of despair.

Elbowing rudely, Jill and Jack,

---

[73] Motto of Sir Richard Burton.

   A nearer view to win,
Youths, men, and women, white and black,
   Pell-mell, they jostled in.

A wretched place of poor resort,
   Far from the world polite,
Few pennies bought the meagre sport
   So fruitful of delight,

And gazing there, each brutish face,
   The godlike stamp resigned,
A tablet seemed whereon disgrace
   Had written thoughts unkind.

"And what," I mused, "will now be fed
   To cater to their mood
Who, as their looks bespeak, have said,—
   "Evil, be thou my good'?

"Order will surely be reversed,
   Judgement will disappear,
The tricks of knaves will be rehearsed
   To catch the plaudits here!"

Yet as I watched the varied throng,
   My theories took flight,
For, lo, they still condemned the wrong,
   They still approved the right!

The "villain" by his better art
   Surprised from them no praise;
They frankly took the hero's part,
   Awarding him the bays;

For they, unlike the wise of earth,
   Slight tribute paid to skill,—
Anhungered for a higher worth,

Lovers of virtue still!

December 9

LOVE, REPROACHFUL

WHEN Love, reproachful, sighed: "Art thou become
   Voiceless, who in my praise wast eloquent?
   To wound my name unto high heaven is sent
A vain lamenting,—the exordium
Of fruitless plaint and chiding wearisome,—
   While they to whom my chiefest joys are lent,
   To worship me in silence are content!"
Love, even so: whom thou dost bless are dumb.

Listen! That strain of ecstasy and pain!
Far-echoing from Thrace, it breathes again,
   Lost Philomela's passion to prolong;
Yet nested near in solitude, the dove—
Beneath thy very pinions, gracious Love!
   Coos to her mate, but sings the world no song!

December 10

THE SINGER[74]

HE came to us with dreams to sell—
   Ah, long ago it seems!
From regions where enchantments dwell,
He came to us with dreams to sell,
   And we had need of dreams.

Our thought had planned with artful care,
   Our patient toil had wrought,

---

[74] Previously published as "A Traveller from Altruria" after the Utopian novel by William Dean Howells.

The roomy treasure-houses where
Were heaped the costly and the rare,—
    But dreams we had not bought:

Nay; we had felt no need of these,
    Until with dulcet strain,
Alluring as the melodies
That mock the lonely on the seas,
    He made all else seem vain:

Bringing an aching sense of dearth,
    A troubled, vague unrest,
A fear that we, whose care on Earth
Had been to garner things of worth,
    Had somehow missed the best.

Then, as had been our wont before,—
    Unused in vain to sigh,—
We turned our treasure o'er and o'er,
But found in all our vaunted store
    No coin that dreams would buy.

We stood with empty hands: but gay
    As though upborne on wings,
He left us; and at set of day
We heard him singing, far away,
    The joy of simple things!

He left us, and with apathy
    We gazed upon our gold;
But to the world's ascendancy
Submissive, soon we came to be
    Much as we were of old.

Yet sometimes when the fragrant dawn
    In early splendor beams,
And sometimes when, the twilight gone,

The moon o'er-silvers wood and lawn,
    An echo of his dreams

Brings to the heart a swift regret
    That is not wholly pain,
And, grieving, we would not forget
The vision, hallowed to us yet,—
    The hope that seemed so vain.

And then we envy not the throng
    That careless passes by,
With no remembrance of the song,—
Though we must listen still, and long
    To hear it till we die!

                                          December 11

IN LONELINESS

ISEULT OF BRITTANY

THEY are at rest.
How still it is—and cold!
The morrow comes; the night is growing old.
They are at rest. Why then, unresting, keep
In vigil lone, a pain that will not sleep—
An anguish, only to itself confessed,
That hushed a moment lies,
Then wakes to sudden eager life, and cries?

At rest?

Ah, me! The wind wails by,
Like to a grief that would but cannot die.
How sore the heart can ache,
Yet beat and beat and beat, and never break!
(Hearken!—Was that a child's awaking cry?)

It was the sea—the ever troubled sea!
My little ones, it was the sea,
That moans unceasingly
One dear refrain repeating o'er and o'er:—
"Tristram returns no more—
Tristram returns, returns—ah, never more!"

Ashen the fire,—
Ashen: like dead desire.
The dawn breaks chill,
The children, sleeping, think their father here.
O Tristram! might I, also, dream you near!—
Mine—mine without regret!
As when I nursed your wound, and taught you to forget
The cruel torment of your love for her,—
The poisoned wine, the still avenging hate,
The ship, the pain, the unrepenting Fate,
The yearning that is death, yet doth not kill!

(Sleep, little ones! your mother guards you still.)

They are at rest,
Their sorrows over.
Forgetful of the tortured past,
They are at rest at last,
Sad lover by sad lover.
Oh, drear to me
The voices of the sea-birds, and the sea—
The sea that moans against the shore,
Repeating ceaselessly:—
"Tristram returns no more,
Returns—ah, never, never more!"

December 12

ROBERT BROWNING[75]

"Never say of me that I am dead!"

GREAT-HEARTED son of the Titan mother, Earth,
    Fed at her breast,
He builded upward from the solid ground,
While listening ever for the heavenly sound
    Of higher voices, to his soul addressed.

The elemental mother, lending might
    With vital breath,
Made him, with her instinctive courage, brave;
And the immortals to his spirit gave
    Their deeper knowledge and their scorn of death.

So evermore with energy and joy,
    He followed Truth:
Still for the message and the vision sought,
Still to the temple of her worship brought
    The imagination of unaging youth;

And in its largeness ever viewing life,
    Perceived its goal
To be beyond the bounds of space or time.
He strove to picture it in powerful rhyme;
    But what he painted ever—was the soul!

Ay, 't was the soul that moved, delighted him,
    Absorbed his care,
From early days in English Camberwell
To that far hour when tolled for him a knell,
    Mournful across the deep, from Venice the all-fair.

---

[75] Robert Browning died on this day in 1889.

Voiceless he sleeps, his giant task performed;
    But in his stead,
Brave Caponsacchi, poignantly alive,
Pippa, beloved Pompilia, and Clive,
    Forbid the world to think of him as dead!

December 13

"POOR LOVE!" SAID LIFE

"POOR love!" said Life, "that hast nor gold,
    Nor lands, nor other store, I ween;
Thy very shelter from the cold
    Is oft but lowly built and mean."
"Nay: though of rushes be my bed,
    Yet am I rich," Love said.

"But," argued Life, "thrice fond art thou
    To yield the sovereign gifts of Earth—
The victor sword, the laureled brow—
    For visioned things of little worth!"
Love gazed afar with dreamt-lit eyes,
And answered, "Nay: but wise."

"Yet, Love," said Life, "what can atone
    For all the travail of thy years—
The yearnings vain, the vigils lone,
    The pain, the sacrifice, the tears?"
Soft as the breath breathed from a rose,
The answer came: "Love knows."

December 14

LOVE IS PASSING

LOVE is passing through the street.
Love, imperishably sweet,

On his silver-sandaled feet
    Draweth near.

Suppliant he came of yore,—
Comes he now as conqueror?
Will he, pausing at my door,
    Enter here?

Once his lips were ruby-red,
And his wings like gold, outspread,
And the roses crowned his head,
    As in story;

And though these he now disguise,
Ever a lost paradise
In the azure of his eyes
    Keeps its glory.

Love is passing through the street—
Love, imperishably sweet,
And were death our way to meet,
    I would dare it.

Come he suppliant, as before,
Come he as a conqueror,—
So he turn not from my door,
    I can bear it!

December 15

VESTAL

SHE dwelt apart, as one whom love passed by,
    Yet in her heart love glowed with steadfast beam;
    And as the moonlight on a wintry stream
With paly radiance doth glorify
All barren things that in its circle lie,

So, from within, love shed so fair a gleam
    About her, that it made her desert seem
A paradise, abloom immortally.

Some rashly pitied her; but, to atone,
    If one perchance gazed long upon her face,
He grew to feel himself more strangely lone—
    Love lent her look such amplitude of grace;
Yet who that would have made that love his own
    Aught worthy had to offer in its place?

December 16

A LOVER'S "LITANY TO PAN"

BY the germinating seed
And the blossoming of the weed,
By the fruitage that doth feed,—
    Oh, hear!

By the light's reviving kiss,
By the law that wakes to bliss
Butterfly from chrysalis,
    Oh, hear!

By the raptures of the Spring,
And the myriad flowers that bring
Incense at her feet to fling,
    Oh, hear!

By the water-lily shrine
And the syrinx that is thine,
By its melodies divine,
    Oh, hear!

By the fragrance of the glade,
By thy slumber in the shade

And thy bed, of mosses made,
    Oh, hear!
By the budding mysteries
And leafy glory of the trees,—
By the human eye that sees,
    Oh, hear!

By the wistful hopes that throng
To thy chantry of sweet song,
By our power to love and long,
    Oh, hear!

By the dawning's tender beam,
By the twilight's westering gleam,
By the soul's enduring dream,
    Oh, hear!

By the summer's ardent quest,
And the balm of winter rest,—
By the calm of Nature's breast,
    Oh, hear!

By the wonder of thy plan,
By thy boundless gifts to man,—
By thy deathless self, great Pan!
    Oh, hear!

December 17

"THE SENSE OF TEARS IN MORTAL THINGS"

WHY does great beauty waken in the soul,
    Together with the pleasure it inspires,
    Sadness and inaccessible desires?—
Why, in our joy anticipating dole,
Ask we for lovely things a lasting goal,
    Though knowing well their destiny requires

That, wasted and consumed by their own fires,
They pay on earth, full soon, Death's heavy toll?
Nay, love! The seed may fail within the sod,
    But beauty fails not; though it seem to die,
    It lights a quenchless torch in Hades' portal:
A gift benignant as a smile of God,
    Through myriad fading forms it mounts on high,
    And at the last creates beauty that is immortal!

                                            December 18

VEILED

IS the promise of day merely darkness,
    Is sleep full fruition for strife,
Is the grave compensation for sorrow,
    Is Nirvana the answer to life?

Is there no unobscured revelation
    The evil of Earth to explain,—
No word of compassion to soften
    The terrible riddle of pain?

In cold, imperturbable silence
    The planets revolve in their course,
And Nature is deaf to entreaty,
    Untroubled by doubt or remorse;

The snows, far outspread on her mountains,
    Dissolve, nor her mandate gainsay,
And the cloud is consumed at her bidding,
    And vanisheth quickly away.

And man?—shall he fade like the cloud-wreath,
    And waste, unresisting, like snow,
Nor learn of the place whence he journeyed,
    Nor guess whereunto he must go?

Alas! after nights spent in searching,
    After days and years, what can he tell,—
What imagine of mysteries higher
    Than heaven, and deeper than hell?

At end of the difficult journey,
    With restless inquiries so rife,
He knows what his spirit discovered
    At the shadowy threshold of life;

He feels what the tenderness beaming
    From eyes bending, wistful, above,
Revealed to his heart when an infant,—
    The care, unforgetting, of love!

The hawk toward the south her wings stretcheth,
    The eagle ascendeth the sky;
They know not the guide who conducts them,
    Yet onward, unerring, they fly:

In the desert the dew falleth gently,—
    In the desert where no man is;
And the herb wisteth not who hath sent it,
    But the herb and the dew,—both are His!

                                        December 19

ALMS

A BEGGAR, bent beneath the weight of years,—
    To wretchedness inured, half reconciled,—
Entreated help, and I could give but tears;
    Yet grateful looked the man on me, and smiled.

December 20

CRIPPLED

WHY hast Thou bound my feet,
Then bade me toil ceaselessly after Thee?
How should a thing so broken, incomplete—
Ah, how should I, Lord! plant these faltering feet
Where shifting sands of Earth so baffle me?

Have I not set thy limits? Who should know,
Better than I, what sloughs I lead thee through?
Mine is the power to hinder—and make free:
      Walk thou with me!

December 21

MARS

IN the blue, cloudless heaven
    A single star,
Lone torch and lamp of even,
    Burning afar;

Not with the radiance tender
    Of other stars,
But with insistent splendor,—
    Celestial Mars!

Above the summits hoary
    Of ancient hills,
It yet pours out a glory
    On lakes and rills,

As when Selene passes
    Across the night
And her fair image glasses,

    Leaving its light.

Strange planet! Thou dost awe me,
    As by a spell;
Thou dost uplift and draw me
    Where thou dost dwell!

Thy mysteries to capture
    Let others guess;
Mine—mine to feel with rapture
    Thy beauteousness.

December 22

TO him who found me sleeping, all my soul
Locked in the dark enchantment of a dream
Of suffering and death: who broke the spell,
And led my faltering steps through twilight paths
Unto the fair, forgotten fields of life,—
To him I dedicate, with timid trust,
Whate'er of worthiest in thought or phrase
May mirror here the visions lent me since.

December 23

THE VIOLIN

HE gave me all, and then he laid me by.
    Straining my strings to breaking with his pain,
He voiced an anguish, through my wailing cry,
    Never to speak again.

He pressed his cheek against me, and he wept—
    Had we been glad together over much?—
Emotions that within me deep had slept
    Grew vibrant at his touch,

And I who could not ask whence sprung his sorrow,
    Responsive to a grief I might not know,
Sobbed as the infant that each mood doth borrow
    Sobs for the mother's woe.

Wild grew my voice and stormy with his passion,
    Lifted at last unto a tragic might;
Then swift it changed in sad and subtile fashion
    To pathos infinite,

Swooning away beneath his faltering fingers
    Till the grieved plaint seemed, echoless, to die;
When, calm, he rose, and with a touch that lingers,
    Laid me forever by.

Forever! Ah, he comes no more—my lover!
    And all my spirit wrapped in trance-like sleep,
Darkling I dream that such a night doth cover
    His grief with hush as deep.

                                            December 24

CHRISTMAS EVE

WOULD Jesus come to me, Mither,
    The morrow's Christmas morn,
Wearin' the bonny smile he had
    That day that he was born,
Around his head a wreath o' light,
    And not a twig o' thorn,—

I'd open wide the doore, Mither,
    The way that he'd come in;
And not to gi' him pain at all,
    I'd keep my heart from sin;
And all I could to pleasure him
    I'd right at once begin.

Not in a stall should he be laid,
    But on me own fine bed;
And half me porridge wi' me own
    Small spoon should he be fed,
The while his Mither smiled, and shared
    Wi' you the bit o' bread.

'T would be a time o' joy, Mither!
    But thinkin' o' they things,
'T is may-be well he should be there,
    Wi' ward o' angel-wings;
I doubt they'd miss him so!—the kine,
    The shepherds, and the kings!

"IN MEMORY OF JEAN"[76]

ALONE, alone in the still, deserted room,
    He knew that she lay dead—that hope was past,
Knew she had left him in her bloom—
    She, of his joys, the last!

Yet warm and tender as the day's caress,
    There lingered in his breaking heart the light
She wore for him, the loveliness
    Death's shadow could not blight;

And in the silence feeling her so near—
    Though wrapped from him in strange oblivion,
Longing that life should hold her dear
    When he, too, should be gone,—

He strengthened for her sake reluctant breath,

---

[76] Jean Clemens, daughter of "Mark Twain," died at 11 A.M. on this day in 1909.

And put away the dread of waiting years,
And wrote the story of her death,
    And sealed it with his tears. . . .

Four little months! and then—ah, seemed it long
    Reft of his treasure, here on earth to bide?—
When April sang its full, glad song
    They laid him at her side.

No partings more! In quiet now they sleep,
    Forgetful of all griefs that came between;
And through his brave, brave love, we keep
    The memory of "Jean"!

December 25

WHEN CHRIST WAS BORN

ON that divine all-hallowed morn
When Christ in Bethlehem was born,
How lone did Mary seem to be,
The kindly beasts for company!

But when she saw her infant's face—
Fair with the soul's unfading grace,
Softly she wept for love's excess,
For painless ease and happiness.

She pressed her treasure to her heart—
A lowly mother, set apart
In the dear way that mothers are,
And heaven seemed nigh, and earth afar:

And when grave kings in sumptuous guise
Adored her babe, she knew them wise;
For at his touch her sense grew dim—
So all *her* being worshiped him.

A nimbus seemed to crown the head
Low-nestled in that manger-bed,
And Mary's forehead, to our sight,
Wears ever something of its light;

And still the heart—poor pensioner!
In its affliction turns to her—
Best loved of all, best understood,
The type of selfless motherhood!

MOTHER MARY

METHINKS the Blessèd was content, her journey overpast,
    Amid the drowsy, wondering kine on lowly bed to lie:
To dream in pensive thankfulness, and happy days forecast,
    While over her the Star of Hope waxed brighter in the sky.

And yet, methinks in Bethlehem her spirit had been lone
    But for the tender new-born joy that in her arms she bore,—
Ay, even though with gifts of gold and many a precious stone
    Great kings had knelt with shepherd-folk about her stable door.

But every mortal mother's heart knows its Gethsemane—
    That lonelier spot whereto no star the light of hope may bring—
Yet even in the darkest hour, amidst her agony,
    Each still remembers Bethlehem, and hears the angels sing.

December 26

SLEEP

To "the Child in us that trembles before death."—Plato.

SAY, hast thou never been compelled to lie
    Wakeful in Night's impenetrable deep,
        Counting the laggard moments that so creep

Reluctant onward; till, with voiceless cry
Enduring, thou hadst willing been to fly
    From Life itself, and in oblivion steep
      Thy tortured senses? To such longed-for sleep
Death is a way; and dost thou fear to die?

Nay, were it this, just this, and naught beside—
    Merely the calm that we have anguished for,
The wayfarer might still be glad to hide
    From grief and suffering!—but how much more
Is Death—Life's servitor and friend—the guide
    That safely ferries us from shore to shore!

                                      December 27

THE POET

IS he alone? The myriad stars shine o'er him,
    The flowers bloom for him mid wintry frost;
He needs not sleep to dream,—and dreams restore him
    Whatever he has lost.

Is he forsaken? Beauty's self is nigh him,
    Closer than bride to the fond lover's arms,—
Veiled, guarding still, to lift and glorify him,
    The mystery of her charms.

Unto his soul she speaks in accents moving—
    In moving accents meant for him alone,
Revealing, past all visioned heights of loving,
    Far-beckoning heights unknown.

December 28

IN MODERN BONDS

EARLY and late, one day but as another,
One night—one dreary night, like to its brother
Silent and songless, empty of desire,—
A numbness after unremitting tire,—
So, in a vicious circle bound alway,
From light to darkness and from night to day
I move: a thing mechanical, I ween,
As this my comrade here—this vast machine
Which seems more of me than my blood and bone;
Which more doth own me than my God doth own.

For what of difference is 'twixt it and me
Lies in myself a vague and nameless sorrow,
Baffling and barren as the flickering gleam
Of starlight fallen on a frozen stream,
Holding no ray of promise for a morrow
Whose moments, as they come and go, must be—
For one who welcomes nor the night nor morn,
Whose weariness scarce knows itself forlorn—
But portions of a dull, unwished eternity.

December 29

THE SUN-DIAL

THEY that read my message clear,
When the sun is shining near,
Know that moments tarry not
Though I keep no record here.

Noiseless as the river's flow,
Onward still the moments go;
Naught delays them—yet they be

Freighted for Eternity!

As the sand drops from the glass,
Unreturning, so they pass;
And the Power that bids them fall
Knows their value—each and all!

December 30

YESTERDAY

MY soul is fain to drink of joy;
    Thy cup is full of tears.
Ah, take it from me, nor destroy
    The dream of future years!
Thy face is fair, but grief is there—
    And grief but wastes and sears.

We two have been companioned long;
    Now straightway let us part!
Another and a dearer song,
    By some mysterious art,
Draws young, sweet breath while thy lips of death
    Yet whisper to my heart.

Ah, joy it is a timid thing,
    And easily 't is slain;
A tender firstling of the spring,
    It shrinks at touch of pain;
Then haste away, dread Yesterday!
    Nor hither come again!

So quickly? But who goes with thee,
    Unrecognized before?
Are hope, alas! and memory
    Thus joined forevermore?
Then must thou stay, O Yesterday!
    Lest joy, too, quit my door.

December 31

BEYOND

HAD we the present—only that, no more!
Were the past, hidden by Oblivion's door,
   Impenetrable to our backward gaze,
   Its lessons lost, its joyful, tearful days!
   Were there no vision of untrodden ways,
No distant fields of morn, no blooms unfound,
No skyey hopes to beckon from the ground,—
   No loves whose waiting welcome ne'er betrays!

Were there no promise of returning Spring
When Autumn preens a migratory wing,
   And on earth's hearth the fire is burning low!—
   Were there no future with romance aglow,
   When the chilled blood within the vein moves slow,
No dream of a fair dawning, in the night,—
No fond expectancy,—no pledge of light
   Fairer than cloud-veiled days of winter know!
  . . . .
To-morrow!—mystic word of the Ideal!
What were all else, wert thou not there to heal
   The deepest hurt that e'er the present gave?
   Friend! Ever wise consoler! We are brave
   Because of thee! Trusting thy might to save,
We journey onward toward an unknown land,
And close, and closer still, we clasp thy hand,—
   Nor will be parted from thee at the grave.

HOLIDAYS

EASTER

REJECTED

THE World denies her prophets with rash breath,
    Makes rich her slaves, her flatterers adorns;
To Wisdom's lips she presses drowsy death,
    And on the brow Divine a crown of thorns.
Yet blessèd, though neglected and despised—
    Who for the World himself hath sacrificed,
Who hears unmoved her witless mockery,
    While to his spirit, slighted and misprised,
Whisper the voices of Eternity!

THE MARTYR JEWS

THEIR fathers wronged thee, Master, long ago:
    Rejected thee, because they knew thee not
Whom it had been their highest peace to know,
    And nobler dreams forgot,
Preferred a kingdom of this world to thee,
And saw thee sacrificed upon a tree.

Yet thou in death—even in death, didst pray:—
    "Father, forgive! They know not what they do!"
But what of those, more culpable than they—
    Oh, more than they, untrue,
Who, in thy name, dear Christ! have tortured men,
And crucified thee countless times since then?

THE LARK

THERE is a legend somewhere told
Of how the skylark came of old
    To the dying Saviour's cross,
And circling round that form of pain
Poured forth a wild, lamenting strain,
    As if for human loss.

Pierced by those accents of despair,
Upon the tiny mourner there
    Turning his fading eyes,
The Saviour said, "Dost thou so mourn,
And is thy fragile breast so torn,
    That man, thy brother, dies?

"O'er all the world uplifted high,
We are alone here, thou and I;
    And near to heaven and thee
I bless thy pity-guided wings!
I bless thy voice—the last that sings
    Love's requiem for me!

"Sorrow no more shall fill thy song;
These frail and fluttering wings grown strong,
    Thou shalt no longer fly
Earth's captive—nay, but boldly dare
The azure vault, and upward bear
    Thy transports to the sky!"

Soon passed the Saviour; but the lark,
Close hovering near Him in the dark,
    Could not his grief abate;
And nigh the watchers at the tomb,
Still mourned through days of grief and gloom,
    With note disconsolate.

But when to those sad mourners came,
In rose and amethyst and flame,
    The Dawn Miraculous,
Song in which sorrow had no part
Burst from the lark's triumphant heart—
    Sweet and tumultuous!

An instant, as with rapture blind,
He faltered; then, his Lord to find,
    Straight to the ether flew,—
Rising where falls no human tear,
Singing where still his song we hear
    Piercing the upper blue!

EASTER

I KNOW the Summer fell asleep
    Long weary months ago;
Heaped high above her grave I saw
    The heavy winter snow;
Say, sparrow, then, what word you bring;
    Is it her requiem you sing?

The meadowlark is mute, the wren
    Forgets his late abode,
No throstle answering fluteth near,
    Yet never prelude flowed
From ivied bosk or verdant slope
    More brimming with delight and hope!

I, listening, seem to see the blooms
    That were whilom so dear,
And voices loved and silent long
    I, listening, seem to hear;
And longings in my breast confer,
    And sweet, prophetic pulses stir.

"Thou lonely one," they seem to say,
  "Lost Summer shall return;
Wreathed in her shadowy tresses shall
  The roses blissful burn;
Wan lilies at her feet shall lie,
  And wind-flowers on her bosom sigh.

"Here, from this rough and lowly bed,
  The little celandine
Shall lift her sunny glances to
  The balmy eglantine;
And flags shall flaunt by yonder lake,
  And fair Narcissus there awake."

I know the Summer fell asleep
  Long weary months ago;
But ah! all is not lost, poor heart,
  That's laid beneath the snow;
There wait, grown cold to care and strife,
  Things costliest, dying into life.

All changes, but Life ceases not
  With the suspended breath;
There is no bourne to Being, and
  No permanence in Death;
Time flows to an eternal sea,
  Space widens to Infinity!

AT EASTER

HE saw the myriad blooming plants
  That mark the hallowed morn;
He thought upon a lowly mound
  In a far land, forlorn,

Where yearning love would never come

    To place or flower or leaf,
Where lonely love would never bring
    Its heartache for relief.

When, lo! athwart his musings, came
    Again that strange appeal
Which he had listened to before,—
    Without the power to feel;

And putting by a vain regret,—
    His fallen foe to save,—
"Ah, love!" he sighed, "lost love!—I lay
    This blossom on thy grave!"

ÉASTRE

    I WHO am ever young,
      Am she whom Earth hath sung
From the far ages when from death awaking
She felt the dawn of life within her breaking—
A strange and inexperienced delight—
That warned the desert places of her night,
      And, after bondage long,
        Left her divinely free
        To worship with an ecstasy,
      Voiceless, that yet was song!

    I am that she, Astarte named,
By proud Phœnicia and Assyria claimed,
Adored by Babylon and Naucratis.
      From the moon, my throne of bliss,
        On famed Hieropolis
Where stood my temple sanctified and hoary,
I poured such floods of silver glory
That mortals—blest my "palest" beams to see—
Fell prone upon the earth and worshiped me!

I am Aurora—goddess of the dawn!
To heaven in my orient car updrawn,
    While wingèd joys fly after,
I part with roseate hand the curtained dark.
    Mid bird-songs and celestial laughter,
I perfume all the æther with my breath,
And putting by the envious clouds of Death,
    With my insistent yearning
Rekindle the sun's fire and set it burning.

    Persephone am I—the Spring!
Whom all things celebrate and sing.
    When glad from Hades' sombre home
    Back to the dear, dear earth I come,
The gods themselves, my way befriending,
    Look down on me with shining eyes benign,
And grant that, to my mother's arms ascending,
    Of miracles the loveliest shall be mine.

    Howe'er men speak my name
    I ever am the same,—
In herb and tree and vine and blossoming flower,
Regenerating, consecrating power.
    Youth am I and delight.
Astarte or Aurora, still the priest
Of mysteries beneficently bright.
The vivifying glory of the East,
The Spring, in vesture of transparent dyes
'Broidered with blossoms and with butterflies,
The door that leads from gloomy vasts of Death,—
I resurrection am!—new life! new breath!

MOTHER'S DAY

MOTHER

AT twilight here I sit alone,
    Yet not alone; for thoughts of thee,—
Pale images of pleasure flown,—
    Like homing birds, once more return to me.

Again the shining chestnut braids
    Are soft enwreathed about thy brow,
And light—a light that never fades—
    Beams from thine eyes upon me even now,

As, all undimmed by death and night,
    Remembrance out of distance brings
Thy youthful loveliness, alight
    With ardent hope and high imaginings.

Ah, mortal dreams, how fair, how fleet!
    Thy yearnings scant fulfilment found;
Dark Lethe long hath laved thy feet
    And on thy slumber breaks no troubling sound;

Yet distance parts thee not from me,
    For beauty—or of twilight or of morn—
Binds me, still closer binds, to thee,
    Whose heart sang to my heart ere I was born.

MOTHER-LOVE

THINK not of love as of a debt—
    Due or in May or in December!
Nay, rather, for a time, forget.
    Life always helps us to remember!

A child whom harmless toys beguile
    To loiter for a little while,
Put heart into your play, and then,
    When you are tired—come home again!

Fair, yet how fragile, pleasure's rose!—
    How vain the toil to make it stronger!
It blooms—it withers,—but love knows
    A sweeter blossom that lives longer!

THE ALL-MOTHER

IN the arid and desolate places of life
    She opens fresh fountains of feeling;
She comforts the spirit o'erwearied with strife;
    For the hurt of the heart she has healing.

She looks on our sorrows with calm that is kind,
    (What recks she of failure or illness?)
And gives, with a smile, to the care-burdened mind
    The relief of her beauty and stillness.

She sings mid the tempest, she wings the storm's flight,
    (There's nothing can life from Life sever!)
To guide the lost wanderer safe through the night,
    She keeps a lamp burning forever.

MADONNA

HE gazed, the little vagrant lad,
    On the Madonna's gentle face;
And all his wistful visage sad
    Renewed its infant grace:
He gazed, reluctant to depart,
    Then kissed her, shyly, as he stood—

Ah, wondrous Art! his lonely heart
    But yearned to motherhood!

FATHER'S DAY

FATHER

HOW should I dream but you were old
    Who seemed so strangely wise?
The truth, had I the truth been told,
    Had filled me with surprise;
But now that you are gone, alas!
    Beyond Death's voiceless sea,
Still, as your birthdays come and pass,
    Younger you grow to me.

COLUMBUS DAY

COLUMBUS

VICEROY they made him, Admiral and Don,
    Wishing—good King and Queen!—to honor him
    Whose deeds should make all like distinctions dim.
Columbus! Other title needs he none.
    And they—in wisdom more than kingship blest—
    Go down to future days, remembered best
For service rendered to that lowly one.

Columbus! With proud love, yet reverently,
    Pronounce that name—the name of one who heard
    A word of life, and, answering that word,
Braved death, unfearing, on the Shadowy Sea;
    Who—seeking land not known to any chart,
    That land by faith deep graven on his heart—

Found justice, truth, and human liberty!

THANKSGIVING

GIVING THANKS

Thou that dost save through pain,
    And dost, afflicting, bless,
We offer Thee from prostrate hearts
    The Greater Thankfulness!

Lord, Thou hast humbled pride—
    Hast shown the world at length
What ruthlessness may dwell with Power,
    What bankruptcy with Strength;

And teaching us the scorn
    Of trifles that beguile,
Hast given us, dear God, to live
    When life is most worth while!

We thank Thee for the dream
    That heroes dreamed of yore,
For the desire of good, the will
    Earth's freedom to restore;

Spoiled children of the Past,
    To-day, more nobly blest,
We thank Thee who hast wakened us,
    And asked of us our best!

God of the young and brave
    Who nothing know of fear,
Who hold the things that life outlast
    Than life itself more dear,

We thank Thee that our souls
    Are strong as theirs to give—
All, all we cherish most on earth,
    That Liberty may live!

That we, O Good supreme!
    Still through our tears can see
On the brow of Death an aureole
    Of Immortality!

THANKSGIVING

NOW gracious plenty rules the board,
    And in the purse is gold;
By multitudes in glad accord
    Thy giving is extolled.
Ah, suffer me to thank Thee, Lord,
    For what thou dost withhold!

I thank Thee that howe'er we climb
    There yet is something higher;
That though through all our reach of time
    We to the stars aspire,
Still, still beyond us burns sublime
    The pure sidereal fire!

I thank Thee for the unexplained,
    The hope that lies before,
The victory that is not gained,—
    O Father, more and more
I thank Thee for the unattained,
    The good we hunger for!

I thank Thee for the voice that sings
    To inner depths of being;
For all the spread and sweep of wings,

From earthly bondage freeing;
For mystery—the dream of things
   Beyond our power of seeing!

POEMS ON WAR AND PEACE

"Heroes with eloquent flags unfurled
  Have trumpeted loudly their just elation,
But the voice that hath sunk to the heart of the world
  Is the voice of renunciation." –FEC

I. WAR

IN the beginning was I born,
    With man from out the dust;
And presently, from earth uptorn,
    Came Cruelty and Lust.
Alway, the vassals of my will,
    They twain go with me still.

Where'er my flashing sword they see,
    Where'er they scent my breath,
Quickly they follow after me,
    Bringing despair and death;
Yet still the mighty wear with pride
My liveries, crimson-dyed!

Once, long ago, in ages gone,
    When man seemed as the brute,
I looked with dread to wisdom's dawn,
    And virtue's ripening fruit:
Now sages wreathe my brow with bays,
And poets chant my praise.

And once, in little Bethlehem—
    Once only, not again—
Peace wore a royal diadem:
    But I could trust to men,
And crucified upon a tree,
Peace is a memory!

II. "VICTI RESURGUNT"

HEROES with eloquent flags unfurled
    Have trumpeted loudly their just elation,
But the voice that hath sunk to the heart of the world
    Is the voice of renunciation.

It nothing vaunts, nor with idle sound
    Perplexes the currents of human feeling,
But speaks with the accent and note profound
    Of deep unto deep appealing.

And Earth—who worships her victims slain—
    To faith's redeeming doth first awaken,
Recalling who, giving themselves in vain,
    Seemed, even in death, forsaken!

III.   "SO WAR HAS BEGUN"

SO war has begun, they say,
    Well, Spring is here before it;
If war takes much away,
    And leaves us to deplore it,—
Yet see! the woody dells once more
Are turning green, in spite of war.

On yonder maple tree
    The misty buds are swelling;
Violets, timidly,
    Peep from their mossy dwelling,
And bluebirds, far and near, outpour
Their brimming hope, in spite of war.

Rumor, with awful tales
    Of death and of disaster,
May clamor through our vales,
    But Spring comes hither faster,
Humming a tender rune of peace—
Breathing of bloom and life's increase.

Old soldiers still relate
    How at Resaca's battle,—
As if to compensate,—

Above the din and rattle
Of musketry, continued long,
A mockingbird sang rapturous song:

And one who lay near death,—
 A soldier sorely wounded,
Drew less distressful breath,
 As clear that music sounded,
And felt to his tired spirit come
The most delightful dreams of home.

Ah, well! we talk of war,
 But peace is so much kinder,
That all our strife is for
 Is just the hope to find her:
And see!—how Spring, with look serene,
 Is garlanding her halls in green!

POEMS OF THE WAR FOR THE LIBERATION OF CUBA

IV. AMERICA

THY children are inspired by thee:
Blest by thy gift of liberty,
They go to make the wretched free,
  Mother-land!

They were indeed not sons of thine
Could they withhold that gift divine.
Of liberty thou art the shrine,
  Mother-land!

Thy children glory in thy name;
They write it, as with words of flame,
In deeds that put thy foes to shame,

>   Mother-land!
>
> In deeds of daring unforecast,
> In deeds of valor unsurpassed,
> In deeds that make thee known at last,
>   Mother-land!
>
> Thy strength it was that made them strong;
> Thy justice taught them hate of wrong;
> They are of thee, to thee belong,
>   Mother-land!
>
> Their lungs are filled with thy sweet breath;
> Thy voice they hear, and what it saith;
> They love thee, and they fear not death,
>   Mother-land!

V.   TO THE RETURNING BRAVE[77]

> COME home! The Land that sent you forth
> From East and West, from South and North,
> Looks wistfully beyond her gates,
> Extends her arms and waits—and waits!
>
> At duty's call she stilled her woe;
> She smiled through tears and bade you go
> To face the death you would not shun.
> Brave hearts, return! Your task is done.
>
> Not as you journeyed come you back!
> A glory is about your track
> Of deeds that vanquished tyranny
> And set a tortured people free:
> Deeds, sprung of manhood's finest grace,

---

[77] Previously published as "Welcome".

That envious Time shall not efface;
Deeds that proclaim a Nation's worth,
And crown the Land that gave them birth.

America but waits to greet
And bless you, kneeling at her feet,
Your standards fair in honor furled,
The proudest mother in the world!

Come home! The Land that sent you forth
From East and West, from South and North,
Looks wistfully beyond her gates,
Extends her arms and waits!

VI.   MEMORIAL ODE

THE peace we longed to keep
   Our fate denied;
Reluctant we awoke, as from a sleep,
And saw the face of duty deified.

We followed with dismay
   The awful hand
That drew us, step by step, along the way,
And pointed to an agonizing land.

Nearer it led and nearer
   To dreadful death,
While ever to the spirit whispered clearer
A voice that promised something more than breath:

A voice that prophesied
   Of victory,
Through mildness and compassion sanctified,—
Of conquest that ennobles and makes free.
   America to-day

        Binds in her hair
The olive and the undecaying bay:
An adult Nation, gloriously fair,

      Who with a mother's pride
          Her children gave,
Who feels their triumph, as her oceans, wide,
And sorrows for her unreturning brave.

     Peace is their martyr-crown:
        No length of years
Can chill her love or lessen their renown!—
But ah! her pæan falters, hushed in tears.

.   .   .   .

   Who are these advancing
     With bugle note and drum,
Their bayonets far glancing?
     Say, who are these that come?
They are thy sons, Great Mother!
   Such sons hath any other?
Be comforted, and bless them as they come!

   Be comforted! Though all
     Respond not to thy voice,
   Though thine impassioned call
     Some answer not, nor hear,
O Mother! with thy valiant ones rejoice,
   Who died for Man, not glory,
   And live in deathless story,
Joined to the names imperishably dear!

   Blessèd who fall for Freedom,
     Where her flag triumphant waves;
   Blessèd who sleep in quiet,
     With her laurel on their graves,
Remembered through the echoing years
And hallowed by a nation's thankful tears!

And blessèd, too, the living,
Who fill our hearts with hope and glad forgiving;
Who mid the battle's deafening roar,
    When fell the ranks like autumn leaves,
    Guarded the standard of the free,
    The ægis of our victory:
Who, fevered and anhungered, bore
The more appalling tests of tragic War,
    And laureate return, and bring to us their sheaves!

    Warriors of the land
        And warriors of the sea,
        Bold to meet adversity
    And constant to withstand;
Heroes of battle, hospital, and tent,
    Men chivalrous and never tired,
    Women devoted, love-inspired,
Who nursed to life the loyal ones you lent;
    And ye—whom all must praise—
        Ye darker children of the nation!
Who with a patriot hope and proud elation,
Faced danger that the stoutest heart dismays;
And in the trench and on the mesa saw,
In memory, the men who fought with Shaw
For freedom, at the parting of the ways:
    Thrice gallant souls! who in the van
    Pressed forward, with one only plan—
        One purpose, to prevail;
        And 'neath the Mausers' burning hail
    Sprang dauntless to the grave,
Your whiter comrades' threatened lives to save:
    Who, stumbling, falling,—forward, onward still,—
    Fought, step by step, up the dread hill,
Up to the crest where red the death-tide ran,—
Up to the high estate and dignities of Man!

Peace! Sound the drums! The great roll call!

Ah, many to Fame's clarion note
    Make answer; but not all!
Yet ye, our brave! have planted seed—
    Not for a day, but distant times remote,
Which priceless from the fruitful earth shall spring,
    In harvest of pure thought and noble deed,
To bless the Land we love, immortal blossoming.

Into the unresponsive past
On wingèd feet the years fly fast:
    Scarcely we pluck the blooms of May,
A shadow on the wold is cast,
And, lo! it is December;
    Yet, as a light to guide our way,
    Some visions of a troubled day
Gone by we still remember.

And one there is, one image, full of rest,
A memory of manhood singly blest,
    The savior of our Nation and her Chief:
Matchless in judgment, love, compassion, power—
    The Man meet for the hour.
    Assailed by ignorance and half-belief,—
Each searching from too near a view
To read the soul of all our souls most true,—
    He went his way, unselfish, minist'ring;
    But in the bud and promise-time of Spring
He died—and then we knew.[78]

So in the years to come, when we shall sleep,
    Tired pilgrims, at life's everlasting goal,
And the hid hands, that faithful minutes keep,
    Shall all the record of our times unroll,
    Our sons shall read, emblazoned on the scroll,
        His name revered and great,

---

[78] Abraham Lincoln, April 15, 1865.

    Who sways our continent with mild control:
Pilot whom war tempestuous could not whelm,
Who stood through every peril at the helm,
    Guiding to peaceful port our Ship of State.
He neither needs our praise nor vindication,
      Who in the coming years shall take his place
      With the wise rulers of the English race;
A leader of the strength that fits a free-born nation![79]

America, my home!—how dear to-day!
    In beauty and augmented splendor,
      With smile of mother-love so tender
    It doth each sacrifice for thee repay,
      Thou standest regnant and secure,
      Thy hands extended to the helpless poor,
Thy war-like brows unbent, thine armor laid away.

    To love devoutly is to pray.
O Land! for thee in thy victorious hour
    We lift our souls in supplication,
That righteousness may sanctify thy power
    And fill thee with that purer exaltation
Which bides with those who highest hests obey.
Oh, may the lips that praise thy strength,
    Laud thee for justice, rather, and for truth,
    Welling immediate from thy heart of youth,
To bless thy children first, and all mankind at length!

---

[79] William McKinley.

WORLD WAR I

VII. WAR

THE serpent-horror writhing in her hair,
    And crowning cruel brows bent o'er the ground
    That she would crimson now from many a wound,
Medusa-like, I seem to see her there—
War! with her petrifying eyes astare—
    And can no longer listen to the sound
    Of song-birds in the harvest fields around;
Such prophecies do her mute lips declare.
Evils? Can any greater be than they
    That troop licentious in her brutal train?
        Unvindicated honour? She brings shame—
        Shame more appalling than men dare to name,
Betraying them that die and them that slay,
    And making of this earth a hell of pain!

VIII. BRITANNIA

I AM calling together my sons—
The children my love gave birth,
    I am arming them
        As the swift sand runs,
    And sending them with their battle guns,
To prove their manhood's worth.

I should have, God knows, less power
To stay them by pleadings poor
    Than the mother who tried
        In woodland bower
    To hold from knighthood—
        His rightful dower—
Her boy, Sir Peredur!

For they know full well, as he knew,
How base is the touch of fear
   When tyrannous wrong
      Would right subdue;
  And they to me
     And themselves are true
When danger draweth near.

Oh, strong with the love I gave,
Their souls have the strength I give,
   Who have taught my sons
     To be pure and brave,
  Nor to fly the chance of a hero's grave,
Where, deathless, heroes live!

IX.   PLACE DE LA CONCORDE

AUGUST 14, 1914

Since the bombardment of Strasburg, August 14, 1870, her statue in Paris, representing Alsace, has been draped in mourning by the French people.

NEAR where the royal victims fell
In days gone by, caught in the swell
Of a ruthless tide
Of human passion, deep and wide:
There where we two
A Nation's later sorrow knew,—
To-day, O friend! I stood
Amid a self-ruled multitude
That by nor sound nor word
Betrayed how mightily its heart was stirred.

A memory Time never could efface—
A memory of grief—
Like a great Silence brooded o'er the place;

And men breathed hard, as seeking for relief
From an emotion strong
That would not cry, though held in check too long.
One felt that joy drew near,—
A joy intense that seemed itself to fear,—
Brightening in eyes that had been dull,
As all with feeling gazed
Upon the Strasburg figure, raised
Above us,—mourning, beautiful!

Then one stood at the statue's base, and spoke—
Men needed not to ask what word;
Each in his breast the message heard,
Writ for him by Despair,
That evermore in moving phrase
Breathes from the Invalides and Père-Lachaise,—
Vainly it seemed, alas!
But now, France, looking on the image there,
Hope gave her back the lost Alsace.

A deeper hush fell on the crowd:
A sound—the lightest—seemed too loud
(Would, friend, you had been there!)
As to that form the speaker rose,
Took from her, fold on fold,
The mournful crape, gray-worn and old,
Her, proudly, to disclose,
And with the touch of tender care
That fond emotion speaks,
Mid tears that none could quite command,
Placed the Tricolour in her hand,
And kissed her on both cheeks!

X. THE NEW MARS

I WAR against the folly that is War,
    The sacrifice that pity hath not stayed,
The Great Delusion men have perished for,
    The lie that hath the souls of men betrayed:
I war for justice and for human right,
Against the lawless tyranny of Might.

A monstrous cult has held the world too long:
    The worship of a Moloch that hath slain
Remorselessly the young, the brave, the strong,—
    Indifferent to the unmeasured pain,
The accumulated horror and despair,
That stricken Earth no longer wills to bear.

My goal is *peace*,—not peace at any price,
    While yet ensanguined jaws of Evil yawn
Hungry and pitiless: Nay, peace were vice
    Until the cruel dragon-teeth be drawn,
And the wronged victims of Oppression be
Delivered from its hateful rule, and free!

When comes that hour, resentment laid aside,
    Into a ploughshare will I beat my sword;
The weaker Nations' strength shall be my pride,
    Their gladness my exceeding great reward;
And not in vain shall be the tears now shed,
Nor vain the service of the gallant dead.
  . . . .

I war against the folly which is War,
    The futile sacrifice that naught hath stayed,
The Great Delusion men have perished for,
    The lie that hath the souls of men betrayed;
For faith I war, humanity, and trust;
For peace on earth—a *lasting* peace, and *just!*

XI. IN WAR-TIME

GAZING SEAWARD

BREAKERS that beat against the shore
    With pulsing throb and angry roar
And multitudinous meanings evermore,—
Ye are to me as souls untaught of pain,
    That bent upon a fruitless quest
Still dash themselves 'gainst barrier laws in vain;
    But, oh, beyond your tumult and unrest,
Is Ocean like the Everlasting Will,—
So vast, so deep, so still!

XII. IN WAR-TIME

AN AMERICAN HOMEWARD BOUND

FURTHER and further we leave the scene
    Of war—and of England's care;
I try to keep my mind serene,—
    But my heart stays there;

For a distant song of pain and wrong
    My spirit doth deep confuse,
And I sit all day on the deck, and long—
    And long for news!

I seem to see them in battle-line—
    Heroes with hearts of gold,
But of their victory a sign
    The Fates withhold;

And the hours too tardy-footed pass,
    The voiceless hush grows dense
Mid the imaginings, alas!

That feed suspense.

Oh, might I lie on the wind, or fly
    In the wilful sea-bird's track,
Would I hurry on, with a homesick cry,—
    Or hasten back?

    XIII.   AN APPEAL

HARKEN, heroic England! Know how near
    To thy life-citadel the foe has drawn!
Abjure complacent counsels; learn to fear;
For Might that wars 'gainst all thou holdest dear,
    Unstayed, is marching on!

Thou, patient ever, be deceived no more:
    Part with delusive dreams that make less strong!
Behold how bold (a ruthless conqueror),
By night and day comes nearer to thy door
    Intolerable Wrong!

Call upon all thy strength—not later, now!—
    Now while the world waits breathless for thy deed,
That it eternally may disavow
The faith that "Might makes Right," nor bow
    To Savagery's brute creed!

Brave in defence of honor and the word
    Which, given freely, binds and maketh free.
Arm, that the weak and helpless may be heard!—
Yea, that the hearts of men may still be stirred
    To Christ's humanity!

From fields of horror, blood-soaked, eloquent,
    From shrines of beauty, waste and desecrate,
From unoffending lips and innocent,

The cry of anguish and of hope is rent:—
  "England! be not too late!"

XIV.   REQUIEM FOR A YOUNG SOLDIER

PEACE to-night, heroic spirit!
  Pain is overpast.
All the strife with life is ended;
  You may rest at last.

The devotion that, amazing,
  Welled from out the deep
Of your being, no more needed,
  Quiet you may sleep:

Sleep, who, giving all for others,
  Battled till the victory nigh,
You, too, toil and heart-break over,
  Had the right to die! . . .

We may guard the grave that holds you,
  As a shrine of Truth
Lighted by the pure devotion
  Of your radiant youth;

We, you died for, may forget you!
  You will have no care,
Who, content, to-night are sleeping—
  Painless, dreamless, there!

XV.   A RUSSIAN'S PRAYER FOR HIS HORSE, BEFORE GOING INTO BATTLE

A PARAPHRASE

ALSO for these that with us bear
   The heat and burden of the day,
These humble creatures of Thy care,
   O Merciful, we pray.

Their guileless lives they offer, Lord,
   To aid their country in distress.
Grant to their virtue the reward
   Of Thy great tenderness.

Have pity also, Lord, on these—
   On these, so docile, faithful, meek!
We supplicate upon our knees
   For them that cannot speak.

XVI.   RHEIMS

AT THE RUINED CATHEDRAL

COVER your face, Humanity, and weep,
   Considering your sorrow and your shame
Where things are writ to keep the eyes from sleep,—
Where sacrilege and horror records keep
   To blemish your fair name!

Hate here betrayed itself, too blind to see,
   Striking with venom at its own heart's core—
Hate, that destroys with dull barbarity
What Time, though long it toil and patiently,
   May not again—ah, not again restore!

The generations yet unborn shall feel
　　This wrong to Beauty, and lament her loss:
Here royal kings, unhappy ghosts, shall steal
Through ruins where no carillon shall peal,
　　Nor altar gleam, nor Christ bend from the cross.

And evermore, haunting this woeful shade,
　　Clothed in white armor a loved wraith shall come;
And here, where she a King and Nation made,
Shall talk again with angels, unafraid,
　　Although her sweet, accusing lips be dumb.

XVII.　THE SMILE OF REIMS

"THE smile," they called her,—"La Sourire"; and fair—
　　A sculptured angel on the northern door
　　　Of the Cathedral's west façade—she wore
Through the long centuries of toil and care
That smile, mysteriously wrought and rare,
　　As if she saw brave visions evermore—
　　　Kings, and an armored Maid who lilies bore,
And all the glories that had once been there.

How like to thee, her undefeated Land!
　　Wounded by bursting shells, a little space
　　　Broken she lay beneath her ancient portal;
But lifted from the earth with trembling hand,
　　Victorious, still glowed upon her face
　　　Thy smile, heroic France, love-given and immortal!

XVIII.　THE KAISER

HE stood alone, in sovereignty sublime,
　　Uniquely great,—the Kaiser! They that feared,
　　Yet honored him, who to the world appeared

Lofty in courage, wise, above his time,
  The Monarch of the hour!—
Using his strength destructive things to bind,
Serving the Fatherland—and, so, mankind,
  Safe-guarding Peace with Power.

He stood alone? How lone today he stands,
  The eyes of all fixed wondering on him!
  His throne ensanguined, his bright ægis dim,
The murderous sword clutched in his lawless hands!
  What spectacle more sad
Than Might by its own folly wounded so?
Are the Gods jealous now, as long ago,
  That thus they make ambitious mortals mad?

    XIX.   THE GODS REMEMBER

THE Gods remember always. We forget,
But they forget not: every debt
Howe'er we palter and evade,
Maturing, must be paid.

They pity us, the Gods, but naught forgive,
Lest we, who slowly learn to live—
Children scarce wiser in our age than youth—
Should come to doubt their truth!

Loving the brave who strive and will not yield
Though hurt and fallen on the field,
They teach us not from death to fly,
Lest we, indeed, should die!

For 'tis their will the soul shall rise
Above its earthly agonies:
Triumphant rise, as from the pyre
A Phœnix, winged by fire!

XX.   ART AND WAR

WAR has its field of blood—heart-breaking War—
    Wherein to rule with undisputed sway
    Throughout its own mad, self-exhausting day.
There, where it rashly sacrifices more
Than laboring Time may ever quite restore,
    Shall it amid red welter and decay
    Strive horribly; but let it not essay
To enter where Peace guards the Future's door!

War has nor right, nor privilege, nor part
    In lives high-dedicate the world to bind
Through love and hope and the great dream of Art!
    All Lands to such are Fatherland; they find
In alien realms love's grateful, welcoming heart—
    They, chosen of the Gods to bless mankind!

XXI.   THE BRAVE

IT is not the desert lonely,
    Nor at the mast-head o'er the wave,
Nor with the climbing fire ascending
    Imperiled life to save,
Nor on the battlefield, that only
    Are found the brave!

Ah, no! Unmarked, pain's passion-flowers,
    Through nights intolerably deep,
They bind in silence; mutely praying—
    Enduring, not to keep
Their watchers wearying through the hours—
    But let them sleep.

Through all the winter chill, ere morning,
    O'er many a frozen trail, I wis,

Fighting their course, that waiting children
    Life's nurture may not miss—
Against the blast they journey, scorning
    As bitter kiss.

From light-towers sending forth at even
    New hope, in place of old despair,
Toiling in mines, in factories toiling—
    But, ah! why seek, why care
To name them o'er? The brave, thank Heaven!
    Are everywhere!

XXII.   HOW LONG?

"'Tis man's perdition to be safe,
    When for the truth he ought to die."

HOW long must we blush for the land of our love—
    We, sons of her honor, who fain would defend her?
How long must we wait, our own manhood to prove,
    While that poor protection she has others lend her?

Oh, heroes there were in the days that are gone,
    Who recked not of danger, who asked but of duty;
Men for whose guidance perpetual shone
    The Patriot Vision, in glorified beauty!

What is our life worth, if life be not living
    Up to the best and the highest we know?
What is life's gain but the glad power of giving,
    To the full measure, the debt that we owe?

God of our fathers, now in our need, hearken!
    Perils that shame us are here at our door;
They who should guide us with tame counsels darken;
    God of our fathers, inspire us once more!

XXIII. BETTER TO DIE

BETTER to die, where gallant men are dying,
  Than to live on with them that basely fly:
Better to fall, the soulless Fates defying,
Than unassailed to wander vainly, trying
  To turn one's face from an accusing sky!

Days matter not, nor years to the undaunted;
  To live is nothing,—but to *nobly* live!
The poorest visions of the honor-haunted
Are better worth than pleasure-masks enchanted,
  And they win life who life for others give.

The planets in their watchful course behold them—
  To live is nothing,—but to nobly live!—
For though the Earth with mother-hands remold them,
Though Ocean in his billowy arms enfold them,
  They are as gods, who life to others give!

XXIV. AMERICA

PATIENT she is—long-suffering, our Land;
  Wise with the strength of one whose soul in calm
Weighs and considers, and would understand
  Ere it gives way to anger: fearing wrong
Of her own doing more than any planned
  Against her peace by others deemed more strong.

Mother of many children alien born,
  Whom she has gathered into her kind arms,—
Safe-guarding most the weakest, most forlorn,—
  The mother's patience she has learned to know,
Which passes trifles by with smiling scorn—
  The mother's hopefulness, to anger slow.

Yet, oh, beware! nor, over-bold, presume
    Upon a gentleness enlikened with Power!
Her torch still burns, to kindle or consume,
    And 'gainst the time when she must prove her might,
Vast energy is stored in her soul's room—
    Undreamed of strength to battle for the Right!

XXV.   THE AMERICAN PEOPLE TO THE ALLIES

IF they tell you that we hold
    Right and wrong are much the same:
    That with equal share of blame
The defender of the fold
    And the ravening wolf we name—
        Don't believe it!

If they tell you that we think,
    When the robber comes by night
    And we see 'neath murderous Might
Innocence unfriended sink,
    We should be "too proud to fight"—
        Don't believe it!

If they tell you we are cold
    When strong men, and maids as brave,
    May not life from bondage save—
We who gave unstinted gold,
    And our heart's blood, for the slave!—
        Don't believe it!

If—O gallant souls and true!—
    If they tell you we judge well
    Ways of Heaven and ways of Hell:
That the honor dear to you
    Also in our souls doth dwell—
        Oh, believe it!

If they tell you our heart's cry:
    That, whate'er the danger near,
    One, one only loss we fear;
And are ready, too, to—die
    For the things that you hold dear—
        Oh, believe it!

XXVI.   UNDER THE FLAG

February 5, 1917

UNDER our own flag, still we will sail her—
    Gallantly sail her, our own Ship of State;
Faiths we have lived by still shall avail her,
    Hope at her prow, wing'd, expectant, elate!

Over the deeps of a perilous ocean,
    Honor compelling, we still will sail on;
Giving, unfearing, a loyal devotion,
    Until, in life—in death, danger is gone.

Deem not that we, whom our fathers before us
    Taught to love freedom and died to make free,
Coward shall fly, while the Heavens are o'er us,
    Craft of the ether or boats under sea.

There is in valor that hearkens to duty—
    Something that dearer may be than long years;
And in man's service may be a beauty
    Higher than glory, and deeper than tears.

XXVII. AMERICA SPEAKS

"For what avail or plough, or sail,
Or land, or life, if freedom fail?"

WE have been sleeping—dreaming. Now,
    Thank God! we are awake!
Awake, and ready with a will
    The nobler part to take!
No more shall a pretended Peace
    Our souls from duty sever;
We dedicate our lives to God
    And Liberty—forever!

We, who have looked with anguished eyes
    On things no eye should see,
Beholding all that may be wrought
    By ruthless Tyranny,
Join hands with you, devoted Lands,
    A liberated Nation
That wills to share your sacrifice,
    That knows your exaltation!

A lofty voice has spoken words
    That bring the world relief;
Our Land has joined the league of Right,
    Led onward by her Chief—
Her Chief who large has writ his name
    With Lincoln's in the story
Of that dear land which still may call
    The flag she loves, "Old Glory!"

XXVIII. THE UNION OF THE FLAGS

May 9, 1917

WE have hung out the flags that we love best—
    The British, the French and our own;
Adoring we see them together,
    That never together were flown!
And we feel in the bond is a blessing
    For every grief to atone.

O flag of my own Land, give welcome!
    Be proud to embrace, fold with fold,
These emblems of service heroic
    Whose measure can never be told:
These banners that speak to the future
    Of honor that shall not grow old!

Across them is "Sacrifice" written;
    They voice peoples generous, brave,
Who, suffering all men can suffer
    This side of eternity, gave
Their best with unflinching devotion,
    The wronged and the helpless to save.

They poured out their hearts' blood for freedom;
    They stood in the terrible way,
And bore the full brunt of the onslaught
    That darkened the sun at noonday.
We gaze with dimmed eyes on their Colors,
    Our souls strong for duty as they!

We will stand with high hearts by our Allies,
    With fear of no evil but shame;
We will face coward Death and outface him,
    In Liberty's eloquent name;
For we're of the brood of the Lion

That Tyranny never could tame!

XXIX. LIVE THY LIFE

LIVE thy life gallantly and undismayed:
Whatever harms may hide within the shade,
Be thou of fear, my spirit! more afraid.

In earthly pathways evil springeth rife;
But dread not thou, too much, or pain or strife
That plunge thee to the greater depths of life!

What though the storm-cloud holds the bolt that sears?
The eagle of the crag, that nothing fears,
Still, still is young after a hundred years!

XXX. AS THEY LEAVE US

BID farewell with pride,
    Show no trace of sorrow;
Smile into their eyes,
    Though your courage borrow;
There will be another day,
    And a time
        To pay!

Gallant is their look,
    But their hearts are tender.
Cry aloud your faith!
    Loyal tribute render!
For they go—the young, the brave—
    Liberty
        To save!

Tell them not of fear;

    Whisper not of sadness;
Overbrim to-day
    With heroic gladness;
Let your love, remembered, shine
    As a light
        Benign!

Simple is their trust,
    But 'tis deep as ocean;
Lofty is their hope,
    Selfless their devotion;
And they go—the young, the brave—
    Liberty
        To save!

Hark! The bugles call!
    Wave your banners!—cheer them!
Happy, let them dream
    All that's valiant near them!
They will know, when far from you,
    That the dream
        Was true!

XXXI.   A SOLDIER

DEAR God, I raised my boy to be a soldier;
    I tried to make him strong of will and true;
I told him many a tale of deeds heroic—
    The noblest and the sweetest tales I knew.

In thought, he shared the charge at Balaclava,
    With the Swiss Guard, o'ermastered coward Death,
With Gordon all renounced, with Scott and Peary
    Breathed in his ardent youth heroic breath.

A little lad, he wept for wounded Sidney,

    For Bayard, sans reproche, who knew no fears,
Yet, hurt himself, if one but said,—"My Soldier!"—
    Straightaway he smiled and swallowed down his tears.

I taught him that the brave are full of mercy;
    That gentleness and love to strength belong;
That honour is the only High adventure,
    And goodness the one everlasting song!

And so I raised my boy to be a Soldier:
    A patriot soldier, brave, devoted, free!
And now, and now,—with grateful trust, O Father!
    I give him to my Country and to Thee!

    XXXII.   FOR FRANCE

SHE had been stricken, sorely, ere this came;
    And now they wrote that he, her boy, was dead—
    Her only one! Through blinding tears she read,
Trying to see what followed his dear name.
    He had died "gloriously," the letter said,
"Guarding the Tricolor from touch of shame
Where raged the battle furious and wild."
    Catching her breath, she stayed despair's advance.
She was a mother; but, besides—a child
        Of France!

And after, though remembrance of past years
    Dulled not to her fond vision nor grew dim;
    Though every slightest incident of him
Was treasured in her breast, she shed no tears.
    Her cup was full now, even to the brim,
And for herself she knew nor hopes nor fears.
So, toiling patiently, with noble pride
    And lifted head she met each pitying glance,
She was the mother of a son who died—

For France!

XXXIII. IN PLAINS OF PICARDY

IN far-off plains of Picardy
   Our country's Flag is flying,
And Life and Death are battling there;
   But no man there fears dying.
So large a hope has set men free
From fear, in far-off Picardy!

To us, across the ocean deep,
   A wondrous strain comes winging;
It is the song of lads who march
   On to the conflict, singing—
Our lads, who so have longed to be
Where heroes strive, in Picardy!

Their strength is tried, their hearts so brave
   Were fed on Freedom's story;
"The coming of the Lord," they sing—
   "Mine eyes have seen the glory!"
The glory all at last shall see,
Rise o'er the plains of Picardy!

O Union Jack! O Tricolor!
   No more you grieve us, calling!
No more we wait, our hearts aflame,
   While brave men there are falling,
Our Stars and Stripes have crossed the Sea,
And we are one, in Picardy!

XXXIV. THE COMRADE

(Among the soldiers of France there is a widespread and touching belief that at Nancy, Soissons, Ypres and in the Argonne a Form in White has passed unharmed through shot and shell, comforting the wounded and the dying.)

WHO is this in raiment white
    Walks across the field,
Midst the terrors of the fight
    Bears nor sword nor shield,
Stays the dying to defend,
Where can come no other friend.

Who is this of whom they tell,
    Beautiful and grave,
As from Heaven, to this Hell
    Come the hurt to save?—
Bearing them with tenderness,
Where can follow no distress?

Who is this that lifts them up
    As they earthward sink,
Bids them, thirsting, from his cup
    Euthanasia drink,
Opens to their closing eyes
Healing visions of the skies? * * *

Is it the supreme Desire,
    Answering their need?—
Is it Faith that doth aspire,
    Lifting them, indeed,
Up, beyond all human strife,
To its own immortal life?

Is it Hope, the deathless one,
    To their broken hearts

Whispering of joys begun,
    E'en as life departs;
Hope, the gift of memories
Garnered at the mother's knees?

Is it, Friend and Healer, Thou—
    Vision pure and pale—
Whom men, sorrowing, look on now,
    As they saw the Grail?—
Is it Thou their yearnings greet,
Unimaginably sweet?

On the blood-stained fields of France
    What the dying view
Who can tell? All, all, perchance!
    But this much is true:
There wherever pain has trod
Comes the pitying love of God!

XXXV.   SEDAN

HOW terrible the victory
    That undermines the soul!
How better, better far to fail—
    To falter from the goal,
And with a brave acceptance meet
The triumph of a high defeat!

France!—generous Land beloved of all!
    More glorious made through pain,
Sedan beheld thy loss,—not fall,
    And taught how men may gain
Conquests that base desires impart,
Corrupt the will, and rob the heart!

XXXVI. CAPTAIN GUYNEMER

WHAT high adventure, in what world afar,
Follows to-day,
Mid ampler air,
Heroic Guynemer?
What star,
Of all the myriad planets of our night,
Is by his glowing presence made more bright
Who chose the Dangerous way,
Scorning, while brave men died, ignobly safe to stay?

Into the unknown Vast,
Where few could follow him, he passed,—
On to the gate—the shadowy gate—
Of the Forbidden,
Seeking the knowledge jealous Fate
Had still so carefully from mortals hidden.
With vision falcon-keen,
His eyes beheld what others had not seen,
And his soul, with as clear a gaze,
Pierced through each clouded maze
Straight to the burning heart of things, and knew
The lying from the true.

A dweller in Immensity,
Of naught afraid,
He saw the havoc Tyranny had made,—
Saw the relentless tide of War's advance,
And high of heart and free,
Vowed his young life to Liberty—
And France!

O Compiègne! be proud of him—thy son,—
The greatest of the eagle brood,—
Who with intrepid soul the foe withstood,
And rests, his victories won!

Mourn not uncomforted, but rather say:—
His wings were broken, but he led the way
Where myriad stronger wings shall follow;
For Wrong shall not hold lasting sway,
To break the World's heart, nor betray
With cruel pledges hollow!

To us the battle draweth near.
We dedicate ourselves again,
Remembering, O Compiègne!
Thy Charioteer—
Thy peerless one, who died to make men free,
And in Man's grateful heart shall live immortally!

XXXVII. SERBIA

WHEN the heroic deeds that mark our time
   Shall, in far days to come, recorded be,
   Men, much forgetting, shall remember thee,
Thou central martyr of the Monster-Crime,
Who kept thy soul clear of the ooze and slime—
   The quicksands of deceit and perjury—
   A living thing, unconquered still and free,
Through superhuman sacrifice sublime.

O Serbia! amid thy ruins great,
Love is immortal; there's an end to hate,
   Always there will be dawn, though dark the night.
Look up, thou tragic Glory! Even now,
The thorny round that binds thy bleeding brow
   Is as a crown irradiating light!

XXXVIII. BELGIUM

I HAD a dream of Greatness; and I saw—
Not one enthroned, before whose golden crown
And jeweled scepter many bowed them down;

Not one full-armored who, more fearful awe
Inspiring, with war's pestilential breath
Sowed havoc as he moved, despair and death;

Nay, in my lofty dream, such greatness paled
Before the image of one nobly fair,
Despite torn raiment and disheveled hair,

The hope within whose eyes had never failed.
Victim of unrelenting Tyranny
That fain would hold her captive, she is free—

Stronger, I wis, than e'en her tyrants be—
Because of something that hath never died:
Her glorious, tameless soul, grief-crucified!

XXXIX. THE INFANTRY THAT WOULD NOT YIELD

AH, yes; the French surprise us constantly;
A something in their spirit is so fine!...
I was in Paris when the famous Line
Went through after Verdun, and so could see
How a whole people, putting by its cares,
Came crowding to the well-loved thoroughfares
To view the men—not all—not all, alas!—
Who, in a fateful hour of fear and woe,
Stood as a wall defensive 'gainst the foe,
And said:—*They shall not pass!*

How surely these had saved her Paris knew—

Heroes who fronting Death turned not aside!
Her heart beat faster as they nearer drew,
And swelled with unimagined love and pride.
Artillery and cavalry went by,—
The plaudits of the people reached the sky!
But for the infantry— At sight of these,
A poignant silence fell upon the crowd:
In reverence the people's heads were bowed,
And they were on their knees.

Ah, yes; the French surprise us constantly!

    XL.   THEIR VICTORY WON

WAN-VISAGED Azrael, in a darkened room,
'Mid stifled sobs and pleadings full of fear,
    I first was made to know thy presence drear;
And I supposed thee dweller of a tomb
Where quickly fade all fairest things that bloom:
    All loves, ambitions, dreams, that men hold dear.
    But now, O Death, beholding thee more near,
How changed thy look! how glorified thy gloom!

In the wide Open, 'neath a summer sky,
Bending above thy chosen, where they lie
    Upon the hard-won fields of Victory,
This have they taught me—these so young, so brave,
Who smiling gave their all, the world to save—
    Life is not lovelier than death may be!

XLI. IN MEMORY OF AN AMERICAN SOLDIER

FALLEN IN FRANCE IN THE GLORIOUS YEAR 1918

HE went singing down to death;
   And the high Gods, who heard him,
Gave something of their breath
   To the melodies that stirred him;
Lending some accents to his dying song
That only to abiding things belong.

His boyish heart had laughed
   For joy of life's completeness—
Life had so brimmed the draught
   It held for him with sweetness;
But when, unlooked for, came the suppliant cry
From tortured Lands, he put the full cup by.

Happy whose soul has wings
   And has the strength to spread them!
Happy whose heart still brings
   Its dreams where truth first led them!
Though he give all, his fellow men to save,
He has a tryst with Life, beyond the grave!

Blithely he took the path
   Appointed him by Duty,
Whose face, viewed nearer, hath
   Such deeps undreamed of beauty,—
Love, hope, ambition—he put all aside,
And for the things that do not perish, died.

. . . .

Soul, was it tragedy to fall like this?
Oh, lovely, lovely, lovely, courage is!
   And death itself may be most sweet,
Though the lips thirst, and empty be the cup,
If won in climbing—climbing up—and up,

To heights where vision and fulfilment meet:
If won at last, by deeds that glorify
Our lowly dust, where 'neath an alien sky,
Their service unforgot,
They sleep who, loving greatly, faltered not,—
   The happy brave, who never knew defeat!

XLII.   OUR LAND

THE gift of an idealist,
She came of vision, and the dream
Of one who saw beyond vast waters gleam
The light of a new world without a name:
   A gift of Life she came—.
She, the renascence from Earth's ancient woe,
With Raphael born and Michel Angelo.

Noiseless, the patient years went by,
And only red-men cared to roam
Her glorious streams, and call her mountains home.
Then came to her, like pilgrims of the Grail
   Whose courage could not fail,
Others, sad exiles, longing to be free—
Seekers of God and human liberty!

A blessèd, blessèd Land! She gave
Ideals, to mankind unknown,
And toiling, taught a wondering world to own
The dignity of toil, despised before:
   She opened a great Door;
Enlarged the human mind, and made men see
That he who shares his freedom is most free.

Oh, strong and beautiful and brave,—
The Titan-Mother of the West,—
Gathering in her arms and to her breast

The hurt, unfriended, weary, and forlorn,
    Outcast, and alien-born!
How should the unfriended poor beyond the seas
Not yearn to her—the new Hesperides?. . .

Full garners were her toil's reward;
But, laboring, alway she dreams.
Mistake her not! Mid clouds her eagle screams,
Emblem of liberty that nothing bars,
    And on her brow are stars—
Stars whose pure radiance is not all of earth,
Enkindled there where Justice had its birth.

Belovèd Land! Apart, she smiled!
But, oh, more glorious to-day,
Life's Larger Summons eager to obey,
Her strength outpoured to succor and befriend
    A World, wide without end,
She waits—how yearningly!—the hour to come
When laurelled Peace shall lead her heroes home!

XLIII. A LOVE-SONG

THIS is the love-song we today are singing—
    The song of her who, blessing, most is blest:
Giver of dreams that set the soul far winging,
    And bring it home to rest.

This is the song of her, our fount of being,
    The pilot of our hope where'er we go:
Of her—the brave, the patient, the foreseeing—
    To whom our all we owe.

The wronged, oppressed,—what poor, unfriended comer
    Has not, with her, found shelter safe from storm?—
A smile of welcoming as sweet as summer,

A heart as deep and warm?

Can we have voice today for others' praises,
    When evil and disaster threaten her?
Ah, no! a passion that man's soul upraises,
    New-born in us, doth stir

At thought of her, belov'd, who shows us living
    Is not the mere continuance of breath,
Giving her favored ones a joy of giving,
    Ineffable in death!

INDEX

INDEX OF TITLES

Ab Humo, *20 Apr*
Achilles, *2 Jun*
Adieu, *6 Jul*
An Adieu, *15 Mar*
Adonis, *7 Feb*
Affinity, *3 Jul*
After, *4 Jan*
After the Paintings by George F. Watts, *2 Jan*
After the Play, *8 Mar*
Against the Gate of Life, *27 Jun*
Alexander III, *9 Sep*
The All-Mother, *Mother's Day*
Alms, *19 Dec*
America (Patient she is—long-suffering, our Land), *Poems on War, XXIV*
America (Thy children are inspired by thee), *Poems on War, IV*
America Speaks, *Poems on War, XXVII*
An American at Lincoln, *14 Oct*
The American People to the Allies, *Poems on War, XXV*
Amor Creator, *22 Nov*
An Appeal, *Poems on War, XIII*
The Angelus—Jean-François Millet, 1814-1875 (*see* Jean-François Millet)
April, *2 April*
Art, *7 Jun*
Art and War, *Poems on War, XX*
As They Leave Us, *Poems on War, XXX*
"Ask what you will", *1 Aug*
At Break of Day, *9 April*
At Dusk, *1 Jun*
At Easter, *Easter*
At Eden's Gate (*see* The Cherubim)
At The Sarah-Bernhardt Theatre, *22 Oct*
Autumn (In her arms unconscious lying), *5 Nov*

Autumn ("We ne'er will part!" Ah me, what plaintive sounds), 23 Sep
A Ballad of a Drum, 17 Nov
The Band of the Titanic, 14 Apr
Base-Born, 14 Mar
Be Thou My Guide, 1 Sep
Beatrice before Death, 12 Oct
Beauty's Path, 22 Aug
Beethoven, 26 Mar
Before the Dawn, 30 Jul
Before the Hour, 29 Feb
Belgium, *Poems on War, XXXVIII*
Benjamin Franklin, 17 Apr
Bereft, 19 Jun
Beside a Pleasant Shore, 3 Feb
Betrothal, 28 Jun
Better to Die, *Poems on War, XXIII*
Beyond, 31 Dec
"Blessèd", 30 May
The Brave, *Poems on War, XXI*
Breathless We Strive, 7 Apr
Britannia, *Poems on War, VIII*
Brook-Song: To the Spring, 6 May
Buffalo, 6 Sep
The Burial of Robert Louis Stevenson at Samoa, 3 Dec
By the Conemaugh, 31 May
Captain Guynemer, *Poems on War, XXXVI*
A Cathedral, 1 Nov
Cendrillon, 3 Aug
"Che Faro Senza Eurydice!" (*see* Eurydice)
The Cherubim, 23 Aug
The Child and the Heart Bereft, 11 May
Child-Fancies, 29 Jul
The Chosen, 7 Aug
The Christ of the Andes, 7 Sep
Christmas Eve, 24 Dec
The Chrysanthemum, 20 May

Civilization, *14 Jul*
The Clouds, *16 Mar*
Columbus, *Columbus Day*
Combatants, *8 Nov*
Compensation, *18 Feb*
The Comrade, *Poems on War, XXXIV*
Conflict and Rest, *26 Feb*
Conscience, *21 Feb*
Cora, *23 Mar*
Coronation—To King Edward VII, *9 Aug*
Courage, *28 Nov*
Cradle Song, *18 Jun*
Crippled, *20 Dec*
Cruel Love—Anacreontic, *9 Mar*
Cupid and the Muses, *15 Feb*
Däi Nippon, *5 Oct*
Daphnis, *12 Mar*
Dawn, *16 Nov*
Dearth, *25 Aug*
Death, *24 Aug*
Deathless Death, *19 Nov*
A Débutante, *11 Mar*
Delilah, *30 Oct*
Demeter, *21 Jul*
A Descant, *4 Jun*
The Difference, *3 Dec*
Didst Thou Rejoice?, *8 Feb*
Ditty: My True Love's Eyes, *7 Mar*
Divination, *18 Mar*
The Dream Beautiful (*see* My Dream)
Dream the Great Dream, *24 Jun*
Dreyfus (If thou art living, in that Devil's Isle), *16 Sep*
Dreyfus (France has no dungeon in her island tomb), *15 Sep*
Dryad Song, *19 Sep*
Du Maurier, *6 Mar*
"Each and All", *7 Oct*
Eagles, *19 Jul*

Earth Has Her Blossoms (*see* Earth's Blossoms)
Earth's Blossoms, *25 Jul*
Earth's Mystery, *6 Nov*
Easter, *Easter*
Éastre, *Easter*
Echo Consolatrix, *13 Nov*
Edmund Clarence Stedman, *11 Nov*
The Empty House, *29 Nov*
Eros, *6 Aug*
Eurydice, *27 Mar*
Every Heart, *3 May*
Every Night at Marathon, *24 Nov*
Exaltation, *24 Sep*
Fairer Than Violets Are, *17 May*
A Farewell, *2 Mar*
Father, *Father's Day*
First and Last, *31 Jul*
For France, *Poems on War, XXXII*
For Joy, *28 Apr*
For the Birthday of William Dean Howells, *1 Mar*
Frederick, *15 Jun*
Friends to Virtue, *8 Dec*
Fritz Scheel, *13 Mar*
The Frogs, *22 May*
Gifts, *29 Jan*
Give Me Not Love, *3 Sep*
Giving Thanks, *Thanksgiving*
"Go not too far", *1 Dec*
The Gods Remember, *Poems on War, XIX*
Le Grand Salut, *18 Sep*
Greatness, *19 May*
He and I, *5 Jan*
The Heart of Love, *9 Feb*
Heimweh, *4 Aug*
Heart-Room, *3 Oct*
Helen Bell (*see* Winter the Nursery for Spring Flowers)
Helen Keller with a Rose, *27 Jun*

Henry James, *28 Feb*
Henry V, *22 Jun*
Henry Wadsworth Longfellow, *27 Feb*
The Hermit, *13 Jan*
A Hero, *15 Apr*
His Face, *12 Feb*
Homeward, *24 Jul*
Honor, *13 May*
"Honor, not Honors", *7 Dec*
The Hospital, *21 Oct*
The House of Pain, *5 Feb*
How Long?, *Poems on War, XXII*
How Wonderful is Love, *8 Jun*
Hylas, *18 May*
I Heard a Voice, *6 Dec*
I know not how to find the Spring, *25 Mar*
"I Longed for Love", *27 Aug*
I Looked on Sorrow (*see* Earth's Mystery)
I Too Have Loved, *23 Apr*
The Ideal, *15 Jul*
An Idle Ditty, *16 Jun*
An Idler, *17 Jun*
Immortal (Life is like a beauteous flower), *4 May*
Immortal (How living are the dead!), *6 Apr*
In a College Settlement, *21 Apr*
In a Tenement, *19 Aug*
In April, *1 Apr*
In Darkness, *9 Nov*
In Dreamland, *10 Jan*
In Loneliness, *11 Dec*
In Memory, *20 Jun*
In Memory of an American Soldier, *Poems on War, XLI*
In Memory of Caroline Furness Jayne, *23 Jun*
In Memory of Henry La Barre Jayne, *10 May*
"In Memory of Jean", *24 Dec*
In Modern Bonds, *28 Dec*
In Pathetic Remembrance, *31 Mar*

In Plains of Picardy, *Poems on War, XXXIII*
In Remembrance: The Antarctic Heroes of 1912 (*see* To Britannia)
In the Maternity Ward (*see* The Hospital)
In the Offing, *7 May*
In the Town a Wild Bird singing, *4 Oct*
In the Wood, *25 Oct*
In War-Time—Gazing Seaward, *Poems on War, XI*
In War-Time—An American Homeward Bound, *Poems on War, XII*
In Winter, *20 Feb*
In Winter-Time, *19 Feb*
India, *13 Apr*
Indian-Pipe, *5 Sep*
The Infantry that Would Not Yield, *Poems on War, XXXIX*
Influence, *17 Aug*
Inheritor, *24 Apr*
Interchange, *27 Apr*
Inviolable, *25 Apr*
The Irish Shamrock in South Africa, *17 Mar*
Israfel, *27 Jul*
James McNeill Whistler, *17 Jul*
Jean-François Millet, *20 Jan*
Jewel-Weed, *4 Sep*
Joan of Arc, *30 May*
John Hay, *1 Jul*
The Kaiser, *Poems on War, XVIII*
Keats, *23 Feb*
Keats to Fanny Brawne (*see* Let Me Believe)
Kenilworth, *12 Sep*
Kindred, *5 Apr*
Lament of Brünhilde, *23 Oct*
L'Amour fait Peur, *1 Feb*
The Lark, *Easter*
The Land of Promise, *17 Feb*
Last Night I dreamed, *26 Sep*
Leaders of Men, *13 Feb*
Leave-taking, *16 Aug*
Let Me Believe, *16 Jan*

The Liberty-Bell, *8 Oct*
Life (Before we knew thee thou wert with us; ay), *2 Oct*
Life (Thou art more ancient than the oldest skies), *3 Mar*
Limitation, *3 Jun*
Lines for a Fiftieth Anniversary, *4 Jul*
The Little Lass, *13 Aug*
A Little Minister, *11 Sep*
A Little Song, *5 Jul*
Live Thy Life, *Poems on War, XXIX*
Longing, *10 Apr*
The Lordly Pines, *26 Oct*
The Lost Gioconda, *21 Aug*
Love and the Child, *19 Apr*
Love Conquers Death, *10 Mar*
Love, Dost Thou Smile?, *17 Oct*
Love Has No Foes, *27 Sep*
Love is Passing, *14 Dec*
Love never is Too Late, *28 Jul*
The Love of Life, *12 Jan*
Love, Reproachful, *9 Dec*
Love Sailed at Morn, *30 Nov*
Love that Faltered, *27 Nov*
A Lover's "Litany to Pan", *16 Dec*
A Love-Song, *Poems on War, XLIII*
A Lowly Parable, *5 Jun*
Lullaby, *9 Jan*
Ma Belle, *30 Jan*
Madonna, *Mother's Day*
A Maid's Defence, *18 Jan*
Man, *28 Sep*
Man, That Will Not Be Beguiled, *29 Aug*
The Man-Soul, *22 Jan*
Mars, *21 Dec*
The Martyr Jews, *Easter*
Masefield, *25 Apr*
McKinley, *14 Sep*
Mediæval, *13 Sep*

A Meeting in the Forest, *27 Oct*
Memoria, *5 Mar*
Memorial Ode, *Poems on War, VI*
Memory, *27 May*
Mid-Ocean, *14 Nov*
Might I Return, *6 Jan*
The Mirror, *11 Jan*
Morning, *4 Nov*
The Morning Glory, *9 May*
Mother, *Mother's Day*
Mother-Love, *Mother's Day*
Mother Mary, *25 Dec*
Motherless, *18 Aug*
The Mourner, *26 May*
Music, *3 Jan*
My Country, *20 Oct*
My Dream, *7 Jan*
My True Love's Eyes (*see* Ditty: "My True Love's Eyes")
Nansen, *10 Oct*
A Narrow Window, *27 Jan*
Natura Benigna, *23 Jul*
Nature, *11 Apr*
Near and Far, *22 Apr*
The Nest, *31 Jan*
The New Mars, *Poems on War, X*
New York, *20 Sep*
No More (*see* No More, Dear Heart)
No More, Dear Heart, *4 Feb*
Nocturne, *23 Nov*
Nothing that can die, *13 Jul*
O Giorno Felice!, *21 Mar*
October, *1 Oct*
Ode to Silence, *22 Jul*
Of Future Days, *8 Jan*
Of Love, *16 Oct*
Old St. David's, *21 May*
Omar, *4 Dec*

On a Poet too early Dead, *24 Mar*
On Finding Buddha's Dust, *10 Aug*
On Re-reading "The Sick King in Bokhara", *26 Jun*
On the Death of Lady Curzon, *18 Jul*
Once in a Still, Sequestered Place, *8 May*
Onward (*see* Per Aspera)
An Optimist, *6 Jun*
The Orchestral Leader, *9 Oct*
Our Land, *Poems on War, XLII*
Paris, *11 Aug*
The "Penseur", *12 Nov*
Per Aspera, *2 Sep*
Perdita, *15 Jan*
Persephone, *20 Mar*
Philistia, *14 May*
Picquart, *17 Sep*
The Pilgrim, *24 Jan*
Pilgrim Song, *16 Feb*
Pilgrimage, *25 Jan*
Place de la Concorde, *Poems on War, IX*
Poems: After George F. Watts (*see* After the Paintings by George F. Watts)
The Poet, *27 Dec*
Poetry, *9 Jul*
The Poetry of Earth, *25 Jun*
Poor Icarus, *3 Apr*
"Poor Love!" said Life, *13 Dec*
President M'Kinley (*see* McKinley)
Privilege, *29 Sep*
Probation, *31 Aug*
Psyche, *30 Mar*
A Realm of Wonder, *12 Aug*
The Red and the Blue (*see* A Song of the Red and the Blue)
Rejected, *Easter*
Renewal, *1 Jan*
Reproach not Death, *20 Nov*
Requiem for a Young Soldier, *Poems on War, XIV*

Retrospect, *14 Jan*
The Return, *15 Nov*
The Return of Proserpine, *22 Mar*
Reveille, *29 May*
Rhapsody, *2 May*
Rheims, *Poems on War, XVI*
Robert Browning, *12 Dec*
Romance, *10 Jul*
A Rose, *8 Jul*
Rouen: In the Prison of Joan of Arc, *23 May*
A Round, *15 Aug*
A Russian's Prayer for his Horse, before going into Battle, *Poems of War, XV*
Saint Theresa, *28 Mar*
Sappho, *22 Sep*
A Secret, *3 Nov*
Secure, *24 Feb*
Sedan, *Poems on War, XXXV*
A Seeker in the Night, *14 Aug*
Self-confident Youth, *22 Feb*
"The Sense of Tears in Mortal Things", *17 Dec*
Serbia, *Poems on War, XXXVII*
Shakespeare, *23 Apr*
She will not hear, *5 May*
Siberia, *8 Sep*
The Singer, *10 Dec*
Sleep, *26 Dec*
The Smile of Reims, *Poems on War, XVII*
"So War has Begun", *Poems on War, III*
So you love me, *15 Oct*
Socrates, *28 Aug*
A Soldier, *Poems on War, XXXI*
Song: "For Me the Jasmine Buds Unfold", *16 May*
Song: "Friendship from its Moorings Strays", *20 Aug*
Song: "Her Cheek is Like a Tinted Rose", *26 Apr*
Song: "If Love Were But a Little Thing", *26 Jul*
Song: "If Love Were Not, the Wilding Rose", *18 Nov*

Song: "My Love is Fairer than the Tasselled Corn" *10 Sep*
Song: "The New-Born Leaves Unfolding Fast", *29 Apr*
Song: "Sweet is the Birth of Love", *12 Jun*
Song of Life, *21 Nov*
A Song of the Red and the Blue (Words and music by Florence Earle Coates), *28 Oct*
The song that is forgot, *15 May*
Stanza, *7 Jul*
The Summer-Time is in the Rose, *21 Jun*
The Sun-Dial, *29 Dec*
Suppliant, *26 Jan*
Survival, *12 Apr*
Tennyson, *6 Oct*
Thanksgiving, *Thanksgiving*
Their Victory Won, *Poems on War, XL*
There's a Spot in the Mountains, *5 Aug*
They live so long, *26 Aug*
They told me, *18 Apr*
Thomas Bailey Aldrich, *19 Mar*
Though Thou Hast Climbed, *24 May*
Through the Rushes, *16 Apr*
Through the Window, *14 Jun*
Time, *8 Aug*
The "Titanic"—Aftermath, *14 Apr*
To a Poet, *19 Jan*
To Alice Meynell, *11 Oct*
To Britannia, *29 Mar*
To England, *6 Feb*
To France, *23 Jan*
To Helen Keller, *27 Jun*
To Henry Mills Alden, *10 Nov*
"To him who found me sleeping, all my soul", *22 Dec*
To Hope, *5 Dec*
To Horace Howard Furness, *2 Nov*
To John Luther Long, on seeing his opera "Madame Butterfly" (*see* To the Author of "Madame Butterfly")
To One in Hospital Pent, *12 Jul*

To Poverty, *30 Sep*
To R. R., *25 May*
To Sappho Dead, *22 Sep*
To Silence (*see* Ode to Silence)
To the Author of "Madame Butterfly", *11 Jul*
To the Muse, *2 Jul*
To the Returning Brave, *Poems on War, V*
To the Tsar (1890), *9 Sep*
To the Victor, *7 Nov*
To William Butler Yeats, *13 Jun*
To-day, *4 Mar*
Together in Way, Together in Heart (for the Transatlantic Society of America) (*see* To England)
To-morrow, *21 Jan*
A Tomb in Tuscany, *19 Oct*
The Tomb said to the Rose, *25 Sep*
Too Late, *2 Feb*
Transition, *25 Feb*
True Love, *9 Jun*
Two Brothers, *26 Nov*
Unbidden, *1 May*
Unconquered, *29 Oct*
The Unconquered Air, *24 Oct*
Under the Flag, *Poems on War, XXVI*
The "Unfinished" Symphony, *10 Feb*
The Union of the Flags, *Poems on War, XXVIII*
United, *13 Oct*
Unpardoned, *21 Sep*
Unrest, *20 Jul*
Vagrant, *18 Oct*
A Valentine, *14 Feb*
Veiled, *18 Dec*
Vestal, *15 Dec*
"Victi Resurgunt", *Poems on War, II*
Victory, *2 Dec*
The Violin, *23 Dec*
Vita Nuova, *30 Apr*

War (In the beginning was I born), *Poems on War, I*
War (The serpent-horror writhing in her hair), *Poems on War, VII*
Water Lilies, *28 May*
Welcome to Dewey (*see* To the Returning Brave)
When Christ was Born, *25 Dec*
When You Came, *31 Oct*
Where Harold Sleeps, *30 Aug*
The White-throated Sparrow, *16 Jul*
"Who Knocks?" (*see* The Return)
Who Walks the World with Soul Awake, *2 Aug*
Why Did You Go?, *17 Jan*
Wings, *11 Jun*
Winter the Nursery for Spring Flowers, *11 Feb*
Winter-Song, *28 Jan*
Winter's Sovereignty (*see* Compensation)
With Breath of Spring, *8 Apr*
Wouldst Thou Learn?, *4 Apr*
Yesterday, *30 Dec*
You, *10 Jun*
The Young Wife, *30 Jun*
The Young Wife Speaks, *29 Jun*
Youth and Age, *12 May*

20241003

ABOUT THE COMPILER, SONJA N. BOHM

During her youth in the 1980s, Sonja N. Bohm frequented a buy-sell-trade bookshop in Plattsburgh, NY. On one visit, after browsing the paperbacks, she ventured into the basement, filled with older, dust-covered volumes, and spied a first edition, two-volume set of poems published in 1916 by an unfamiliar author. Pasted inside the front board of Volume I was a platinum print photograph of a woman whose gaze seemed to reach out to her across time. Intrigued, she purchased the set and brought it home. For over two decades the identity of the woman remained a mystery, until an internet search revealed it to be that of Florence Earle Coates, the poet herself.

This discovery ignited a determination in Bohm to delve into Coates' life and times, and a desire to ensure that the poet's work would not fade into obscurity. She gathered all available information at her disposal and created Coates' Wikipedia article. She also transcribed the poet's works to Wikisource—the free online library—giving the poet a voice in the digital age so that her words might endure for future generations. To the best of Bohm's knowledge, the poems in this daybook represent the complete works of Mrs. Coates, excluding any prose.

In addition to her efforts to preserve Coates' legacy, Bohm crafts bilingual verses inspired by her two-year stay in Portugal. Her poems, written in Portuguese and English, serve as bridges between distant lands, carrying the hope of finding a home in kindred hearts.

www.ingramcontent.com/pod-product-compliance
Lightning Source LLC
Chambersburg PA
CBHW070748230426
43665CB00017B/2293